CREATING

THE PATH TO SUSTAINABLE

CUSTOMER

COMPETITIVE ADVANTAGE

 # VALUE

BY

EARL NAUMANN

Naumann and Associates Consultants
Boise, Idaho

TP THOMSON EXECUTIVE PRESS
A Division of South-Western College Publishing

Library of Congress Cataloging-in-Publication Data

Naumann, Earl
  Creating customer value: the path to sustainable competitive
advantage / by Earl Naumann.
   p. cm.
  Includes index.
  ISBN: 0-538-83847-7
  1. Consumer satisfaction. 2. Customer service. I. Title.
HF5415.5N33 1994
658.8'12--dc20   94-159
                                  CIP

1 2 3 4 5 6 7 D 0 9 8 7 6 5 4

Printed in the United States of America

I⊤P
International Thomson Publishing

Thomson Executive Press (a Division of South-Western College Publishing) is an ITP
Company. The ITP trademark is used under license.

 This book is printed on recycled, acid-free paper that meets Environmental
Protection Agency standards.

PREFACE

Dramatic events have changed the world order in the past few years. Five or ten years ago, who would have predicted the unification of Germany or the deterioration of communism all across Eastern Europe? Who would have predicted the disintegration of the Soviet Union? Who would have predicted that the United States would be embroiled in the Gulf War, a war watched around the world live on television? Virtually no one would have predicted such visible, powerful changes.

Even more powerful changes are taking place, changes that have gone largely unnoticed, even here in the United States. These more subtle changes are forcing businesses to change their fundamental orientation. For businesses that don't change, long-term survival is unlikely. What are the events that are causing some organizations to change their fundamental beliefs? What are the forces at work in virtually all advanced economies that are being ignored by so many?

Quite simply, there has been a fundamental power shift within all industrialized economies. That power shift has occurred in all portions of the Triad, in Europe—in North America, in Asia. The power shift deals with changes in the distribution of power *within* economies. The relative power of each portion of the Triad is simply a reflection of how well each responds to the change in power. In general, the economic success of Japan is a direct result of better responsiveness to the redistribution of power.

The power involved is neither military power, nor political power, nor bureaucratic power within organizations. The power shift has occurred in *economic* power. Economic power has shifted from the producers and suppliers of goods and services to the consumer. Unfortunately, many firms act as if they still have power, as if they need to only give lip service to customers. But it is the customer who now clearly dictates what constitutes appropriate product quality, appropriate service, and reasonable prices.

As power has shifted to customers, those channel members closest to consumers have also increased in power, and the more consumers that a channel member serves, the more powerful they are. Does anyone doubt the economic power of Wal-Mart, K-Mart, or Target? Does anyone doubt the power of L. L. Bean? The economic power of such firms flows from their proximity to consumers and from their role as gatekeepers. The slotting allowances necessary to buy shelf space, particularly in the grocery industry, are a graphic indictor of where the power now rests in a channel.

But these retailers derive their channel power not only from their proximity to customers; they derive power also due to their ability to satisfy customer needs. The more customers that a channel member serves and the more satisfied those customers tend to be, the greater the power of that firm. These concepts apply not only to retailers but to all types of businesses in all industries. Xerox derives its economic power from 2.2 million highly satisfied customers. Merck is an industry leader because it has a large, highly satisfied customer base. Firms in economic difficulty have usually not done as good a job as their competitors have in satisfying their customers. In essence, when a firm is in a weak or declining market position, customers have exercised their economic power and *fired the firm*!

That is fundamentally what this book is all about: how to not be fired by your customers. Chapter 1 focuses on the primary cause of the inability, or unwillingness, to become more responsive to customers, a pervasive complacency in business. Chapter 2 explains the concept of customer value, and Chapters 3, 4, and 5 discuss the importance of each component of customer value: product quality, service quality, and value-based prices. The subsequent chapters discuss both the high costs of delivering low value and the various aspects of customer satisfaction, the scorecard by which delivered customer value is measured. Chapter 8 stresses that customers must be integrated throughout a firm's decision-making process to achieve true customer orientation. Chapter 9 addresses the need to build closely integrated, value-added chains. The final chapter makes the point that "good enough" never is.

Virtually all successful firms are learning these lessons, although some of them very recently and very painfully. Ultimately, any firm that does not learn these lessons will not survive. The speed of their demise will be dictated by how fast their competition learns.

ACKNOWLEDGMENTS

Many business professionals and academics contributed to the development of this book. I am especially grateful to the reviewers who made many helpful comments and suggestions.

Diann Cox
ChoiceCare

George L. Dershimer
George L. Dershimer Consulting

Andrew J. DuBrin
Rochester Institute of Technology

Douglas L. Fugate
Western Kentucky University

Kathleen Giel
Boise Cascade Corporation

K. Douglas Hoffman
The University of North Carolina at Wilmington

Steve Jacobs
The OSD Alliance
A Division of Franklin Quest Co.

Ray Kordupleski
AT&T Customer Service Director

Dennis J. Krause
Formica Corporation

Diane Krause
Formica Corporation

Timothy S. Mescon
Kennesaw State College

Frank W. Rudolph
James River Corporation

Sue Russell
ChoiceCare

Susan Smyth
Smyth Management Resources

BRIEF
CONTENTS

CONTENTS

APPENDIX C;
HOW TO DESIGN A CUSTOMER SATISFACTION
MEASUREMENT PROGRAM   253

1

Complacency: Success Sows the Insidious Seeds of Failure

"American workers are illiterate and lazy."
—*Yoshio Sakurauchi, Speaker of the Japanese House of Representatives*

Virtually every aspect of the business environment is experiencing accelerating change, particularly the consumers, customers, technology, and globalization of markets. The increasingly turbulent environment places a severe penalty on complacent management, as knowledge of all types is subject to rapid obsolescence and erosion. Out of this chaos, maximizing delivered customer value is emerging as the dominant success factor.

Is Mr. Sakurauchi correct? Are all, or even a significant portion of, American workers lazy and illiterate? The answer to both questions is an emphatic "No!" American workers are clearly among the most productive in the world, based on labor productivity statistics, although the differences between the United States, Germany, and Japan are minor. The United States has had the best educational system in the world for the past 140 years. Public education in the United States is more comprehensive and accessible than in any other country in the world. Our leading academic institutions attract students from all over the world, including Japan. Would Japanese

1

students study in U.S. universities if our schools were so bad? Of course not!

Is Japan, instead then, the cause of our current economic malaise? The answer is also an emphatic "No!" For the most part, Japan bashing is unwarranted. Sure, Japan has protected industries through tariff and nontariff barriers and that protectionism has hurt some industries in the United States, most notably the auto industry. However, most of the auto industry's problems are a result of years of poor managerial decisions that have only recently been corrected. The plain truth is that Japan's trade balance with the United States is a minor, but highly visible, issue in the overall economic scheme of things. We must remember that the Japanese economy is about half the size of the U.S. economy. To have balance of trade equality, per capita consumption of U.S. imports in Japan would need to be twice the level of per capita consumption of Japanese imports in the United States. That is a very unrealistic scenario.

What country consistently ran a balance of trade surplus with its trading partners for about 100 years? What country is the source of the largest amount of foreign direct investment in the world? What country continually bought and controlled assets throughout the world? What country is viewed by its trading partners as having a complex array of protectionistic barriers? What country provides extensive protection for its domestic agricultural industry? What country has extensive protectionistic barriers to assist its auto industry? What country grants hundreds of millions of dollars to its domestic industries to assist in export activities? The answer to these questions is neither Japan nor Germany. The answer to these questions is the United States.

We Americans certainly don't view our economic activities as being detrimental to other countries. The United States played an important role in the reconstruction of Europe and Asia after World War II. Former Prime Minister Miyazawa acknowledged that Japan's current economic prosperity is due largely to U.S. postwar assistance. The current economic boom in Mexico is due largely to U.S. activities. Much of Canada's economic development was due to U.S. investment. Much of the economic growth in Southeast Asia is due to access to U.S. markets. The same could be said of many industrial economies. The current trade situation between the United States and Japan is only slightly different from the traditional trade position of the United States with many countries, and the trade imbalance with Japan has been, by historical standards, very brief. Most of us can recall back to the 1960s and early

1970s, when "made in Japan" was synonymous with cheap, low-quality merchandise. Overall, the United States did not damage the economies of its trading partners. Japan is not the cause of economic problems in the United States; Japan is merely a convenient whipping boy.

COMPLACENCY IS THE ENEMY

The root cause of most problems facing business is not Japan. Neither is the problem caused by laziness and illiteracy as Mr. Sakurauchi contends, although he is not far off the mark. The fundamental cause of our current economic malaise is found within each of us to some degree. It is found in our schools, in our government, and in our businesses. It is something that can be cured, but there is no apparent quick fix. The fundamental, root cause of most problems facing organizations is the pervasive complacency of workers and managers.

If we subscribe to the view that things around us are static, that we have arrived, that this is the "best of all possible worlds," as Voltaire would say, then there would be no need to change, to improve. Unfortunately, if we buy into such a static view, we are as out of touch with reality as Cervantes's Don Quixote was by chasing imaginary knights. Not only is change certain, but it also appears that an *accelerating* rate of change is even more certain. Complacency, among us as individuals or organizations, is guaranteed to lead to mediocrity. If we don't change as rapidly as other countries, as rapidly as our competitors, as rapidly as the environment, we will simply fall farther and farther behind. We won't be getting any *worse* at what we do; we simply won't be getting better fast enough. And not getting better will absolutely, positively lead to economic decline for us individually, for our businesses, and for our economy.

The *American Heritage Dictionary* defines "complacency" as "contentment to a fault; self-satisfaction." Examples of how contentment to a fault can lead to mediocrity illustrate why complacency is such a fundamental problem.

Complacency in Business Schools

There are about 1,300 colleges and universities in the United States that grant business degrees in one form or another. Of those 1,300, about 20 percent are accredited by the American Assembly of Collegiate Schools of Business (AACSB). AACSB accreditation is commonly viewed as a stamp of approval that a program meets a minimum quality level. Unfortunately, the accreditation criteria evolved very slowly over the period from 1975 to 1990, certainly much more slowly than the rapidly changing business environment.

The result was that by the late 1980s, many of the accredited business schools were teaching topics that were necessary for accreditation but of little relevance to real-world businesses. And the situation was even worse in most business programs that were not AACSB accredited. This gap between academia and business practice led to a good deal of controversy in the popular press regarding business education.

One pervasive problem is that universities are not well suited for rapid change. Promotion and tenure guidelines normally reward publication in accepted journals, not innovative, applied research. Changing a business curriculum significantly is a process that takes years in most universities: There are departmental, college, and university committees that must approve changes. When finally approved, changes appear in the next catalog, often a year later. And then the changes are often phased in over several years.

The same situation exists in in the field of college textbooks. Texts in a subject area evolve incrementally. Radically different texts don't sell well because they normally don't fit with an instructor's traditional approach to a course.

For example, a recent (1992) survey of the best M.B.A. programs found that, on average, quality issues were discussed for one or two weeks in one class—normally a production management class of some type. Quality was generally neglected as a topic of discussion in other classes. Recently, the dean of one of the most respected and well-known M.B.A. programs in the United States was asked where quality was addressed in the program. His response? "I'm not sure. In the production class, I think."

Unfortunately, many business graduates of both graduate and undergraduate programs feel that they have arrived when they get their degree. Many graduates feel that their business knowledge will last them for years. Most graduates do not understand how fast an existing, "current" knowledge base will become obsolete—typically within five to ten years, especially for M.B.A. graduates. A colleague who received a doctorate in business ten years ago from a well-recognized university decided recently that the knowledge acquired in that doctoral program was now 90 percent obsolete. Micron Technology, a computer chip manufacturer, feels that workers' "current" knowledge base has about a four-year life in Micron's rapidly changing industry. What graduates of bachelor's, master's, and doctoral programs must understand is the need to continually replenish their knowledge base, to recognize that complacency will render their knowledge base obsolete very quickly.

Complacency in Business

Business success tends to reinforce complacency. Those businesses that were successful in the 1960s and 1970s tended to reinforce the things that made them successful during that period of time. Managers who did well by those standards were promoted, not for the radical changes they made, but for doing things "the right way." Corporate cultures emerged that reinforced the appropriate way to do things. Very few individuals, even at the CEO level, could make significant, short-term changes in the corporate culture. It is far more common for the individual to adapt to the corporate culture, which, in most firms, changes very slowly. If you examined the Fortune 500 from 50 years ago, you'd find that over 50 percent of those firms no longer exist in their previous form. Some have gone bankrupt, many have been acquired by stronger firms, some were liquidated in one way or another, and some have simply atrophied. The common trait that most of these corporate casualties shared was the inability to adapt to or anticipate environmental change. Their corporate cultures reinforced complacency—the status quo. The environment simply passed them by.

The firms that survived were better able to change and adapt. Their corporate cultures were less tolerant of complacency. Some even encouraged creativity and innovation. Pursuing that logic a bit further, the firms that performed at the top of their industry did so because they were not complacent: they tended to seek new products, new markets, new production techniques, new organization structures (usually flatter), and new ways of managing. In a word, the industry leaders were responsive. Somehow they overcame the trap of complacency. Somehow they identified the emerging new trends.

Complacency at Xerox

Xerox, one of the 1989 Malcolm Baldrige National Quality Award winners, perfected and then overcame complacency. Without question, Xerox created an industry, owned the market, and set the standards by which all products were compared. For about 15 years, Xerox was simply unbeatable; it dominated the industry. But its overwhelming success sowed the insidious seeds of complacency. Xerox paid only superficial attention to customers; product quality remained unchanged; and the rate of innovation slowed. Why bring out new products quickly to replace old ones? After all, those old products had produced handsome profits. Xerox pursued the nonsensical strategy of "milking cash cows." The best word to describe Xerox's corporate culture was "complacent."

During the mid-1970s, Japanese competitors entered the market. Xerox initially shrugged the competition off. There was no need to worry about those distant, low-quality, low-price competitors. Remember—the prevailing view at that time was that "made in Japan" was synonymous with low quality in most industries. Certainly mighty Xerox didn't have to worry about those competitors at the bottom end of the market. Losing market share in low-price, low-margin products didn't have much effect on profits anyway. For more than five years, the competition gained market share, ratcheting up the product mix with higher-price, higher-margin products. And Xerox was asleep at the wheel.

The wake-up call for Xerox came in 1981. Xerox had lost over 50 percent of its market share in the previous five years, but profits in 1980 remained strong due to the number of copiers in place and the sales of top-end machines. Profits in 1981 fell almost 50 percent, a decline of $500 million to $600 million. CEO David Kearns finally acknowledged that status quo business as usual would be completely unacceptable.

Unlike at most firms, the solution to Xerox's complacency came from within. At the time, a Fuji-Xerox joint venture in Japan had just won the Deming Quality Award. After an initial evaluation, top management at Xerox decided that adopting a similar corporate-wide quality focus was probably a pretty good idea. In 1983, Xerox formally launched its Leadership Through Quality program.

The program consisted of six major elements: First, an executive-level transition team was created to oversee implementation of the program. Second, all of Xerox's 100,000 employees had to complete quality improvement training. Third, management behavior had to become proactive and customer oriented and had to encourage innovations that improved customer satisfaction. Fourth, employee empowerment and involvement had to happen to achieve real cultural change. Fifth, an open environment that encouraged the free flow of communication in all directions, including communication with customers, was necessary.

Sixth, a performance appraisal, reward, and recognition system that reinforced customer-oriented quality improvement was created. Xerox's success at overcoming complacency through this program is evidenced by the fact that only six years after starting the quality focus, Xerox won the 1989 Baldrige award.

Xerox now has regained the number one position in all six major segments in the copier industry. From 1985 to 1989, Xerox's customer satisfaction level increased 38 percent. The 1990 goal was to achieve "satisfied" or "very satisfied" ratings from 90 percent of its 2.2 million customers around the world. The 1991 goal was 94 percent, and the 1993 goal was 100 percent satisfied customers!

Many are undoubtedly skeptical of a goal of "100% customer satisfaction." It is probably simply a marketing gimmick—good fodder for the corporate public relations folks. Wrong! Some business units within Xerox achieved and maintained 100 percent customer satisfaction in 1990, well ahead of the 1993 corporate target.

Complete customer satisfaction is attainable in a responsive, innovative firm. The dominant market position that accompanies it is also attainable. High levels of customer satisfaction are *not* attainable by a firm that is mired in the status quo approach to management. Complacent firms will never respond quickly enough.

Was Xerox's real enemy the competition? Was it those Japanese firms? No! The competition simply exploited a weakness that had resulted from Xerox's complacency. Was the turnaround at Xerox a miracle, something few firms could hope to achieve? Of course not. Such thinking is nonsense! Thousands of American firms excel, are very responsive to customers, and can compete head-to-head with the Japanese or the Germans. Unfortunately, the majority of the 15 million businesses in the United States are complacent to some degree and are not really customer driven. The easy response is self-denial, to use foreign competition as the scapegoat, and to clamor for more protectionistic barriers. The real enemy lies in the pervasive complacency that dwells within each of us and that permeates far too many businesses. Success and long-term survival will come only to those firms that learn how to overcome and conquer the real enemy.

Other examples of complacent firms abound: the primary cause of problems at IBM, General Motors, and Sears is complacency. Those firms, over a number of years, failed to change and adapt as fast as the environment and the competition did. Now they face the unenviable task of changing faster than the competition just to catch up. And such rapid change is always a very painful process in organizations.

COMPLACENCY IS MORE OF A PROBLEM THAN EVER

The price of complacency has skyrocketed. In ancient times in business (the 1960s and 1970s), a firm could get away with a status quo approach to management. Compared to today, that was a period of relative tranquillity. However, the rate of change accelerated during the 1980s. Corporate bankruptcies, mergers and acquisitions, and declining profits were the rewards bestowed upon firms for their complacency. The most frightening prospect for many managers is what the 1990s and beyond will be like. As Jack Welch, CEO at General Electric, noted, "Compared to the 1990s, the 1980s were a cakewalk." And the business environment beyond 2000 will be even more challenging.

Three predominant, environmental areas have led to the turbulent, chaotic environment of the 1990s: the rapid changes in consumers and customers, technology, and globalization increased the cost for complacent management. And these areas show no sign of slowing; indeed, every indication suggests that the rate of change in these areas will accelerate.

Consumers and Customers

The most significant impetus for a shift in management orientation is clearly the change in consumers. Consumers in industrialized countries worldwide are older, better educated, more informed, and far more demanding than ever before. Consumers lack tolerance for products that fail to meet their expectations. Brand loyalty is valid for consumers only as long as their expectations are met. Fail to deliver product quality or service quality, and few consumers will display allegiance; they will simply switch to a competitor's products. These trends are certainly evident in the United States, but they are equally evident in all industrialized economies. With only a few exceptions found in countries such as states of the former Soviet Union, consumers globally have very significantly increased their economic power.

These changes are not restricted to consumers though. The term "customers" often includes those channel intermediaries or organizations that buy products. Organizations are more and more demanding of their suppliers, just as consumers are. As many organizations reduce the numbers of suppliers, the evaluative criteria are far more sophisticated. For example, British Petroleum (BP) drastically reduced the number of its suppliers for its Prudhoe Bay operation in Alaska. A key factor in the supplier reduction process was the supplier's commitment to total quality management. Whereas in the past suppliers were wary and distrustful of one another, they must now work closely together to optimize delivered value to BP. The remaining suppliers not only had to be committed to continuous quality improvement, but they each also had to view themselves as part of a supplier "team." Five years ago, such practices were almost unthinkable.

The consumers and customers—whether individuals or organizations—will continue to be innovative, creative, and more demanding of business. Much of this change is due to the mushrooming supply of information made available by technological advances.

Technology

The ubiquitous spread of technology permeates and shapes every aspect of business. Technology has changed *how we manage business*. We need fewer managers as computing power enables data to be processed into usable information that is easily diffused throughout the organization. No longer can managers maintain their power base by simply controlling the flow of information. The dispersion of information and the technological advances in telecommunications have resulted in changed, flatter, more decentralized organizational structures. Worker empowerment and increased participatory decision making flow more from the effective utilization of technological advances than from any other factor.

Technology has changed *what we produce*. The use of synthetic materials and the applications of computer technology influence virtually every industry, be it cameras, clothing, electronics, health care, or grocery items. Five- to ten-year-old "state-of-the-art" products in virtually any industry are still functional but technologically obsolete by current standards. Ten years ago, hypalon, a tough, heavy material, was the fabric of choice for white-water rafts. Today, rafts are made of synthetics that are lighter, stronger, just as durable, and less expensive. Kayaks used to be made of fiberglass; now they are plastic or Kevlar composites. The current high-quality cameras make the 35-mm single-lens-reflex models of ten years ago look like antiques. The light, powerful camcorders of today bear little resemblance to the big, bulky, VHS recorders of only a few years ago.

The continuous, accelerating spread of technology drastically shortens product life cycles. Competitors are often able to quickly clone technological breakthroughs and put competing products on the market in a few months. Successful products in Germany or Japan find their way quickly to the United States or vice versa. The differences in technological choice between one country and another have largely evaporated. The same, or very similar, products can be found throughout the world. The ability to milk a technological breakthrough throughout its product life cycle is a historical myth, a vestige of 1970s and 1980s thinking in business.

Technology has changed *how we produce things*. Computer-assisted design, computer-assisted manufacturing, and flexible manufacturing systems have caused the end of much mass manufacturing. As manufacturing economic order quantities approach one, customization to perfectly match customer needs has become common. Take, for example, the National Bicycle Industrial Company in Kokubu, Japan. A customer can get a custom-fitted bicycle based on that customer's measurements, intended use, and price range. The customer pays only about a 10 percent price premium and can have delivery within two weeks. The same customization is already available in rifles and fly rods in the United States. In the 1990s and beyond, such customization to perfectly match customer needs will become commonplace. The enabling factor is technology.

Technology has changed *the way we sell things*. Mass advertising is becoming less important because there are cheaper, more effective ways of reaching increasingly fragmented market segments. The proliferation of internal customer databases and external databases of potential customers allows more clearly focused, customized promotional campaigns. Personalized direct contact with customers will promote interactive, long-term relationships, not the one-shot transaction view that still predominates.

Technological advances mean more than issuing sales representatives a laptop computer for good record keeping and customer databases. Using technology also means that the laptop will have a modem and interactive software so that customers' questions and problems can be solved quickly. Customization will be achieved by sales reps' offering superior service by their development of creative solutions to customer needs.

Technological advances permeate virtually every aspect of every business and our daily life. As consumers, all we have to do to find new technological applications is to walk through our home. Our dishwashers and ovens often have computer controls, and our microwaves and other appliances are even much more advanced. Personal home computers, printers, VCRs, compact disc players, Nintendo games, handheld computer games, and television remote controls are far different from those of five or ten years ago. And the rate of change will absolutely, positively increase as a result of the increasingly competitive business environment. The accumulated base of knowledge in the world will double in the next 10–20 years. Product life cycles will continue to get shorter. Speed to market will become even more important. Customers will be faced with a continually wider array of product choices. Competition will be even more intense and the winners will be those firms that learn quickest how to use technology to satisfy customers' needs.

Globalization

In addition to changes in consumers and technology, global economic integration is the third major factor that has shifted power squarely into the hands of the consumer. Stated quite simply, consumers in every industrialized economy are faced with a diverse array of product choices. Increasingly, the product choices include those products produced either in a foreign country or by a domestic firm based in a foreign country. However, country of origin is of concern only to politicians and beleaguered executives in noncompetitive industries. Consumers are displaying an increasing disregard for the place where a product is made. Consumers worldwide are seeking to maximize the value they get whether they are spending dollars, pounds, francs, deutsche marks, yen, or won.

The annual rate of growth in international trade is more than twice the average rate of economic growth within industrialized countries. Stated differently, international trade is becoming more and more important to every industrialized country, a trend that will continue indefinitely and will eventually overwhelm protectionistic sentiments. An open flow of trade is in everyone's best interest. Ironically, international trade has increased the economic gap between the rich and the poor countries.

What is traded internationally has changed considerably in the past 25 years. The big changes in merchandise trade consist of the relative decline of food products and primary commodities and the big increase in manufactured goods, which now constitute about 70 percent of all merchandise trade. The decline in food and agricultural products has negatively impacted both the United States, which has rich agricultural resources, and the less developed countries reliant on specific crops as countries became more self-sufficient. The big decline in primary commodities, such as copper, lead, zinc, and silver, has hurt less developed countries that traditionally exported their natural resources. Use of synthetic materials has displaced the need for primary commodities in many industries. However, the biggest change in world trade is clearly the huge increase in manufactured goods, which has benefited both industrialized and newly industrialized countries, particularly those in Asia. From a consumer's viewpoint, the increase in manufactured goods simply means a wider array of competitive products from which to choose.

As you might suspect from these trends, industrialized economies are capturing a larger portion of world trade—over 70 percent in 1990. This has resulted in a concentration of world economic growth in the industrialized countries. The four largest economies account for 60 percent of world gross domestic product (GDP) (U.S., Japan, Germany, and France). The ten largest economies (add the United Kingdom, Italy, China, Russia, Brazil, and Canada) account for 70 percent of world gross national product. The remaining 230 or so countries divide the rest of world GDP, and the Asian newly industrialized countries capture a good portion of it.

Although the figures are ambiguous at best, international trade in services is growing faster than merchandise trade and now is estimated at about 30 percent of world trade flows. As the largest and most advanced service economy, the United States has an obvious comparative advantage in international services. But the U.S. service industry is not immune from foreign competition. Examining world financial flows is a real eye-opener. Currently, world trade in goods and services is about $3 trillion annually. However, the annual volume of international currencies traded is estimated at about $75 trillion annually, 25 times greater than trade in goods and services. The annual volume of foreign exchange transactions is about $35 trillion, ten times greater than merchandise trade. The implication is clear: Capital movements are causing industrialized economies to become increasingly integrated. Merchandise and service trade will follow the same trend, although more slowly than capital, which knows no nationality.

SUMMARY

In the face of such rapid, turbulent changes in the business environment, complacency of any type will lead first to mediocrity and then failure. The increased speed of technological change has dramatically shortened product life cycles. Concepts such as milking a product throughout the product life cycle and planned obsolescence are archaic vestiges of a different business environment.

Increasing global competition virtually ensures that a window of technological superiority will be short-lived. Sustaining a competitive advantage based only on technical superiority will not guarantee long-term success. Customers simply demand more and more of their suppliers, regardless of where they are in the supply chain.

As increased competition fuels commensurate increases in the expectations of customers, the penalty for complacency grows. The real danger is in thinking of complacency only in technological terms, say, measuring the rate of product modifications or new product introductions. Complacency is far more pervasive than that.

Every aspect of the business must continually be reevaluated, in the search for a better, more efficient way to operate. Business must realize that *all* managerial knowledge is subject to obsolescence and must develop a culture that encourages and rewards change instead of fighting it every step of the way.

The key success factors are shifting, from having an efficient, well-managed firm to having a creative, innovative, responsive firm that tries to anticipate the market and the customers years in advance. These more enlightened firms realize that the ultimate measure of success consists of delivering better value to the customer than the competition and that that value is much more than just product quality.

APPLICATION IDEAS

1. Examine the mission statement and major operating policies of your organization. Do these statements reinforce the traditional way of doing things? Or do they encourage creativity, innovation, and change? Have these documents changed as the environment changed?
2. Has the training and development budget remained constant? Are the training programs about the same as a few years ago? Or has the commitment to training and composition of training programs kept pace with the changing environment?

3. How have the needs and expectations of your consumers or customers changed in the past several years? Does your organization simply react to changes? Or does it proactively anticipate changes in the customer? Does your organization have a formal system for using customer expectations to drive organizational change? Or does change just gradually happen?

4. What changes has technology made in how your organization is managed, what is produced, and how your products are sold? Does your organization actively seek out new technology to improve? Or does the organization wait until the current technology is fully depreciated? What technological changes will impact your customers? How will those changes alter or influence your business?

5. How do the changes in global competition influence your organization? What threats or opportunities are presented by the accelerating rate of global economic integration? How does your organization increase the global awareness of employees?

2

The Customer Value Triad: Product Quality Alone Is Not Enough

"Product Quality and Service Quality are the pillars that support Value-based Prices."

The most important success factor for a firm is the ability to deliver better customer value than the competition. Good customer value can be achieved only when product quality, service quality, and value-based prices are in harmony and exceed customer expectations. Delivering only good product quality will never guarantee survival.

The environment in which business operates is far more turbulent, chaotic, and rapidly changing than ever before. Those big, beautiful mass markets are being shattered into fragments and splinter groups. Customers in every niche are less tolerant, less forgiving, less loyal. Their product expectations are soaring to ever higher levels—levels many managers feel are totally unrealistic.

Technological change simply makes matters worse. There is always a new material, new machine tool, and new computer hardware and software with more capability. The new product breakthrough of six months ago is now being cloned by competitors. It feels like somebody turned up the speed on the treadmill. You run

15

faster and faster, but you just aren't going anywhere. If you slow down, though, you'll be thrown off, left behind by the constant changes.

And then there is the competition. A few years ago, you knew who most of the competitors were, but every year now there are more competitors trying to steal your customers. The Germans and the Japanese have been there for quite a while, but nowadays there are firms from Taiwan and Korea that have an unfair advantage by virtue of their lower labor costs. There are those "maquilladoras"—manufacturing firms—located just across the border in Mexico, where the workers are paid one or two bucks an hour with almost no fringe benefits. And there is even more competition from within the United States, in the form of those pesky start-up firms that have low overhead and are willing to accept those low profit margins. And firms from another city or another state are trying to steal your customers. You long for the good old days.

Remember the era of "strategic planning"? You simply evaluated the environment, set those long-term goals, and allocated your resources based on financial formulas. You used your three- or four-year sales forecast as input to those formulas, feeling pretty comfortable with the results. Now you worry about a 12-month forecast!

What is the appropriate response to such a bewildering but common-place situation? Is it *more* marketing and advertising, simply cranking up the volume? Is it more couponing and discounting, simply shaving prices and margins? The answer is an emphatic "No!" That is what Peter Drucker refers to as "doing things right." You can do a great job of advertising, or couponing, or price cutting. Unfortunately, doing these "things right" is very different from doing the "right things."

THE CUSTOMER VALUE TRIAD

The "right thing" for the 1990s and beyond should be the dominant, overarching goal of business. The number one goal of business should be to "maximize customer value and strive to increase value continuously." If a firm maximizes customer value, relative to competitors, success will follow. If a firm's products are viewed as conveying little customer value, the firm will eventually atrophy and fail.

Whereas there are prerequisites to maximizing customer value, there is no single quick-fix, easy solution. No simple series of steps will cure complacency and create customer value. Maximizing customer value must flow from a firm's culture, beliefs, values, management style, re-

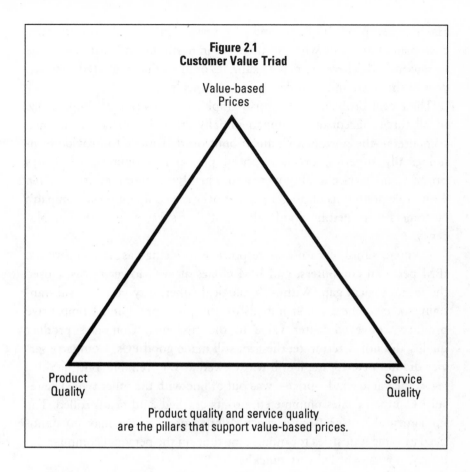

Figure 2.1
Customer Value Triad

Value-based
Prices

Product
Quality

Service
Quality

Product quality and service quality
are the pillars that support value-based prices.

ward systems, and structure. Some of the ways of achieving customer value are addressed in detail in later chapters of this book. First, we must identify the ingredients of customer value.

As a concept, customer value is fairly simple. But since it is defined by the customer, it is inherently ambiguous. The Customer Value Triad (Figure 2.1) consists of only three things: product quality, service quality, and value-based prices. Customer value is created when customer expectations in each of the three areas are met or exceeded. Fail to meet customer expectations in any one of the three areas, and you have not delivered good customer value.

Product quality and service quality are the foundation that supports price. Produce poor-quality products, and the value-based price will fall. Provide lousy service, and the value-based price will fall. Set prices too high for a given level of product and service quality, and sales will suffer.

Having great product quality and poor service quality will not maximize customer value. Only when all three are in harmony will customer value be maximized. There are many examples of firms that neglected some aspect of the triad and paid dearly for their neglect.

The recent problems at Compaq graphically illustrate the importance of all three ingredients. Compaq initially created a niche in personal computers—the portable. Compaq built on that niche to provide technologically superior, premium-priced personal computers. Compaq's product and service quality were good, justifying premium prices. Even with price premiums of 30–35 percent over the competition's, Compaq's customers were getting good value. But that success spawned complacency.

Compaq simply was not as responsive to change as its competitors. IBM personal computers, and IBM clones at even lower prices, closed the technological gap. With technological superiority gone, or substantially so, customers could not justify the price premium. Competitive products conveyed better value to the customer. Compaq's product quality did not deteriorate; the firm still made good PCs. Compaq's service did not deteriorate; it still was viewed as very reliable. But the third leg of the value triad—price—was out of line with the other two. The result? Compaq's sales plummeted, profits crashed, and heads rolled. The fundamental cause? Complacency. While complacency may go unnoticed in some industries for quite some time, in the personal computer industry, it gets exposed very quickly.

Product Quality and Service Quality are Inseparable to the Customer
The customer value triad applies to virtually every type of business—even government organizations. Although product quality has received a good deal of attention in the past ten years, almost every tangible product has some service associated with it in some fashion, even a product as mundane as a pack of gum or a candy bar. If we find a stick of gum that doesn't meet our expectations, a small percentage of us will complain but the vast majority will not. However, the manufacturer should plan a response for those who do complain. This is not the primary application of service for this mundane product though. In order for that pack of gum to get to the vending machine, the supermarket, or the convenience store where we bought it, it had to pass through a long, complex distribution channel, and service is a major issue to every one of those channel intermediaries.

Likewise, it is hard to think of a service that doesn't include product quality. A restaurant is certainly a service industry, but does anyone doubt that product quality is important? The same can be said for health care, hospitality and tourism, insurance, and so forth. Virtually every service business has a product as well as related services. Anyone who has ever had a "bad" haircut, hairstyling, or permanent can readily discuss the product quality of a service.

The differences between products and services are not discreet, at least from a customer's viewpoint. The customer tends to roll up into a big bundle the price, product attributes, perceived product quality, service attributes, perceived service quality, and expectations of these variables throughout the product's life and to attach some value to the bundle. The bundle is then compared to competitive alternatives, and the "best value" is selected. Firms that focus on only one or two dimensions of the customer value triad and neglect the third will experience difficulty the way Compaq did. Product quality is necessary to get onto the customer's playing field; it alone is not sufficient to win. Service quality is also a necessary prerequisite, not a guarantee, for success. Pricing strategy must be appropriate given the quality, service, and competitive alternatives.

Back to the Xerox example again: Xerox had problems with two of the three legs of the customer value triad. The quality of Xerox copiers did not deteriorate; in fact, there were product improvements and new product introductions while market position was declining. The *relative* quality of Xerox copiers, compared to competitive products, was declining, however. Competitors not only closed the technological gap but also passed Xerox in some product lines and created a technological gap of their own. Since the relative quality of Xerox copiers had deteriorated, there was no longer any justification for premium prices. Customers exercised their economic power and bought the products that represented the best value. The result for Xerox was a 50 percent loss of market share and a $500-million decline in profits. Once Xerox corrected the problems and maximized customer value, it regained a leadership position in the industry.

THE FIVE BASIC CUSTOMER VALUE LESSONS

There are several lessons to be learned from these examples. The following five lessons apply to virtually any firm in any industry. Firms in rapidly changing industries must learn these lessons very quickly. Firms in stable industries have a bit more time. But eventually every firm in every industry will learn these lessons or pay the high price for complacency.

Lesson One

The customer defines the appropriate product quality, the appropriate service quality, and a reasonable price. If a firm is guessing at what the customer thinks is appropriate, the guess is probably wrong. There is a saying regarding customer expectations that is very appropriate: "In God we trust, all others bring data." It is completely possible to translate customer expectations into usable data. Indeed, it is imperative to do so. Therefore a firm must implement an organized system to capture customer expectations of product quality, service quality, and reasonable price.

Most of the classic product failures have been a result of firms ignoring customer expectations. The Edsel car was produced because Ford wanted to produce it, not because customers expected it. The U.S. auto industry kept producing gas-guzzling V-8 cars because the manufacturers wanted to fully depreciate their factories, not because customers expected them. Coca-Cola introduced New Coke because it wanted to, not because of customer expectations. The list is endless. But every product failure shares the common trait of not meeting the customer's expectations of value.

Lesson Two

The second lesson is that customer expectations are formed relative to competitor alternatives. Simply determining what customers think of *your* products without reference to alternatives really tells you very little. A firm can steadily improve product and service quality and reduce price and still convey less value than competitors. The competitors may simply be improving faster. Such relative standing would not be determined by surveying only your own customers. This is precisely why competitive benchmarking is so important. You must be able to empirically validate what customers—both yours and your competitors'—think of you compared to the competition.

Cadillac provides an example of this lesson. For a number of years, Cadillac surveyed Cadillac owners to determine customer satisfaction. The results were consistently good. It wasn't until Cadillac started surveying potential customers and buyers of other luxury cars that Cadillac realized the competition was getting much faster.

Lesson Three

The third lesson is that customer expectations are dynamic. Surveying your customers once will give a snapshot of one point in time. However, customer expectations continually ratchet upward. The rate of increase is determined largely by competitive activity. If a firm has a monopoly, the rate of technological change is almost totally under control. However, as markets become more competitive, competitors contribute to changes in alternatives, which in turn influences customer expectations. Therefore, determining customer expectations of product quality, service quality, and price—relative to the competition—should be part of a continuous, ongoing program. One-shot, ad hoc investigation of customers will not enable a firm to mold continuous improvement around changing customer expectations.

A public utility (an electric company) had been monitoring customer satisfaction for a number of years. Each year the satisfaction levels steadily decreased even though the firm could document that its quality of service had actually improved each year. But customer expectations were going up faster than the firm was improving, so customer satisfaction levels decreased. Simply maintaining the status quo is unacceptable in today's business environment.

Lesson Four

The fourth lesson is that product and service quality must extend throughout the channel. Upstream, suppliers must adhere to higher and higher quality standards. Downstream, all of the channel intermediaries must be coordinated to deliver maximum value to the end user. Achieving channel coordination is easier in a vertically integrated channel, or in a vertically coordinated channel such as a franchise, but the intermediaries in all types of channels must be committed to maximizing customer value.

Toyota's successful introduction of the Lexus provides an example of how to maximize value to customers in a highly competitive industry. With the European luxury nameplates of Mercedes, BMW, and Porsche; Scandanavia's Volvo and Saab; and North America's Cadillac and Lincoln, the marketplace is fiercely competitive. Who needs another luxury car?

Not only is competition fierce, but the consumer is extremely quality conscious and demanding. The target market for Lexus is 45- to 50-year-old and college-educated consumers with a median income of $160,000. Twenty percent are company presidents or CEOs. Those in this niche are as knowledgeable and demanding as virtually anyone in any segment anywhere.

To successfully penetrate this market, Toyota's Lexus division adopted a customer-driven approach to all three legs of the customer value triad, with particular emphasis on service. Lexus stressed product quality by using a zero defects or six sigma approach to manufacturing quality. The service quality goal was to treat each customer as one would treat a guest in one's home, to pursue the perfect person-to-person relationship, and to strive to improve continually. Maximizing customer value would be achieved by achieving superior product and service quality at a price competitive with the competition. The integrating theme was "The Relentless Pursuit of Perfection."

In the auto industry, the individual dealer is the face of the company. Therefore, Lexus was highly selective in its dealer selection process, evaluating dealers' customer satisfaction performance, management experience, capitalization, and willingness to meet the high standards of luxury. For example, the average dealer spent between $3 million and $5 million on facilities, with 80 percent of the dealers building new facilities.

Lexus assisted dealers with design of the dealership, just as McDonald's offers design expertise to its franchisees. Layout, decor, landscaping, and furnishings were integrated into a high-quality, luxury image. Diagnostic equipment and computer information systems were customized for Lexus and integrated into a national computer database. A dealer can access the full service record of any Lexus sold anywhere in the United States and update the information on that individual car. Dealers are empowered to achieve customer satisfaction on any concern without any prior approval, regardless of the cost.

In 1990, when one customer contacted Lexus twice about a problem, Lexus immediately recalled the LS400 model. Dealers personally contacted most owners and made arrangements for the pickup and repair of their car. If the customer lived more than 100 miles from a dealer, a technician was sent to the customer to perform the work on-site so as to reduce customer inconvenience. In one case, a technician flew from Los Angeles to Anchorage, Alaska, to service a car.

This relentless pursuit of perfection has a direct impact on customer satisfaction. In *Car and Driver*'s annual buyers survey, the LS400 received a score of 9.7, on a 10-point scale—the highest ever for any car. The J. D. Power Quality Survey, conducted during the LS400 recall, rated the Lexus highest of any car. The result? Lexus has established a clear, quality image and captured a significant share of the luxury car market in just a few years by maximizing customer value.

Lesson Five

The fifth lesson is that to maximize customer value through high product and service quality, the whole organization must be involved. Top management rah-rah or directives alone will have little impact. Delegating responsibility to functional departments such as marketing, or sales, or customer service will have only superficial impact. To maximize customer value through product and service quality, everyone in the organization must share responsibility.

Jan Carlzon, energetic CEO of Scandinavian Airline System (SAS), is widely acknowledged as the mastermind behind the spectacular turnaround of the airline. In 1981, SAS was struggling, and the airline lost $8 million. The former CEO resigned and was replaced by Carlzon. Profits for 1983 were $71 million! In less than two years, SAS had experienced an $80-million swing in profits—fortunately, in the right direction.

Very simply, the astounding reversal was accomplished by paying close attention to customers and satisfying their needs fully. Product quality—getting from point A to point B both on time and with your luggage—had improved the best of any European airline. However, service quality is what really distinguished SAS from competitors.

Carlzon coined the term "moments of truth" to capture the continual contacts between customers and SAS. With over 50,000 moments of truth occurring every day, *every* employee, from the reservation agent to the pilots to the CEO, had to be committed to improving service quality. To enable employees to improve service quality, a comprehensive training program was instituted, policies and programs revised, performance and reward systems changed. In essence, the entire organization became extroverted, focusing on the customer.

These five lessons, summarized in Table 2.1, constitute the basic core issues of customer value. All five basic issues must be recognized and explicitly designed by management. If a firm is complacent about any of

Table 2.1 Customer Value Basics

1. The customer defines the appropriate product quality, service quality, and reasonable price.
2. Customer value expectations are formed relative to competitive offerings.
3. Customer value expectations are dynamic, always moving higher.
4. Product quality and service quality are delivered by and are the responsibility of the whole channel, not just the manufacturer.
5. Maximizing customer value requires total organizational involvement and commitment.

the five areas, then maximizing delivered customer value becomes very unlikely. These five issues will be recurring themes throughout the remainder of this book.

BRANDS AND VALUE

Much of the current literature suggests that brands are in decline, a vestige of mass markets. The logic contends that as markets fragment, the importance of brands will be reduced. That is nonsense. As markets fragment and choices proliferate, brands, if nurtured properly, help consumers both determine value and make choices. Essentially, a strong brand is a product that conveys certain value to the customer. Product quality and service quality are assumed, by consumers, to be good and thus worthy of a price premium. Managed properly, brands will become more important in the future. However, a brand is an asset that requires continual replenishment.

Economic Darwinism

Charles Darwin's theories on evolution were highly controversial when introduced and still can be the source of spirited debate. Darwin's theories also may be applied in a business context. At the heart of Darwin's theories was the idea of survival of the fittest. For eons, the earth has been constantly changing and evolving, as most recently evidenced in the retreat of the last ice age. The environmental changes were the fundamental contributor to evolution. Both plants and animals had to change to survive. Those that could not change, for whatever reason, became extinct, going the way of the saber-toothed tiger and the mammoth. The species that survived were those that had evolved most appropriately for the environment, hence the term "survival of the fittest." To Darwin, a rapid change meant one that took place over a period of a few thousand years.

Although the time horizon is considerably shorter—just a few years in some cases, and 30 or 40 at the outside—Darwinism is very applicable to business in general or to brands in particular. The firms that survive over an extended time period are those that change most appropriately to fit the evolving environment. On a narrower business level, the brands that survive are those that are fittest for the new marketplace. If a brand is unfit, based on the survival criteria of customer value, it will become extinct. Let's apply Darwinism to some recent business evolutions and see how well it applies.

AT&T

AT&T, parent of the former Bell Telephone System, went from a virtual monopoly in some products into a highly competitive environment in about ten years. When the Bell System was split up in 1984, only 18 percent of American consumers realized that AT&T was a long-distance phone carrier. Although most of the battles in the long-distance wars involved AT&T, MCI, and Sprint, there are also about 500 other competitors nationwide. In this newly competitive marketplace, AT&T stressed customer value. Quality, integrity, and service were the themes of its promotional campaign. AT&T invested heavily in its promotional effort and in 1989 was fourth-largest advertiser in the United States. Building and sustaining its brand image were necessary to long-term survival. The company had to become adaptive and responsive to rapid changes in the past decade in order to convey customer value. The current financial strength of AT&T is a result of rapid evolution toward the goal of maximizing customer value.

Pillsbury

Pillsbury Dough Products were progressing toward extinction in 1980. Sales of Pillsbury Dough Products (they make those cook-and-serve biscuits), had nearly doubled during the 1960s, peaking in 1970. Competition was low, traditional families sat down to dinner every night, and most women were not employed outside the home. The baby boom consisted of teenagers. But something happened on the way through the 1970s.

More women started working outside the home, family size reduced, dining out became more common, convenience became a concern, and health consciousness emerged. Consumers started buying already baked products that were more convenient. And what was Pillsbury's response to this situation? About the same as that of a dinosaur stuck in the La Brea tar pits! There was much floundering around, but Pillsbury sank deeper and deeper. By 1980, sales had declined 30 percent from 1970, and the dinosaur still couldn't touch bottom.

During 1980 and 1981, Pillsbury Dough Products found the path out of the tar pit. Pillsbury finally recognized the consumer changes, realized competition must be more broadly defined, invested in new technology, and brought out new products supported by increased promotional expenditures. In short, Pillsbury dramatically invested in the brand and improved quality. The result? Sales and profits steadily increased during the 1980s, capped by the 1989 introduction of the firm's most successful new product ever—Cornbread Twists.

Hellmann's Mayonnaise

The food industry provides other examples of economic Darwinism. From 1988 to 1989, new product introductions increased 14 percent. Microwavable foods grew from 278 in 1986 to nearly 1,000 in 1990. The battle for shelf space is intense, with more and more new products trying to dislodge existing products or preempt other new entrants. Yet most new products are not a real commercial success although they may survive for a while. The rapidly changing consumer presents challenges to survival for some products while simultaneously providing boundless opportunities for others. The common denominator of successful products? High customer value.

Hellmann's Mayonnaise, known as Best Foods Mayonnaise west of the Rockies, is the market share leader and is increasing its position. Consistent with the health consciousness of consumers, a new product— Hellmann's Cholesterol Free Mayonnaise—was introduced supported by an initial annual promotional campaign of $15 million. As consumers' health consciousness emerged, Best Foods reduced the cholesterol, fat, and sodium content of its products. Failure to evolve would mean extinction.

ConAgra

ConAgra's frozen prepared food division also demonstrates the ability to rapidly evolve and adapt. ConAgra entered the frozen prepared food market with the acquisition of Banquet Foods—the marketer of TV dinners in 1980. Since 1981, ConAgra has introduced over 300 new frozen prepared foods, 80 percent of which are still on the market—an astounding success rate. Even more amazing is the fact that 25 percent of ConAgra's sales consist of products less than two years old. One of the firm's biggest success stories is its Healthy Choice product line.

After ConAgra's chairman, Mike Harper, suffered a heart attack and had to modify his diet in 1985, he realized the difficulty of maintaining a flavorful, healthy diet. High levels of cholesterol, fat, and sodium eliminated many foods from his consideration, including most Banquet meals at that time. Soon Harper became a champion of healthy, nutritional, flavorful products. And Healthy Choice was the first obvious result.

Healthy Choice entered the premium meal market, a market that had been declining for several years. In late 1990, the category rose over 8 percent (a $2.6-billion market), and Healthy Choice dinners were approaching a 40 percent share after only 12 months on the market. Nutritional products, not even in existence in 1987, represented 25 percent of the premium meals category in 1991 and clearly constitute the fastest-growing segment.

What was happening with the competition while this was going on? The Weight Watchers product line, previously a portion of Heinz's Ore-Ida division, took a direct hit. Much of the share gains at Healthy Choice had come at the expense of Weight Watchers and Stouffer's Red Box. At Ore-Ida, a major corporate restructuring took place. The new Ore-Ida CEO resigned after only about a year on the job and Weight Watchers was spun off as a separate division. The goal was to make Weight Watchers more responsive and innovative due to ConAgra's competitive pressure. The Weight Watchers product line had to become more customer focused and convey increasing customer value or become extinct.

Survival of the Fittest

Examples of economic Darwinism are everywhere: in the food industry, in the auto industry, in the computer industry. Survival of the fittest has never been more appropriate than in the rapidly changing business environment of the 1990s. The fittest is decided by the ever-changing, all-powerful consumer.

The survival of a business is dependent upon delivering higher and higher levels of customer value. Being complacent and content regarding any of the three legs of the customer value triad will place a firm's survival in jeopardy. Product quality must get better because the competition will get tougher and consumer expectations will get higher and higher. Service quality, long neglected by many firms, will become more and more important as consumers become less tolerant. Price must be consistent, from the consumer's perspective, with product and service quality and with competitive offerings. The next three chapters explore each leg of the customer value triad in more detail.

SUMMARY

Delivering high customer value should become a dominant goal for all businesses. The reason for this is very simple: the customer makes decisions based on delivered customer value. In other words, the customer is *imposing* delivered customer value on firms. And failure to respond will lead to loss of competitive position.

Unfortunately, many firms still believe that product quality and customer value are the same thing. Their assumption is that if product quality improves, delivered customer value automatically increases as well. That assumption is fundamentally incorrect and incomplete.

Delivered customer value consists of three things: product quality, service quality, and value-based pricing. Of the three components, only product quality has received much attention. Service quality and value-based pricing have been largely ignored. Firms disappointed with the market results of their quality improvement efforts have probably neglected service quality and value-based pricing. All three areas must be in harmony, from the customer's perspective.

There are five key issues related to the concept of customer value. First, the customer defines what is or is not good value. This is at the heart of being customer driven. The customer's perceptions and expectations in all three areas must be clearly understood and quickly acted upon.

Second, the customer's expectations for all three areas are strongly influenced by competitive alternatives. The more competitive a particular industry, the stronger the competitive influence on the customer's development of expectations. Hence, a firm *must* conduct customer-based, competitive benchmarking.

Third, customer expectations of good value are dynamic and always increasing. What is good value this year may be totally unacceptable in only a year or two. Therefore, a firm must continually measure the customer's perceptions of value (usually called "customer satisfaction measurement") and use the data to drive continuous improvement efforts.

Fourth, few firms fully control all value-added activities. Virtually all firms rely on suppliers and/or downstream intermediaries. Therefore, all members of the value-added chain must work together to maximize delivered customer value to the end user. The survival of each channel member depends on the collective success of *all* channel members. Channel partnerships and alliances are becoming mandatory.

Fifth, delivering high customer value is the responsibility of the entire organization; it cannot be delegated to one or two departments. Therefore, *all* employees must become customer focused, understanding exactly how each job contributes to customer value. This usually requires a significant change in corporate culture.

Only when a firm has successfully integrated all three components of customer value and recognized the importance of these five issues will market leadership be achieved. And these concepts are precisely what the rest of this book is about.

APPLICATION IDEAS

1. How does the delivered value of your organization's products compare to competitive alternatives? Do the organization's perceptions of delivered value match those of the customer?
2. Has your organization developed an explicit strategy to improve all three legs of the customer value triad? Or has the focus been predominantly on one portion, such as price cutting or improving tangible product quality?
3. Does your organization have a specific strategy to address each of the five concepts in Table 2.1? Or does the organization simply react when it is forced to do so?
4. Which legs of the customer value triad are changing most rapidly in your industry? Which legs hold the greatest potential for creating a comparative advantage over your competitors?

3

The Quality Imperative: Creating Value through Product Quality

"Quality is when our customers come back and our products don't."
    —*Siemens quality motto*

High product quality is no longer sufficient to create a competitive advantage—that era has passed. But high quality is absolutely essential to deliver good customer value, and customers have come to expect high product quality as a minimum requirement. And product quality, as a concept, is becoming far more complex than a simple "good" or "bad" continuum. There are now several ways of categorizing quality attributes.

Of the three elements of the customer value triad, product quality has received the most attention by far over the past ten years. Quality gurus have become well-known throughout the world—Deming, Juran, Crosby, Ishikawa—each touting the virtues of their approach to quality improvement. The quality movement was easily the most important strategic issue of the 1980s and has been probably the most important business concept of the past 20 or 30 years.

Yet, despite the acknowledged importance of the total quality management (TQM) approach, amazingly few firms—probably less than 10 percent of all businesses—have embraced quality as a strategic, cultural philosophy. Instead, most firms continue to pursue the traditional business-as-usual approach, making small incremental changes and evolving very slowly. And some firms still view the quality movement as a fad that will eventually go away.

THE AVERAGE FIRM

The average, business-as-usual firm might be described as follows. Over the past ten years, sales have steadily increased, and, although the firm is profitable, profit margins have become narrower and narrower. The primary cause of the lower profit margins is the increasingly intense price pressure by competitors. There are more and more competitors battling for market share in a slow growth market. In order to hit break-even points, it seems everyone is willing to sell for less and less, so the firm simply has no choice but to follow the trend and shave margins.

The quality of products is relatively good, due largely to the experienced workforce and modern production processes. Since the employee turnover rate is pretty low, the average number of years of experience for each production worker is well above the industry mean and everyone receives about a week of training each year. With regard to the capital base, the firm has been very committed to steadily improving its technology with new and better tooling and computer applications.

The quality standard for each individual operation is higher than 99 percent (about four sigma), which seems pretty good. After all, everyone makes mistakes once in a while. It is troubling to the firm that about 15 percent of sales goes to reworking and correcting errors, however. The vast majority of defects are stopped by quality control inspections and corrected internally so they don't usually reach the customers, but defects are still a problem. The firm has heard about Zero Defects and Six Sigma quality efforts but feels such programs are unrealistic. While Zero Defects and Six Sigma may work in certain precision production situations, this firm's products have too much variability.

Once reason that quality can't be changed much is the suppliers, who collectively constitute about 50 percent of total value added. To keep from becoming too dependent on just a few suppliers, the firm has a general policy that multiple sources most items. Unfortunately, the suppliers produce at various quality levels, and keeping them straightened out is a real challenge. As a result, incoming products are also subject to quality control inspection. One of the sources of finished product defects has been the components and subassemblies purchased from suppliers, despite the quality control checks.

The firm has been soliciting customer satisfaction information for a number of years. Response to its ten-question survey sent to customers once a year has been disappointing at times, but about 85 percent of customers appear satisfied. External benchmarking of customer satisfaction is something that the firm would like to do, but the tight budgets of the past few years have precluded funding the project. The firm loses about 15–20 percent of its customers each year, but management prefers to be optimistic and look at the bright side of the picture: 80–85 percent of customers are retained each year despite the intense competition.

Over the years this firm has consistently tried to hire the best workers at all organization levels. Salaries are at or above the industry average, and profit-sharing incentives have been implemented to encourage employee buy-in. The firm has consistently updated its capital base so it won't fall behind technologically. Yet the firm remains just average.

The firm's market share, financial performance, and product quality are all acceptable but not spectacular. The primary concerns of top management are externally oriented, toward the competitive environment. As profit margins narrowed, management embarked on a cost-cutting campaign, complete with some layoffs and managerial downsizing. But profits still haven't improved much yet.

This firm could be typical of those in almost any industry. It could be in light or heavy manufacturing, in construction, or in services, such as insurance or banking. It could be in the airline industry or in forest products or in food processing. It really doesn't make much difference, because the average firms—those stuck in the middle—are about the same in any industry.

STRATEGIC REASONS TO PURSUE TOTAL QUALITY

The average firm has not fully embraced the TQM concept although its product quality has probably improved. Failure to adopt the total quality approach is a strategic weakness for several reasons. First, the leading firms in many industries are pursuing six sigma quality. Thus, the competitors of those leading firms will be at a competitive disadvantage. Second, as quality improves, costs and cycle times typically go down.

Hence, quality pays. And third, fully embracing quality improvement requires that the voice of the customer be heard. Therefore, customer-driven quality improvement is absolutely essential.

Six Sigma Quality

The first strategic reason to pursue total quality is competitively based, and high product quality is the necessary ticket for admission to the dance. High-quality products don't guarantee success, but low-quality products guarantee failure. If product quality is not up to customer expectations, the firm is assured of mediocrity, at best. And the four sigma quality of the average firm is no better than average in any industry. But in most industries there is one firm, possibly the industry leader, that has fully adopted a total quality approach and is stalking five or six sigma quality.

The quality differences between four and six sigma can be shocking. First, some basic definitions are necessary. A sigma is a standard deviation around a mean of some type. If the mean is designed to be perfect quality, a four sigma quality standard means that the acceptable quality limits range from four standard deviations below the mean to four standard deviations above the mean as depicted in Figure 3.1. If the process is normally distributed, a common assumption, then 99.7 percent of the production will fall within the acceptable quality limits. You might reach the conclusion that that is pretty good quality. And it would be if you had a product that was simple and took only one operation to produce.

Unfortunately, few products are that simple. The average television set requires completion of about a thousand different operations, counting all components and subassemblies from installing a screw to manufacturing a picture tube. If each operation were performed at four sigma quality, which again is pretty average, a minority of television sets would be defect free. The reason for that low quality level is that the overall quality level is the multiplicative result of each individual operation.

If a product requires a hundred parts or operations to complete, the quality standard must be multiplied times itself a hundred times. With the number of opportunities for error (parts, operations, etc.), a chart such as Table 3.1 can be developed. Table 3.1 assumes that a process mean has shifted slightly (1.5 standard deviations) but is still well within the quality control limits—a fairly realistic assumption since few processes stay in perfection.

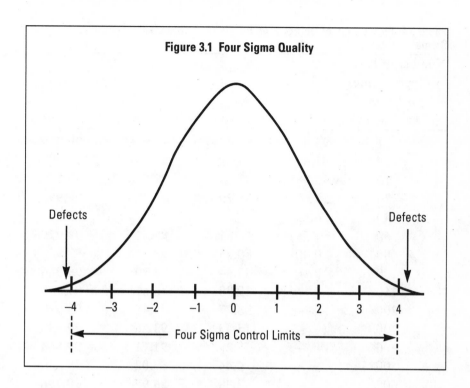

Figure 3.1 Four Sigma Quality

Defects   Defects

−4   −3   −2   −1   0   1   2   3   4

←——————— Four Sigma Control Limits ———————→

Back to the television set again. At three sigma quality and assuming a thousand parts or opportunities for error, no TVs are defect free, at four sigma quality, 20 percent are defect free; At five sigma, overall quality improves so that 79.24 percent of the sets are defect free. However, at six sigma quality, 99.66 percent of TVs are defect free.

At a six sigma quality level, the defect rate is three to four per million opportunities for error. At a four sigma quality level, the defect rate is calculated per hundred or per thousand. The difference is on the order of one hundred times improvement in quality level. And amazingly, there are firms that are now pursuing eight sigma quality.

Certainly, all defects don't render a TV set inoperable. However, some defects will. Further, customers may not even notice some defects, but you can be assured that they *will notice* some of the defects. If the average firm is operating at four sigma quality and the industry leader is operating at six sigma quality, the industry leader will create a quality image for its products. Therefore, six sigma quality can create a significant competitive advantage.

Table 3.1 Percentage of Defect-Free Products at Three, Four, Five, and Six Sigma Quality

Number of Parts or Opportunities for Error in the Product	±3σ	±4σ	±5σ	±6σ
1	93.32	99.379	99.9767	99.99966
7	61.63	95.733	99.839	99.9976
10	50.08	93.96	99.768	99.9966
20	25.08	88.29	99.536	99.9932
40	6.29	77.94	99.074	99.9864
60	1.58	68.81	98.614	99.9796
80	0.40	60.75	98.156	99.9728
100	0.10	53.64	97.70	99.966
150	–	39.38	96.61	99.949
200	–	28.77	95.45	99.932
300	–	15.43	93.26	99.898
400	–	8.28	91.11	99.864
500	–	4.44	89.02	99.830
600	–	2.38	86.97	99.796
700	–	1.28	84.97	99.762
800	–	0.69	83.02	99.729
900	–	0.37	81.11	99.695
1000	–	0.20	79.24	99.661
1200	–	0.06	75.88	99.593
3000	–	–	50.15	98.985
17000	–	–	1.91	94.384
38000	–	–	0.01	87.880
70000	–	–	–	78.820
150000	–	–	–	60.000

However, if a firm is not in the leadership position in its industry in terms of product quality, quality improvement may have little strategic impact. Stated differently, quality improvement will not create a competitive advantage. This is because the average firm would just be playing catch-up. While some internal benefits, such as cost savings, are certain to result from quality improvement, market performance may not change at all. Customers will evaluate a firm's product quality relative to competitive alternatives and possibly conclude that, although product quality is better, it is still inferior to the "best" product.

Catching up to the quality level of the industry leader is a challenging task. The industry leader probably achieved its leadership after three to five years of concerted effort. If a follower firm is ever to close the gap, it must improve quality faster than the leader. And this process typically takes four or five years, testing the commitment of top management.

Quality Pays

A second strategic reason for adopting the total quality approach is the cost savings. The most common perception is that as quality goes up, costs also go up. If you compare across products or brands, the contention is often true. A Mercedes does cost more than a Volkswagen to produce, a Rolex does cost more than a Timex to produce, and so on. However, such views are of little value to a manager. Mercedes competes very little with Volkswagen; Rolex competes very little with Timex.

The proper base of reference is what happens to costs for a specific product when quality goes up. This requires calculating the costs at some benchmark level of quality and then tracking subsequent changes in cost as quality increases. The evidence from this type of quality/cost study is overwhelmingly clear: as quality goes up, costs go down. For a given product, increases in quality generate cost savings, a fact apparently overlooked by many firms.

The primary area of cost savings is the reduction in waste and rework. In the average four sigma firm, 15–20 percent of sales dollars go toward the reworking of previously produced products. The rework could take place when a worker damages a component inadvertently during the assembly process. The rework could result from an improperly completed order form or an incorrect invoice. The rework could take the form of a defective product returned by a customer. Rework is pervasive in all manufacturing and nonmanufacturing operations.

As Motorola neared six sigma quality, rework costs plummeted. For example, the mean time between failure for Motorola's pocket pagers is 150 years. Cycle time for product modifications in pagers had dropped by a factor of 300:1. Rework and even quality control inspection to detect defectives became almost nonexistent.

Costs go down for reasons other than a reduction in rework, however. Worker productivity typically increases as employees become more involved in the total quality effort. Costs associated with customer dissatisfaction due to defective products also decline. In firms achieving TQM success, benefits accrue in virtually all areas of the firm, not just the assembly line.

Customer-driven Quality

A third strategic reason for adopting a total quality philosophy is the explicit recognition that the customer is the alpha and omega of quality. Quite simply, quality starts and ends with the customer. The customer decides whether a product is or is not of high quality, and the opinions of top management, engineering, or quality assurance are of little importance to customers.

There are two primary determinants of quality: design quality and conformance quality. For a product to create a high level of value, both must exist in a product. Unfortunately, the traditional view of quality by most firms is conformance quality. Conformance quality means a firm strives to produce a product that consistently meets engineering standards with few or no defects. Most quality control efforts match product characteristics against some set of standards and monitor the degree of conformance. This approach is at the heart of the do-it-right-the-first-time mentality. The Edsel was a classic example of a car with high conformance quality but with poor design quality.

Design quality occurs when the product matches, or exceeds, the customer's expectations or needs. Hence, for a firm to deliver design quality, customer expectations must be known and translated into product characteristics. The current term that describes this process is "quality function deployment" (QFD). QFD is just a fancy term that describes staying close to customers and building their expectations into the product. From the customer's perspective, if a product lacks either design quality or conformance quality, it lacks quality. Both must be present. Ironically, although this view is simple, logical, and fundamental to being customer oriented, it is routinely ignored in many, if not most, firms.

A large, well-respected, high-technology firm makes disc drives for computers. The engineers have developed a new disc drive that is more capable and carries higher profit margins because of its uniqueness. Ideally, the firm would like to discontinue the old model and replace it with the more profitable new version.

As is often the case in the computer industry, however, customers still aren't fully utilizing the old model. The customers, therefore, don't see a need to replace currently underutilized hardware with a more expensive version that will have an even lower utilization rate. The firm making the disc drive has become driven by its engineers' capability to design a product instead of by customers' expectations and needs. In the computer industry, the line between technological capability and customers' perception of value is very fine as well as difficult to find. But if a firm becomes engineering driven rather than customer driven, the firm will be producing fantastic products with all sorts of capabilities that no customers want.

Although there are other reasons for adopting a total quality philosophy, probably the most compelling are competitive advantage, cost reduction, and customer focus. Even if top management buys in to the TQM philosophy and starts the transformation from being an average firm to being a TQM firm, the road is typically long and arduous. Most of the Baldrige National Quality Award winners for the past several years began their quality improvement efforts five or six years prior to winning. Embarking on the TQM effort is not an easy task by any means, but several stages in the transformation process are becoming apparent.

THE EVOLUTION TO TOTAL QUALITY

The first stage in the evolutionary process is a focus on conformance quality (Figure 3.2). Initially, this is often manifested by "better" quality control techniques, particularly the use of statistical process control charts and acceptance sampling. The acceptable quality standards are probably developed by engineering or quality control or, in a service industry, top management. Unfortunately, it's almost certain that none of the definers of quality are basing their decisions on accurate customer data. At this stage, management is certain it knows what quality the customer should want and have.

As a result, the focus for quality improvement is internal. And the do-it-right-the-first-time slogan commonly emerges, because reducing scrap and rework are important goals. Resource allocations will be made to prevent defects and to help workers avoid errors. Although the stage 1 firm probably wouldn't admit it, it is pursuing the build-a-better-mousetrap-and-the-world-will-beat-a-path-to-your-door fallacy. The stage 1 firm may produce a defect-free mousetrap that exceeds internally defined standards and yet simply not realize that the customer would rather dispose of mice in other ways.

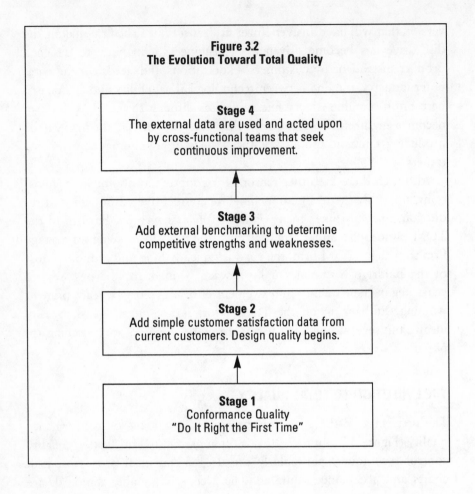

Figure 3.2
The Evolution Toward Total Quality

Stage 4
The external data are used and acted upon
by cross-functional teams that seek
continuous improvement.

Stage 3
Add external benchmarking to determine
competitive strengths and weaknesses.

Stage 2
Add simple customer satisfaction data from
current customers. Design quality begins.

Stage 1
Conformance Quality
"Do It Right the First Time"

The stage 2 firm adds customer satisfaction data to its established conformance quality programs. Someone in the customer service or marketing research department probably put together a fairly brief, one-page questionnaire that is routinely distributed in some fashion to current customers. The questions, around ten or so, focus on the key attributes that management thinks are important. While it is unlikely, it is possible in a few instances that the questions may have been developed in focus groups or by depth interviews with current customers. Former customers aren't included in the customer satisfaction surveys because they are too hard to find and would probably give negative, biased responses anyway, skewing the data. Potential customers aren't included because they are even harder to survey and all that could be obtained is merely their perception of quality. And those vague perceptions aren't nearly as good as current customers' opinions based on actual experiences.

For a good portion of the early 1980s, Cadillac exemplified a stage 2 firm. Cadillac was trying to improve quality by stressing quality control standards. To measure how well it was doing, Cadillac regularly surveyed Cadillac owners. And to no one's great surprise, the results were pretty good. Cadillac buyers are highly brand loyal, often owning four or five Cadillacs during their lifetime. It would have probably been surprising if the Cadillac buyers were dissatisfied.

Although it was getting good customer satisfaction scores, Cadillac was losing market share very steadily for two reasons. First, the competition was getting better faster. Both Mercedes and BMW were achieving much higher levels of customer satisfaction. So while Cadillac was improving, the quality gap was widening. The second reason for loss of market share consisted of the perceptions of first-time luxury car buyers. The perceptions of potential customers were much more negative than those of Cadillac's brand-loyal customers. And those potential customers simply took their business elsewhere. The result was a tough financial situation for Cadillac in the mid-1980s.

The stage 3 firm adds external benchmarking to conformance quality and the surveying of current customers. Though there are a variety of specific types, external benchmarking normally requires comparing the performance of a firm's products against those of key competitors. And the comparison is made by customers, not by management.

Customer focus groups, including past customers, current customers, competitors' customers, and potential customers, are used to generate a list of specific attributes that contribute to quality. The attributes are translated into a series of questions included in the customer satisfaction questionnaire, which is administered to past customers, current customers, and competitors' customers. The data generated constitute a customer-driven, competitor analysis that identifies priorities for the quality improvement process.

Comparison of a firm's performance on each attribute, relative to competitors', pinpoints strategic strengths and weaknesses. When competitive strengths and weaknesses are combined with customers' perceptions of the importance of each attribute, the priority becomes one of improving quality, so the more serious weaknesses are corrected first.

When a firm reaches stage 3, the most difficult problem is achieving comprehensive buy-in to the effort throughout the organization. It is not uncommon to generate more customer-driven data than many areas really want to see. It is also not unusual for a firm to use only about 20 percent of benchmark data when this stage is reached. Perhaps it is because of priorities—only so many things can be done at once. Perhaps it is because of skepticism—many areas of the firm have never really relied on customer-driven data. But gradually, the firm learns how to use the data and that is the major difference between stage 3 and stage 4. A stage 4 firm combines stages 1, 2, and 3 with strategic implementation and response.

The customer satisfaction data drive the development of cross-functional teams that are responsible for quality improvement. The budgeting and capital investment decisions are driven by quality improvement efforts intended to improve customer satisfaction. The performance evaluation and reward systems are customer oriented. The planning process is oriented toward customer performance measures, not just share price and return on investment, although those typically do improve, as will be discussed later in this chapter.

Examples of stage 4 firms are numerous. All of the Baldrige award winners such as Xerox, Motorola, Milliken, and Solectron have reached stage 4. Many other firms are capable of meeting the Baldrige criteria but have not yet applied. Most of these firms share a common transformation. The initial goal for quality improvement is typically to improve product quality. After four or five years of evolution toward TQM, the goal is no longer to improve product quality. Rather, the goal becomes one of achieving customer satisfaction. To really create a high-quality product, the firm must become thoroughly customer driven.

To recap a bit, as the average firm moves from average, four sigma quality to five or six sigma, a variety of benefits result. First, because most firms aren't there yet, five or six sigma quality will often yield a competitive quality advantage. As quality improves, costs go down, so a cost advantage often results as well. As a firm becomes more concerned with quality, a customer-driven orientation normally emerges due to the need to improve both design and conformance quality. The transformation from an average firm to a TQM firm is gradual, with at least four fairly distinct stages. The transition from being average is arduous and challenging, normally requiring five or more years of solid effort and continual improvement. Furthermore, there is no preset, ready-made mix that can simply be added to a firm to yield total quality. Having said that, let's examine case examples of acknowledged quality leaders to see what elements must be present.

QUALITY LEADERS

The Malcolm Baldrige National Quality Award has emerged as probably the most recognized and admired quality award in the world. While the Deming award in Japan has been in existence much longer, the Deming award places predominant emphasis on conformance quality. The Baldrige award addresses a much broader range of customer-driven evaluative criteria, particularly customer satisfaction. Therefore, all the Baldrige winners share the common trait of a very powerful customer focus.

Because of their customer-driven cultures, all of the Baldrige award winners would make interesting case studies. Throughout this book, specific examples of Baldrige winners, such as Xerox, Solectron, IBM-Rochester, and Milliken, are cited. However, four additional winners are briefly profiled at the end of this chapter. These firms were selected not because they were better than other winners but because they represent large and small businesses in a variety of industries. Also, each firm pursued a somewhat different approach to quality improvement, but all of them achieved outstanding results.

Motorola was a 1988 winner and won the award on the basis of the entire organization rather than a specific division. While some readers may be familiar with the Motorola story, Motorola was included because firms have copied the Motorola quality improvement process more than any other approach.

Globe Metallurgical was a winner in the small business category, also in 1988. Of the winners so far, Globe is the most smokestack type of business in the group. There is a tendency to think that Baldrige winners are all high-technology businesses.

Zytec Corporation was a winner in the manufacturing category in 1991. A fairly new business, it is a high-technology firm that achieved spectacular success very quickly. The firm's success is due partly to the high expectations of its customer base.

Graniterock was a 1992 winner in the small business category. Whereas other winners operated in industries conducive to rapid quality improvement, the building materials industry is much less quality focused. But in spite of little industry precedent, Graniterock also has achieved outstanding success.

There is clearly no one best way to embark on the road to continuous quality improvement: Motorola had no domestic U.S. role model so it visited Japanese firms, learned what it could, and developed its own approach to quality improvement. Globe Metallurgical patterned its quality system after the Ford Motor Company's. Zytec started with Deming's 14 Points of Management Obligation and supplemented it with Hoshin Planning. Graniterock used the Baldrige award criteria as a quality guide, the way many other firms are now doing. But all Baldrige winners share a customer commitment, a commitment to employees, and a commitment to continuous quality improvement.

As one of the requirements of the award process, Baldrige winners are required to tell their story to others. In order to spread the gospel of quality improvement, award winners typically have a packet of materials available to interested parties. They also offer site visits to firms interested in conducting best-in-class benchmarking studies.

For readers wishing to see how their firm compares to Baldrige award criteria, Appendix A of this book contains a 100-item self-diagnostic questionnaire. The questionnaire covers most of the Baldrige criteria, and the weightings for each section are approximately the same as the actual evaluative criteria. The questionnaire will not predict the exact Baldrige score, but the results will give a rough indication. To be most effective, the questionnaire should be completed by a vertical and horizontal slice of employees. Then a composite profile should be developed from the various respondents, preferably in a group meeting or workshop of some type.

The real purpose of the questionnaire is to quickly identify areas for improvement. It should definitely not be used as an evaluative assessment for a business unit. But the results typically provide an excellent starting point for more detailed discussions regarding *why* a specific score emerged.

GAO REPORT

In a 1991 report, the Government Accounting Office (GAO) presented the results of a study of firms applying TQM. Though the sample was fairly small—20 firms—and the measures of performance a bit general and imprecise, the study found a consistent and positive link between quality improvement and performance measures. The sample consisted of firms that were finalists for the 1988 and 1989 Baldrige National Quality Award (Table 3.2). The 1988 and 1989 finalists were included to allow a sufficient time for benefits to flow from the quality improvements. The finalists consisted of both large and small firms from the manufacturing and service sectors.

The study examined four types of operating results: improved employee relations, improved operating performance, greater customer satisfaction, and increased financial performance. From three to eight performance indicators were examined in each area, although all firms did not respond with data for each measure. The firms were asked to indicate what happened to the performance indicators as the firms evolved toward a TQM philosophy. Since the Baldrige award application requires empirical support, the firms in the sample had empirical data to evaluate these performance measures. Hence, the study was based on actual results, not managerial perceptions. As we shall see, the results were consistent.

Employee Relations

Eighteen companies responded with data on five performance indicators (Table 3.3). Overall, 39 observations were positive, 9 were negative, and 4 were unchanged. In terms of magnitude of change, suggestions received had the biggest improvement followed by a decrease in turnover. Both safety/health and employee satisfaction showed moderate improvement; attendance improved only slightly. The one company with a decline in employee satisfaction attributed it to merger activity and speculation in its industry. Employee turnover was usually lower (10 of 11 firms) than the industry average, with an average annual decline of 6 percent. The number of lost workdays due to occupational injury or illness declined in 11 of 14 companies and was below the industry average in 12 of 14 firms. The average annual increase in the number of suggestions was over 16 percent, although some firms experienced a decline due to use of quality improvement teams. Overall, employee relations evidenced a notable improvement due to TQM.

Operating Performance

Twenty companies responded with data on the eight performance measures indicated in Table 3.4. Of the 65 observations, 59 improved, 2 became worse, and 4 were unchanged. All measures improved annually between 5 and 12 percent. Order processing time, reliability, errors or defects, and costs of quality showed the biggest improvements. On-time delivery of orders, new product cycle time, and inventory turnover all showed significant improvement also. When some of the measures were

Table 3.2 1988 and 1989 Baldrige Finalists and Participants in GAO Review

Corning, Inc. Telecommunications Products Division Corning, NY	International Business Machines Corp. Endicott, NY
Digital Equipment Corp. Maynard, MA	L. L. Bean, Inc. Freeport, ME
Eastman Kodak Company Eastman Chemicals Division Kingsport, TN	Milliken & Co. Spartanburg, SC
Ford Motor Company North American Auto Division Indianapolis, IN	Motorola, Inc. Schaumburg, IL Paul Revere Insurance Group Worcester, MA
General Motors Corp. Allison Transmission Division Detroit, MI	Seagate Technology Small Disk Division Oklahoma City, OK
Globe Metallurgical, Inc. Beverly, OH	Timken Company Bearing Division Canton, OH
Goodyear Tire and Rubber Company Akron, OH	USAA Insurance Company Property and Casualty Division San Antonio, TX
GTE Corporation Telephone Operations Irving, TX	Westinghouse Electric Corp. Commercial Nuclear Fuel Division Pittsburgh, PA
Hoechst Celanese Corp. Chemical Group Dallas, TX	Xerox Corporation Business Products and Systems Fairport, NY
International Business Machines Corp. Rochester, MN	

Source: GAO/NSIAD-91-190 Management Practices.

Table 3.3 Employee-Related Performance Indicators

Performance Indicator	Number of Responding Companies	Direction of Indicator		
		Positive (favorable)	Negative (unfavorable)	No Change
Employee satisfaction	9	8	1	0
Attendance	11	8	0	3
Turnover	11	7	3	1
Safety/health	14	11	3	0
Suggestions received	7	5	2	0
Total	18[a]	39	9	4

[a]Indicates the total number of companies providing data and not the total number of responses for all performance indicators.

Source: GAO's analysis of company-provided data. GAO/NSIAD-91-190 Management Practices.

Table 3.4 Operating Performance Indicators

Performance Indicator	Number of Responding Companies	Direction of Indicator		
		Positive (favorable)	Negative (unfavorable)	No Change
Reliability	12	12	0	0
Timeliness of delivery	9	8	1	0
Order processing time	6	6	0	0
Errors or defects	8	7	0	1
Product lead time	7	6	0	1
Inventory turnover	9	6	1	2
Costs of quality	5	5	0	0
Cost savings	9	9	0	0
Total	20[a]	59	2	4

[a]Indicates the total number of companies providing data and not the total number of responses for all performance indicators.

Source: GAO's analysis of company-provided data. GAO/NSIAD-91-190 Management Practices.

Table 3.5 Customer Satisfaction Performance Indicators

Performance Indicator	Number of Responding Companies	Direction of Indicator		
		Positive (favorable)	Negative (unfavorable)	No Change
Overall customer satisfaction	14	12	0	2
Customer complaints	6	5	1	0
Customer retention	10	4	2	4
Total	17[a]	21	3	6

[a]Indicates the total number of companies providing data and not the total number of responses for all performance indicators.

Source: GAO's analysis of company-provided data. GAO/NSIAD-91-190 Management Practices.

negative, there were logical explanations. For example, one firm had a better inventory turnover than the industry average but experienced a decline in its turnover rate due to weak industry demand.

Customer Satisfaction

Customer satisfaction increased in 12 of 14 firms and remained at a high level in the other two (Table 3.5). Customer complaints decreased in 5 of 6 firms, and the remaining firm developed and implemented a better system to identify and correct customer complaints, which resulted in an initial increase. Customer retention improved in 4 of 10 firms, and 4 firms were unchanged at a high level. The two firms that had a decline in customer retention had an average negative change of about .7 percent, so the decline was very slight.

Financial Performance

Quality improvement is typically pursued because it pays off financially (Table 3.6). For 9 of 11 firms, market share increased. The reason for the decline in the two firms was international competition; both firms subsequently reversed the decline and recaptured the lost share. The average annual increase in share of 13.7 percent was the strongest performance

Table 3.6 Financial Performance Indicators

Performance Indicator	Number of Responding Companies	Direction of Indicator		
		Positive (favorable)	Negative (unfavorable)	No Change
Market share	11	9	2	0
Sales per employee	12	12	0	0
Return on assets	9	7	2	0
Return on sales	8	6	2	0
Total	15[a]	34	6	0

aIndicates the total number of companies providing data and not the total number of responses for all performance indicators.

Source: GAO's analysis of company-provided data. GAO/NSIAD-91-190 Management Practices.

improvement and was followed by sales per employee, with an 8.6 percent annual increase. Seven of 9 firms had an improvement in return on assets, and the 2 firms with a negative change had only slight decreases. Six of 8 firms had an increase in return on sales; 2 had a decline of 1–2 percent.

Many factors can influence these four categories of performance measures. Each industry has a different competitive structure, and some are more exposed than others to international competition. Economic conditions affect industries differently. Rates of technological advancement and demographic shifts affect industries differently. But in spite of those differences, the firms showed consistent performance improvement in the GAO study. The GAO report results are similar to other studies linking quality improvement and corporate performance.

OTHER EVIDENCE

A Conference Board survey of 111 firms implementing TQM found that 47 reported noticeably increased profits due to quality improvement. A study by the American Society for Quality Control found that 54 percent of respondents were pleased with the results of their quality improvement efforts, and half of those reported significant results including increased profitability and market share. A study of Japanese firms that had won the Deming Quality Award also showed improved overall corporate performance. However, one of the strongest empirical studies supporting the quality payoff is the PIMS study.

PIMS Study

One of the largest empirical studies of business performance is the Profit Impact of Market Strategy (PIMS) program. Started in the early 1960s by General Electric, the program has grown to include over 450 firms with over 3,000 strategic business units (SBUs). Each firm reports on an extensive array of variables in a format consistent among the SBUs.

The objectives of the PIMS program were to help firms evaluate their financial performance, analyze strategic choices' impact on profits, and identify the relationship of certain variables to profitability. Although several short- and long-term financial performance variables are monitored, the most widely used is return on investment (ROI). ROI is evaluated with respect to three categories of variables: prevailing conditions in the market, competitive position of the firm, and strategy employed by the firm. Table 3.7 gives a sample of some of the variables examined.

The dependent variables, such as ROI, were linked to independent variables, such as those in Table 3.7, through the use of regression analysis. The results of various empirical tests have shown that the three best predictors of ROI are market share, product quality, and investment intensity.

PIMS uses a multiattribute approach to measure quality. Executives list the attributes that consumers view as important; the relative importance of each attribute is determined; and the firm's performance, relative to competitors' performance, is calculated for each attribute. Multiplying the importance weight by the rating gives an estimate of relative product quality. Obviously, this approach is based on managerial perceptions rather than customer perceptions but the results are profound. At low relative quality levels, ROI is around 15 percent, but at high relative quality levels, ROI is over 30 percent. The financial impact of high quality becomes even more pronounced when combined with market share data.

Market share and relative product quality are complementary to one another. For those SBUs with low relative quality and low market share, average ROI is only 7 percent. For firms with high relative quality and

Table 3.7 A Sample of PIMS Variables

Market growth rate	R&D expenditures
Product differentiation	Inventory expenditures
Product quality	Exports to imports
Market share	Fixed capital intensity
New product introductions	Plant age
Pricing	Capacity utilization
Rate of price inflation	Vertical integration
Employee productivity	Unionization

high market share, ROI is 38 percent. The relationship between product quality and share is no accident; around 50 percent of firms with high quality also have high share. More recently there is some indication that the rate of improvement in relative product quality is also a good predictor of ROI.

The conclusion reached by virtually all studies attempting to link product quality and corporate performance is the same: quality pays and it doesn't make much difference how you measure quality. Or which performance indicators are examined. Or how they are measured. Improvement in quality leads to improvement in other areas, particularly financial performance.

Why, then, don't all firms adopt a quality improvement culture? The only apparent reasons are ignorance or an unwillingness to put out the effort. Since it takes years to produce major results, some managers and executives may simply be too short term oriented and myopic. Whatever the reasons, those firms that don't adopt a strategic quality improvement effort probably won't have to worry about the business environment after the year 2000. They won't be in business long after!

TWO-FACTOR MODEL OF PRODUCT QUALITY

Research in the area of customer satisfaction and customer turnover reveals some interesting insights into the role of product quality in creating customer value. First, as discussed previously, every product consists of a bundle of attributes. Some of those attributes are tangible product characteristics and some are the more intangible service attributes. Since service quality is the topic of the next chapter, discussion of service attributes will be deferred until then for the most part. For now, the discussion will be restricted primarily to tangible product attributes.

When an analysis of the factors that contribute to extreme customer dissatisfaction is conducted, customers can consistently identify why they are dissatisfied. When an analysis of the factors that contribute to extreme customer satisfaction is conducted, customers also can identify why they are satisfied. In most cases, the factors contributing to dissatisfaction are quite different from the factors that contribute to customer satisfaction. When considering product and service attributes simultaneously, product attributes tend to be associated more frequently with dissatisfaction whereas service attributes are associated somewhat more frequently with satisfaction. However, both product and service attributes contribute to both satisfaction and dissatisfaction.

Most important, the factors that cause customer dissatisfaction, whether product or service characteristics, tend not to cause customer satisfaction. The absence of, or low performance on, some product attributes will quickly cause customer dissatisfaction. High performance on those same attributes contributes very little to high levels of customer satisfaction. Low performance on these attributes will prevent a firm from ever reaching high levels of customer satisfaction, however.

Conversely, the factors that cause extreme customer satisfaction are usually not identified as factors that cause customer dissatisfaction. Thus, low performance on those attributes causing high satisfaction does not usually cause customer dissatisfaction.

Therefore, there appear to be two general categories of factors: One category consists of the hygiene factors that contribute to customer dissatisfaction. The other category consists of the satisfiers that contribute to extreme customer satisfaction. This relationship is depicted in Figure 3.3.

If a firm performs at a very high level in delivering the hygiene attributes, customers will perceive the product as being acceptable but not spectacular. Even if a firm is delivering hygiene attributes at the six sigma quality level, high levels of customer satisfaction will never be achieved. But a firm must deliver hygiene attributes with a reasonable level of proficiency before the satisfiers become important.

Hygiene attributes collectively constitute some threshold level of product characteristics for customers. Failure to meet that threshold level will cause customers to become dissatisfied. Performing at a very high level on hygiene attributes might yield the customer response "So what? You're expected to do that."

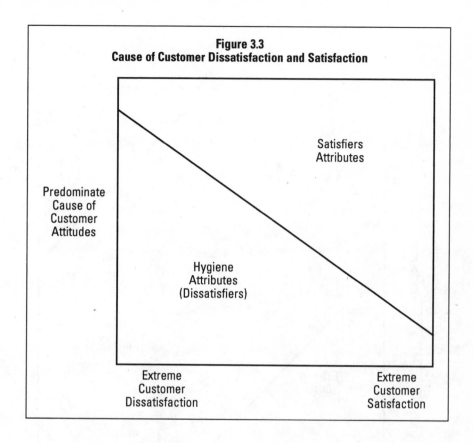

Figure 3.3
Cause of Customer Dissatisfaction and Satisfaction

Satisfiers
Attributes

Predominate
Cause of
Customer
Attitudes

Hygiene
Attributes
(Dissatisfiers)

Extreme
Customer
Dissatisfaction

Extreme
Customer
Satisfaction

Let's assume that a customer expects a 40,000-mile life from a set of tires. If the tires last only 25,000 or 30,000 miles, the customer will be dissatisfied. It won't matter how good the traction of the tires is, how quiet the tires are, or how smoothly they ride. Failure to deliver on the hygiene attribute of 40,000 expected miles will lead to customer dissatisfaction.

The hygiene attributes must be delivered at an acceptable level of performance before the satisfiers become important. Once the customer's expectations on hygiene elements have been met, then the satisfiers have the potential to create high levels of customer satisfaction. In the tire example, if the tire lasts 40,000 miles, then traction, ride, handling, and noise may each contribute to high satisfaction levels.

The relationship between performance levels, hygiene attributes, and satisfier attributes is depicted in Figure 3.4. Firms in the lower left corner of the figure (close to 1,1) are almost certain to be in a crisis situation. Their products would be substandard on both hygiene and satisfier at-

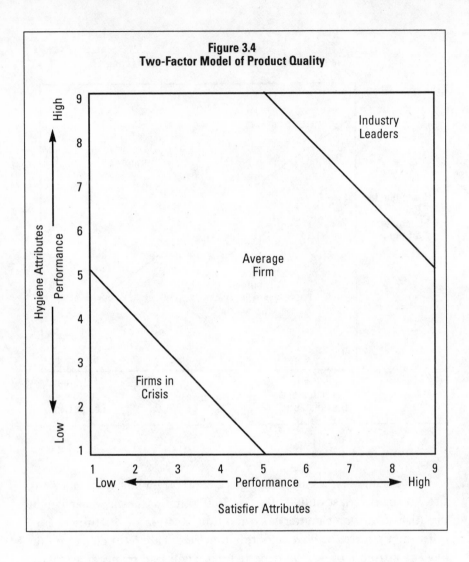

Figure 3.4
Two-Factor Model of Product Quality

tributes, and customer satisfaction would be low. Customer turnover is likely to be high, and this firm has bleak prospects of surviving. Firms in the upper left corner (near 9, 1) may be improving *conformance* quality and delivering on the hygiene attributes. In spite of quality improvement efforts, however, these firms will still not attain a strong market position because they are achieving only a very average customer satisfaction level. The upper right corner is where the industry leaders are found (around 9,9). These firms are exceeding customer expectations on both hygiene and satisfier attributes. In essence, these firms have stressed design quality, which means the product is designed to meet or exceed customer needs.

A word of caution is necessary for now. It is a bit myopic to exclude service attributes from the discussion, because customers certainly evaluate service quality. However, service issues will be integrated into this framework in subsequent chapters for more complete treatment.

Until now, product quality has been viewed as a linear concept. Products were viewed as either high or low quality. What is becoming increasingly apparent is that high quality and low quality are not just opposites; perceptions of low quality are caused by some product characteristics, and perceptions of high quality are caused by other product characteristics. We need to be a bit more sophisticated in how we think about product quality.

Virtually all products consist of some bundle of attributes. However, those attributes are seldom viewed uniformly by customers. Not only are there differences in importance among attributes, but some attributes are undoubtedly hygiene factors and some are satisfiers. Beyond some expected level of performance, the satisfiers are where resources should be allocated in order to achieve 100 percent customer satisfaction.

SUMMARY

Quality improvement should be an explicit portion of a firm's corporate strategy. This is not because it is a fad or "the thing to do" in the 1990s. Quality improvement must be part of corporate strategy because customers demand it!

Some managers dismiss TQM, TQC, Kaizen, Zero Defects, or Six Sigma as part of the continuous flow of business jargon. And they may be right! But it makes no difference what you call it—improvement of product quality is essential and the quality improvement process is an arduous journey. Firms must evolve from a rather smug, knowledgeable, internal focus to an innovative, creative, external focus. Only when a firm uses good, customer-driven data—almost to the point of information overload in order to drive continuous improvement effort—will the changes be visible. Corporate culture must evolve almost to the point where there is a pervasive fear of losing contact with customers.

Product quality, as a concept, is becoming far more complex. It is not just a linear, "good" versus "bad" issue. That, too, is a vestige of 1980s thinking in business.

For a product to have both design and conformance quality, all of the relevant attributes important to the customer must be identified. Some of those attributes are simply hygiene factors—attributes that customers expect to be there. High quality on these attributes may have little impact on a firm's market position or customer satisfaction levels.

The satisfier attributes are where high product quality can create real customer delight and high customer satisfaction levels. But the hygiene attributes must first be delivered at some threshold level of quality. Unfortunately, most firms don't understand which product attributes are hygiene factors and which are satisfiers.

Regardless of how quality is thought of or how it is improved, quality pays. It pays in cost reduction. It pays through improved efficiency. It pays through more satisfied employees. And, probably most important, it pays through higher customer satisfaction levels, especially when service quality is also high.

APPLICATION IDEAS

1. Does your firm fit the description of the average firm described at the beginning of the chapter? What strategies are being implemented to move away from the stuck-in-the-middle position? Do the strategies include strong TQM commitment?
2. Where in the evolution to TQM is your firm (Figure 3.2)? What strategies are being used to move to the next level? In which stage of evolution are your key competitors? At what rate are they improving?
3. What is the cost of poor quality in your organization? Calculate the actual savings or the potential savings that can be gained by quality improvement. Does your organization use such data when establishing priorities for investment decisions?
4. Does your estimate of cost savings from improved quality include the various items in the four categories of the GAO report? Or is the focus only on waste and scrap?
5. How do your customers rate the quality of your products compared to the competitive alternatives? Which product attributes are most important, and how is your firm doing on each—again from the customers' perspective?
6. Of the quality attributes, which are hygiene factors and which are satisfiers? Which attributes hold the greatest potential for creating a comparative advantage? How are your key competitors doing on the hygiene factors? What are the satisfier attributes that those competitors are using to differentiate their products?

THE MOTOROLA STORY

Motorola, based in Schaumburg, Illinois, won a Baldrige award in 1988, the first year of the award program. However, Motorola had started its strategic emphasis long before then. Quality was first discussed at Motorola as a strategic issue in 1979, when the vice president of marketing indicated quality was becoming a primary concern of customers. During the next eighteen months, additional research on quality was conducted, including site visits to Japanese firms.

Although quality had been important to Motorola and many other U.S. firms for years, Motorola, in 1981, was one of the first to establish quality as a dominant, strategic issue. There were several reasons for Motorola's early quality commitment. First, all of Motorola's seven business units were linked somehow to high-technology electronic products. High-technology electronics were industries subject to early, intense, international competitive pressure, particularly from Japan. Thus, Motorola, unlike some other U.S. firms, was sensitive to the early competitive changes in their markets, and a strategic response was developed and implemented without too much delay.

The second reason for adopting a quality commitment consisted of rapidly changing customer expectations. Motorola management found that customers expected significant increases in quality continually. If Motorola were going to maintain a leadership position in its various businesses, it had to respond to the increasing competitive pressure and the changing customer expectations. The response was the five-year, tenfold increase in quality by 1986.

The response from lower levels of management was about what you would expect. Most managers agreed that quality improvement was important but were skeptical about a tenfold increase. Many viewed the goal as unrealistic, an impossible dream. Despite that skepticism, however, Motorola was on its way to quality improvement.

The major problem experienced by Motorola during the first three years of its quality improvement effort was lack of a common measurement of quality. A good deal of diversity existed across business units in terms of the nature and complexity of products. Even within a business unit, tremendous diversity existed between the manufacturing and nonmanufacturing operations. The result of this diversity was that upper management couldn't really measure quality improvement accurately or uniformly across different activities within the company. The solution came in 1985, after more than three years of quality improvement effort.

The Communications Sector of Motorola developed a common quality metric of "defects per unit of work." A defect was defined as anything that caused customer dissatisfaction. A unit of work was any logical unit of output, defined by the division or department. It could be a piece of equipment, a circuit board assembly, a page in a manual, a line of software code, an hour of labor, or a wire transfer of funds, for example. While the definitions of a defect and a unit of work would vary, a common metric existed to measure quality improvement.

The Communications Sector implemented the common metric in 1986. During 1986, the Communications Sector's quality improvement was greater than the previous four years' total improvement with inconsistent quality definitions. This result graphically illustrated the importance of a common quality measurement and caused Motorola to restate the corporate quality goal.

In January 1987, Motorola's quality goal was stated as follows: "Improve quality 10 times by 1989, improve quality 100 times by 1991, and achieve six sigma capability by 1992." The "unrealistic, impossible" goal in 1981 of a ten times quality improvement had given way to far more ambitious goals by 1987. Ironically, due largely to earlier success and an improved quality awareness, the far more challenging goals established in 1987 were met with much less skepticism by the workforce.

Also in 1986, CEO Robert Galvin initiated a formal program of management visits to customer locations. Essentially, Motorola management asked two questions of its customers at all organization levels: What do you like about Motorola? What don't you like about Motorola? Each manager prepared a formal report that included recommendations for improvement. The program of management visits led Motorola to restate its fundamental objective as achieving Total Customer Satisfaction, also in 1987.

As Motorola moved toward achieving Total Customer Satisfaction, three other goals were stated:

1. increase global market share;
2. be best in class in terms of people, technology, marketing, product, manufacturing, and service; and
3. achieve superior financial results. To attain these goals, Motorola identified five key operational initiatives.

Motorola's Five Key Initiatives

First, and most important, was reaching six sigma quality levels for all products and services by 1992. This required an emphasis on improving the design quality to meet customer needs. Next, the processes to produce those products were designed to yield six sigma conformance quality. And, although the six sigma goal was ambitious, most manufacturing and nonmanufacturing activities were at that quality level by 1992.

The second key initiative was cycle time reduction. For existing products, cycle time was defined as the length of time from the receipt of an order until the delivery to the customer. For new products, cycle time was the length of time from the conception of the product idea to the shipment of the first unit. To illustrate their success, the cyclical time reduction for portable pagers was reduced by a factor of 300:1.

Cycle time reduction applied to nonmanufacturing processes as well. The length of time to close the books annually on nonmanufacturing processes' consolidated financial statements had previously been three to four weeks. It was reduced to four days, resulting in an annual saving of $20 million.

The third initiative was product and manufacturing leadership. Product development and manufacturing jointly worked together to solve customers' problems so that six sigma quality could be delivered with the first unit. Essentially, Motorola was committed to satisfying customer needs rapidly with innovative, leading-edge technological solutions.

The fourth initiative was profit improvement. Although this largely flowed from the first three initiatives, Motorola was committed to identifying and capturing leadership in those markets holding the greatest long-term profit potential. The goal was not just to satisfy current customer needs but also to anticipate customer needs several years in advance so that Motorola could gain the financial advantage of first-in-market pioneer.

The fifth and final key initiative was participative management within and cooperation between organizations. The "within" portion was intended to mobilize Motorola employees at all levels with a synergistic, organization-wide effort. The "between" portion was intended to link different business units within Motorola to one another and to build suppliers into the process as well. Motorola management felt that internal and external participation would yield greater potential to achieve corporate goals.

These key initiatives are certainly neither distinct from one another nor mutually exclusive. Each initiative is related to various aspects of the others, but the first, six sigma quality appears more pervasive than the others. Therefore, a more detailed discussion of the six sigma efforts is warranted.

Motorola's Six Steps to Six Sigma

Motorola developed two related programs—one for manufacturing processes and one for nonmanufacturing processes. Both are referred to as "Six Steps to Six Sigma."

The six steps for manufacturing are:

1. Identify the product you create or the service you provide.
2. Identify the customer(s) for your product or service, and determine what those customers consider important.
3. Identify your needs (to provide product/service so that it satisfies the customer).
4. Define the process for doing the work.
5. Mistake-proof the process and eliminate wasted effort.
6. Ensure continuous improvement by measuring, analyzing, and controlling the improved process.

At first glance, the steps appear pretty straightforward and a bit simplistic. Most firms have probably already made some progress on each step; some firms may actually do very well on several steps. However, few firms do very well on all steps, and to achieve six sigma quality, a firm must continually improve and get better on every step.

Step 1. Identifying your product or service is the easiest step and probably the one accomplished by most firms. The danger lurking here is that the producer might define the product in the producer's terms instead of in the customer's terms. For Motorola, the concept of "product" applied to internal customers as well. *All* activities were linked somehow to their "customer" group. So the definition of "product" had to recognize both the external customers as well as the internal customers for activities such as accounting or human resources.

Step 2. Identifying your customers and their needs is probably something that most market-driven firms feel they've been doing for years. For Motorola, this meant more direct contact and feedback. Customers were asked to evaluate Motorola's strengths and weaknesses. A wide variety of employees began making customer visits. The results of each customer site visit were compiled into a report that indicated areas for improvement and strategies to be pursued. For internal customers, this process began to break down many of the functional silos that had existed previously.

Step 3. Identifying what the firm needs to do to satisfy the customer is often described as translating the "voice of the customer" into the "language of the firm." The translation requires building customer needs and expectations into design specifications so that the delivered product is what the customer expected. In some cases, employees needed additional training to learn new techniques. In other cases, new machine tools or production processes were necessary. But the voice of the customer was the key driver for most of the changes at Motorola. In many cases, this required Motorola to anticipate customers' needs and expectations several years in advance.

Step 4. Charting the steps and tasks for doing your work is an internally focused effort. The first three of Motorola's six steps are externally oriented, that is, toward customers. The last three are internally oriented—toward improving the value creation process.

Often policies, procedures, and the way things get done in organizations gradually emerge and evolve over time. But these accepted ways of behaving may be behaviorally or technologically obsolete and result in significant inefficiency.

By breaking down the value added tasks, step 4 becomes a complete organizational audit or diagnostic evaluation. Once the task is broken down, defect rate and cycle time can be calculated accurately. This allows those sources of error to be isolated for corrective action. The process also facilitates the determination of "value added" by each operation, linking all internal customers into a value-added chain.

Step 5. This step is a logical extension of step 4. Activities that don't contribute value to the process are eliminated, reducing waste. Activities that do add value are analyzed to determine how they can be done better. It may require job redesign or simplification. It may require new methodologies or technology. It may require significantly different training programs. This is where the six sigma conformance quality comes into play, as the process becomes mistake proofed.

As with step 4, this step requires the inclusion of suppliers and downstream channel members when appropriate. The internal focus is on the entire value-creating chain, not just on a firm's manufacturing or production systems.

Motorola found that about 20 percent of quality problems were caused by the employees themselves. Mistake-proofing for this area required better training, worker empowerment, participation, and cross-functional teaming. However, 80 percent of the quality problems were the result of the systems and processes that were being used. Mistake-proofing this required redesign, new technologies, and supplier partnering.

Step 6. The final step is to monitor the value-creating processes in an effort to ensure continual improvement instead of drifting back to the old way of doing things. Statistical process control is used to track key criteria such as tolerance levels, defects, or cycle time. The goal at Motorola was for everyone in the organization to evaluate his or her own job and strive for continual improvement. The measurement and analysis system is essential to provide individual feedback on the value of changes and modifications.

Defect-per-unit targets are established at the start of the design process. Each new product or design must have a specified defect rate significantly lower than the existing product it replaces. This forces the design of quality to explicitly recognize customer needs and continuous improvement at the start of the process. Since the product design and production systems are concurrently designed with a goal of six sigma quality, manufacturability becomes an early design issue.

The last step is a check to ensure that design and process quality goals have been met. The measurement of the relationship between product design and process capability is the capability index (CP). In all new designs, Motorola strives for a CP of 2, which means that the design limits for every critical product characteristic will be at least twice the normal variation of the process that produces that characteristic. Thus, design quality and conformance quality are explicitly linked early in the development process.

The Quality Payoff at Motorola

The benefits accruing to Motorola from its quality improvement programs during the past five years are pervasive. Paul Noakes, Vice President and Director of External Quality Programs, estimated that for the first four years of the six sigma effort, a cumulative savings of $1.5 billion was realized in manufacturing operations because of defect reduction alone. Comparison of the defect rate of the early 1980s with the rate in 1990 revealed that defect reduction in one year, 1990, had resulted in $550 million in savings. There is an estimated potential savings of $1 billion in nonmanufacturing operations that has not been realized yet. The success stories come from throughout the company.

Many of Motorola's examples of success come from manufacturing. In producing a cellular phone—the mini TAC—the quality improvement team achieved a 4:1 reduction in defects, a 30:1 reduction in cycle time, and a 10:1 improvement in reliability. The Government Electronics Group, producing strategic secure communications systems for manned spacecraft missions for more than ten years, has never had a failure. The computer group had a 75 percent reduction in cycle time for its circuit boards and systems, going from four and a half days to one day and reducing inventory by 16:1. One work group of

27 people producing microwave equipment recorded 255 operator months without a defect. Examples like these are numerous, but the bottom line was a cost savings of $550 million in 1990.

Successes have also occurred in nonmanufacturing operations. In the processing of orders for semiconductor equipment, a quality improvement team attacked the problem of order entry errors. The team designed a computerized order entry system to reduce the incidence of incomplete orders and incorrect part numbers, quantities, prices, and shipping locations. The result was a decrease from 525 return material requests per quarter in 1985 to 63 requests per quarter in 1987, generating a savings of $1.7 million.

Because Motorola had reached six sigma quality goals in many operations, one might think the firm would relax a bit. But that is hardly the case. Motorola's latest quality goal is to achieve eight sigma quality levels.

THE GLOBE METALLURGICAL STORY

Globe Metallurgical, based in Beverly, Ohio, was a 1988 Baldrige award winner in the small business category. Globe's foundries are not the image of cleanliness. The workplace is unheated, smoky from molten metals, and usually very hot. But Globe's quality systems are outstanding.

One of the most unusual facts about Globe's winning the award was that the firm had found out about the Baldrige award only two weeks before applying. Four individuals pulled the necessary information together, and one person wrote the entire application, about 80 pages, in one weekend.

Globe is one of the largest producers of silicon metal products in the United States and a significant factor in the ferrosilicon market as well. It produces 120 or so different products tailored to fit the needs of its customers, which include General Motors, Ford Motor Company, and Dow Corning. Overall, the industry has been in steady decline as synthetics replaced metals in the auto industry. Imports have consistently increased and now account for over half of silicon-based alloy sales in the United States. With declining industry demand and increasing foreign competition, competitive intensity is quite high.

The major shift to a quality emphasis was not a strategic response to the competitive environment, however. Like at Motorola, initial impetus had come from customers. For Globe this occurred in 1985, which is the watershed point in the company's evolution to TQM. Globe describes its history as either "pre-1985" or "1985 to now."

Pre-1985

Prior to October 1985, Globe was the epitome of a stage 1 firm. The company's whole quality system was based on detection of finished product defects. Because Globe conducted 100 percent inspection, it developed a reputation as a reliable, high-quality supplier. Globe used state-of-the-art X-ray and atomic absorption inspection techniques and helped to develop many of the industry standards.

Because of conducting 100 percent inspection, Globe could grade finished products into different lots based on the needs of particular customers. The most demanding customers got the better-quality output, while less demanding customers got products that met the lower-quality specifications.

1985 to Now

In October 1985, Ford Motor Company informed its suppliers that it was implementing a quality certification program called "Q-1." Since Ford was one of Globe's major customers, Globe listened very carefully. Globe's management quickly realized that, while the Q-1 program was voluntary, the criteria would have to be met to keep Ford as a long-term customer. In October 1985, therefore, Globe formally embarked on its quality improvement effort.

The first step in the certification process was a quality audit. Ford's "Q-101" audit is completed first by a supplier as a self-assessment and then by Ford personnel. If the audit meets a designated cutoff score, the supplier then becomes eligible for an internal Ford review of its performance history at all Ford locations using that supplier's products. If the supplier is acceptable to the various locations, Q-1 certification is granted by Ford.

The Q-101 self-assessment audit of Globe indicated that Globe would not meet the certification criteria. Although Globe had developed a reputation as a high-quality supplier over the years due to its 100 percent inspection practices, its quality systems were deficient. The primary deficiencies were that Globe's quality system focused on detection rather than prevention, it lacked statistical process control techniques, quality planning was absent, and there was no employee involvement in the improvement process.

To overcome these deficiencies, Globe implemented three key initiatives simultaneously. First, the entire workforce was trained in statistical process control. Second, a quality manual describing a new quality system was developed. Third, Globe's suppliers were educated and trained in the design of quality systems and statistical process control.

Quality Training

Globe's initial training was done by a trainer from the American Supplier Institute, affiliated with Ford. Globe's managers initially watched a series of videotaped lectures by Dr. Deming. Then the managers and employees received a minimum of six hours of fundamental statistical process control (SPC) techniques. Actual historical data from Globe were used in the training so that employees would be able to maintain, read, and interpret SPC charts.

From this beginning, Globe gradually developed in-house training capabilities in more advanced techniques. Employees were continually provided with additional quality training program. Both management and employees attended off-site training and brought the new knowledge back into Globe's internal training. Continual training in the most advanced quality improvement techniques remains a critically important issue at Globe.

Designing the Quality System

To design a quality system, several committees were formed at Globe. The name given to each committee was QEC, short for Quality-Efficiency-Cost. The QEC steering committee is chaired by the president and CEO and consists of all top management. This committee meets monthly to discuss the broader issues of the quality system such as allocation of resources and quality planning.

Each of Globe's two plants also has a QEC committee. The plant QEC committees are chaired by the plant managers and consist of all department heads. Each committee meets daily to discuss specific projects and implementation issues. Since the plant managers also serve on the QEC steering committee, they are the conduit that links the two levels of committees. The plant QEC committees had the initial responsibility of designing the quality system; subsequently, those committees shifted their focus to continuous quality improvement. The quality system was then codified into a quality manual.

Quality Manual

The quality manual was designed to be a reference manual for employees on the shop floor or in the various departments. The manual has five, major distinct segments that provide guidance for all employees.

Procedures. This section describes the nature of the interaction between different work groups at Globe. Procedures are based on workflow analysis that shows how each activity influences other activities. Essentially, this applies the concept of the "next operation as customer" so that every employee knows how his or her job contributes to the overall quality of Globe products.

Job Work Instructions. Job work instructions (JWIs) are basically very detailed job descriptions that describe exactly how each job should be done. JWIs are intended to ensure consistent employee performance at each activity because Globe plants operate 24 hours a day, using three shifts. Also, the JWIs ensure consistency when turnover occurs so new employees can be quickly trained.

Critical Process Variables. Critical process variables (CPVs) are the key product characteristics or attributes. CPVs have been identified for all control points in the production process. The primary technique used to track CPVs is the $\bar{x}$ and R chart. The QEC committee monitors processes to determine how process capability can be improved.

Product Parameters. Product parameters are the customer's expressed quality requirements. Most of Globe's customers now require a control plan that ensures product quality. The control plan includes both technical specifications and Globe's plan for quality assurance. Often both Globe and the customer sign off on the control plan, and any changes are jointly negotiated. Most of Globe's customers now require that SPC data and control charts accompany each order.

Failure Mode Effects Analysis. Failure mode effects analysis (FMEA) is undertaken for every process to determine the risk of failure. The likelihood of failure, the ability to detect failure, and the cost of failure to the customer all are calculated. When high risk of failure is identified, the process is redesigned or reengineered with better controls. FMEA is used in the development of new processes, in improvement of existing processes, and in analysis of complaints.

As Globe's internal quality system matured, Globe became much more sophisticated in its process control. For example, Globe purchased a new $60,000 computer system to monitor processes. The new system allowed hourly employees to customize each product to each customer's different specifications. Each personal computer on the shop floor was linked to the laboratory where quality tests were done. As customers became aware of the capability of the system, the requirement of 100 percent inspections was relaxed. The reduced inspections saved Globe $600,000 annually.

Supplier Development

The third cornerstone of quality improvement at Globe was supplier development. The management personnel of key suppliers were invited to attend the initial quality training held in October 1985. Of the large number of suppliers who attended, many lacked the knowledge and resources necessary to implement SPC in their company. Therefore, top management at Globe decided the best approach was for Globe to assist its suppliers.

QEC teams were formed that visited each supplier location and trained the suppliers' hourly employees in SPC basics. As the suppliers became more knowledgeable, increasingly sophisticated training was done. Globe provided training materials, calculators, and blank control charts. Globe personnel acted as consultants to Globe's suppliers by identifying critical processes and process variables. This training of suppliers remains a critical part of Globe's quality improvement effort, with significant results.

For example, the cost of sending a QEC team to a particular supplier was about $2,500. The QEC team helped to implement an SPC procedure that improved the quality of the supplier's products. The quality improvement among all its suppliers saved Globe $250,000 annually through reduced labor costs and improved efficiency.

All of Globe's suppliers are now trained, and each supplier annually undergoes a quality audit by Globe personnel. Globe has its own supplier certification program and has entered into long-term partnerships with numerous suppliers. Many suppliers now operate on a just-in-time inventory basis. Overall, Globe's supplier development has reduced supply costs, reduced inspection costs, reduced inventories, and improved efficiency.

Employee Involvement

Traditionally, hourly employees at Globe had never been involved in improvement efforts. After 1985, however, employees were involved in quality circles and various planning committees. Hourly employees were given the same benefit and pension package as salaried employees. A profit-sharing program was installed, and the average hourly employee now receives over $5,000 annually in profit-sharing bonuses.

The transition was not always smooth for Globe. As Globe began to implement improvements, the changes were met with distrust by many of the unionized workers. A yearlong strike occurred and many new workers were hired at the Beverly, Ohio, plant. The union was ultimately decertified. At Globe's Selma, Alabama, plant, which is still unionized, the improvements were welcomed and the union played an important role in the implementation.

Results

Globe's rapid and successful quality improvement led to its approval as a Ford Q-1 supplier in June 1986. Globe subsequently received General Motors' Mark of Excellence Award, which utilized somewhat different criteria from those that Ford used. Globe has received ISO-9000 certification. And, in 1988, Globe won the first Baldrige award given to a small business.

Globe has experienced tremendous increases in productivity since beginning its quality improvement process in October 1985. It has documented over $10 million in annual savings through quality improvement. And Globe has developed much closer relationships with both its customers and its suppliers, which continue to yield significant improvements annually.

THE ZYTEC CORPORATION STORY

Zytec Corporation, based in Eden Prairie, Minnesota, won a Baldrige award in 1991 in the manufacturing category. Prior to its creation in 1984, Zytec had been a unit of Magnetic Peripherals, Inc., a joint venture of four electronics firms. In 1984, Zytec was almost totally dependent on sales to its former owners.

Today, sales to its former owners account for only a fraction of total revenues. Customized power supplies for original equipment manufacturers of computers, office electronics, and medical and testing equipment account for 90 percent of Zytec's sales. The remaining 10 percent of sales come from repairs to cathode-ray-tube monitors and power suppliers, now the largest repair business of this type in the United States.

Immediately following the leveraged buyout that had created Zytec, Ronald Schmidt (chairman, president, and CEO) sought to establish a quality culture rather than a quality program. Thus, Zytec's approach to quality improvement consisted of a broad-based, cultural orientation which began with the company's inception in 1984.

As a template for building a continuous quality culture, Zytec chose Deming's 14 Points of Management Obligation (see the list of the points at the end of this section). Deming's 14 points focus on allowing workers to be all they can be, contending that management's real responsibility is to coach and support workers by way of the creation of an open, trusting, team-oriented environment.

Management by Planning

Combined with this quality culture, Zytec implemented a type of Hoshin Planning, which it calls Management by Planning (MBP). Long-range strategic plans are developed first. Then plans for each of the 33 departments are derived from the strategic plan. And then each job is linked to a departmental plan. At first glance, this seems to be the old strategic planning process that has been around for years. But it is really quite different.

Each year, Zytec holds a two-day planning meeting that involves about 150 employees, or 20 percent of the workforce. These employees represent virtually all of the horizontal and vertical areas in the company. The employees review and critique five-year plans that have been developed by six cross-functional teams. The cross-functional teams represent marketing, technology, manufacturing, materials, the product renewal center, and the corporation.

Concurrent with the internal review, Zytec invites customers and suppliers to evaluate and critique the long-range plan. This invariably leads to further refinement as the external partners often offer different perspectives and information.

Based on both the internal and external reviews, top management at Zytec then finalizes the long-range plan. Within the plan are the company's objectives for all aspects of the business, including quality planning. From these objectives, top management derives four key, one-year objectives. These objectives drive the MBP process.

In each department, a team develops a departmental plan. This plan must include annual goals and strategies for contributing to each of the four corporate objectives. Then, CEO Schmidt reviews each departmental plan, including goals, action plans, performance measures, and monthly progress targets. The CEO meets personally with the entire team or a representative and discusses the plan, offering advice when necessary. Then, each department reports at monthly operations meetings the progress it has made toward the departmental goals. In this way, each job is linked directly to the departmental plan, which is linked to the long-range plan. And employees are actively involved at each step. Employee involvement is not restricted to the planning process, however.

New Product Development

The design and development of new products are assigned to interdepartmental work teams. These cross-functional teams "own" the new product development process from start to finish. The teams work with both suppliers and customers and are empowered to make decisions regarding process development, specifications, and quality standards. This team approach extends through all four development stages: predesign initiation, design initiation, prototype delivery and testing, and preproduction certification. Once the new product is fully ready for production, the team relinquishes control.

Autonomous Work Teams

Some of the 33 departments at Zytec are managed by self-directed teams of workers. The workers themselves decide how the jobs will be allocated, designed, and evaluated. A key part of this autonomous work group is the Multi-Functional Employee (MFE) program. Through the MFE program, employees are evaluated and rewarded for the number of skills they acquire. The more skills each employee possesses, the better each employee understands the whole process. But even more important is that a larger number of skills per employee creates within each autonomous work group more flexibility in designing and allocating activities in the department.

Training

To support the various team efforts, participation, and involvement, Zytec places heavy emphasis on training. Most employees receive at least 72 hours of training annually, some receive much more. The internal environment also encourages employees to learn on their own as well. Much of the training is on analytical and group problem solving linked directly to quality-related issues.

Suggestion Program

Zytec has implemented a recognition-based suggestion program called the Implemented Improvement System (IIS). Each employee who has an idea for improvement must get approval from the supervisor to investigate the idea further. Once approval is given, the employee assumes all responsibility for researching and implementing the idea. The employee can use input from suppliers, engineering departments, or research departments, for example.

If the idea is not implemented, the employee gets no credit for trying it. If the idea is implemented, the employee gets one dollar. However, each month all suggestions are reviewed and rated. The first-place winner gets $100, second place gets $75, and third place gets $50.

In addition, the names of all employees who implement suggestions go into a hat each month. The name of one employee is drawn and that person gets a paid day off. And the selected employee has the right to ask anyone in the company to do his or her work on that day. Occasionally, the one selected to do the work has been the CEO. And sometimes the employee will come into work on that day off just to watch the replacement doing the work.

Benchmarking

Zytec actively engages in all types of benchmarking. The company conducts competitive benchmarking whereby its products and services are compared to its competitors' and to industry leaders'. The company conducts best-in-class benchmarking for processes such as employee involvement, just-in-time manufacturing, and supplier management. Zytec's goal is to continually search out the world's best practices and integrate them into the Zytec culture.

Results

Zytec has achieved a wide array of positive results from its quality culture. Sales per employee are 25 percent above the industry average. From 1988 to 1991, Zytec achieved a 50 percent improvement in manufacturing yields, a 26 percent reduction in cycle time, a 50 percent reduction in the design cycle, and nearly a 40 percent reduction in product costs. The mean time between failure rate for a Zytec power supply has increased to over 1 million hours. And the company's on-time delivery rate had improvement to 96 percent in 1990. These results led 18 of Zytec's 20 customers to make Zytec a sole source supplier.

Through Zytec has achieved notable quality improvement, it still has room for improvement. Zytec is improving its continous improvement system, investing in computer-integrated manufacturing technology, and increasing employee training. Its current goal is to reach the six sigma quality level for most of its activities in 1995.

Deming's 14 Points of Management Obligation

These 14 points were developed by Dr. W. Edward Deming to guide management in developing the proper organizational environment for a quality transformation.

1. Create constancy of purpose toward improvement of product and service, with the aim to become competitive and stay in business, and to provide jobs.
2. Adopt this new philosophy: We are in a new economic age created by Japan. Transformation of Western management style is necessary to halt the continued decline of industry.
3. Cease depending on inspection to achieve quality. Eliminate the need for inspection on a mass basis by building quality into the product in the first place.
4. End the practice of awarding business on the basis of price tag. Purchasing must be combined with design of product, manufacturing, and sales to work with the chosen suppliers; the aim is to minimize total cost, not merely initial cost.
5. Improve constantly and forever every activity in the company in order to improve quality and productivity and thus constantly decrease costs.
6. Institute training and education on the job for everyone, including management.
7. Institute supervision. The aim of supervision should be to help people and machines do a better job.

8. Drive out fear so that everyone may work effectively for the company.
9. Break down barriers between departments. People in Research, Design, Sales, and Production must work as a team to tackle usage and production problems that may be encountered with the product or service.
10. Eliminate slogans, exhortations, and targets for the workforce that ask for zero defects and new levels of productivity. Such exhortations only create adversarial relationships; the bulk of the causes of low quality and low productivity belongs to the system and thus lies beyond the power of the workforce.
11. Eliminate work standards that prescribe numerical quotas for the day. Substitute aids and helpful supervision.
12a. Remove the barriers that rob hourly workers of the right to pride of workmanship. The responsibility of supervisors must be changed from sheer numbers to quality.
12b. Remove the barriers that rob people in management and in engineering of their right to pride of workmanship. This means, among other things, abolition of the annual or merit rating and of management by objective.
13. Institute a vigorous program of education and retraining. New skills are required for changes in techniques, materials, and service.
14. Put everybody in the company to work in teams to accomplish the transformation.

THE GRANITEROCK COMPANY STORY

Graniterock is a 1992 Baldrige award winner in the small business category. Based in Watsonville, California, just south of San Francisco, Graniterock produces rock, sand, and gravel aggregates, ready-mix concrete, asphalt, and road treatment, and it also has a highway paving operation. In addition, the company sells a wide range of building materials, such as brick, concrete block, wallboard, and decorative stone, which are manufactured by outside suppliers.

The industry in which Graniterock competes is fiercely competitive, and most competitors are now large, publicly traded firms. Traditionally, the industry has consisted of a commodity business, with most customers buying from the lowest-bid supplier. Further, the industry has been adversely affected by recession, and the overall demand has decreased. Despite that highly competitive, shrinking industry, Graniterock has achieved notable success.

Graniterock has significantly increased market share. Productivity has steadily increased and revenue per employee has risen to about 30 percent above the national industry average. Turnover and absenteeism have steadily decreased. Due to the extensive amount of attention paid to safety, Graniterock's worker's compensation rates have declined to less than half of the industry average. Costs of resolving customer complaints are .2 percent of sales—one-tenth of the industry average. Some key production processes have the achieved six sigma quality level. And Graniterock has nearly a 10-point lead over the customer satisfaction level of its best competitor.

Graniterock's evolution to its current level of quality performance is typical of many firms. For the first few years after starting its total quality program in 1985, progress was slow and uneven. However, quality improvement really gained momentum in 1988, when Graniterock adopted the Baldrige award criteria as a process template, which several other recent Baldrige winners also have done. Graniterock applied for the Baldrige award in 1989, 1990, 1991, and 1992. It received a site visit in 1991 and won an award in 1992, seven years after embarking on the quality journey. By using the Baldrige criteria as a *process*, quality issues permeated every area of the company.

Graniterock's Nine Corporate Objectives

The comprehensive approach to quality is illustrated by Graniterock's nine corporate objectives. From these 9 objectives, 57 annual baseline goals are derived, with about 6 goals for each objective. These baseline goals are identified by senior management, and the goals define the quality improvement strategies for all 400 of Graniterock's employees at its 15 or so plants and facilities. The goals specify the measurements to be used, and progress is monitored quarterly and annually. The results of the performance reviews are shared with all employees and also are used in the compensation system.

The nine objectives drive the long-term planning process. Graniterock has developed the Quality by Design Timeline, which is a large chart that traces improvement in all nine objectives since 1985. The chart also includes projections for several years into the future. The intent of the chart is to graphically link long-term planning, annual planning, and the contribution of each employee.

The Team Approach

The management at Graniterock adopted a matrix structure in 1986 to flatten the organizational hierarchy and to foster team development. There are ten corporate quality teams that align improvement efforts across the various divisions. The corporate quality teams consist of a comprehensive vertical and horizontal slice of employees, from top management to hourly employees. In addition, there are about a hundred quality teams that involve nearly all employees. These lower-level teams are fully empowered to make local improvement decisions that contribute to each of the 57 annual baseline goals. The company's team-oriented structure has resulted in much faster responses to customers' needs and requests. The goal of all teams is to develop a proactive approach that anticipates customers' needs before the needs arise.

Information Systems

As a result of this proactive approach, the information system monitors changes over time in key areas of importance to customers. For example, on-time delivery of ready-mix concrete is a factor critical to customers. As this criterion has become more important, customers' expectations about on-time delivery have increased. Since Graniterock could not find a firm that measured on-time delivery of concrete, Domino's Pizza was used as a benchmark. Both concrete and pizza are perishable products, and on-time delivery is important to customers of both products. Domino's tracks on-time delivery worldwide and for local operations in traffic conditions identical to those faced by Graniterock. By benchmarking Domino's processes, Graniterock improved its on-time delivery from 70 percent in 1988 to 93.5 percent in 1991. Graniterock uses similar comparisons for linking internal measurement of a variety of processes to best-in-class benchmarks.

Human Resource Development

A key element in Graniterock's quality improvement has been the development of its human resources. Each employee can voluntarily participate in the Individual Professional Development Plan (IPDP). The IPDP is a process whereby an employee and the employee's manager separately develop a professional development plan for the employee. The two then jointly meet to discuss the similarities and differences and to develop a consensus plan. The individual's aspirations, abilities, and skills are integrated with each of the quality objectives. This process identifies an individual human resource, training, and development needs. The process also allows the manager to emerge as a coach, who assists in the development of employees and facilitates clear identification of education and training needs for divisions and the overall company.

The education and training needs are then translated into specific courses, seminars, and programs offered by "Graniterock University." Over 50 subjects are offered. The five categories of offerings are quality process skills; maintenance skills; sales and service skills; product or technical skills; and health, wellness, and personal growth. In 1991, Graniterock spent an average of $1,697 on training per employee, which is over 3 times the average in the mining industry and over 12 times the average in the construction industry.

Although Graniterock spent about $700,000 on training in 1991, the training *saved* money. The $2-million annual savings in workers' compensation premiums was directly related to safety training. The savings in that one area paid for all of Graniterock's training.

Process Quality

The construction industry is project oriented. Each project may require products with unique designs, applications, and specifications to fit a particular situation. This is true for all three major product categories of aggregates, concrete, and asphaltic concrete. Therefore, Graniterock has developed a four-step process to ensure product quality.

First, the needs are determined through project requirements, customer requirements, or specification changes. Second, the production and delivery process is designed based on approaches consistent with high quality, reliable production techniques, and service considerations. Third, evaluative criteria are developed that include testing procedures, benchmark comparisons, and customer or government agency approval. And fourth, the process is implemented, including documentation of having met improvement goals through statistical process control.

When a product or service discrepancy (PSD) occurs, Graniterock conducts root cause analysis. This allows the cause of the PSD to be identified and redesigned to prevent future problems.

An example of process improvement is the Granitepress automatic load-out system. A customer uses a billing card to activate an automated loading system, much as a customer uses an automated teller machine. A truck is weighed, loaded over the scale, and reweighed. The facility is open 24 hours a day, seven days a week, and the customer receives an automatic detailed billing statement.

Supplier Partnering

Graniterock has developed a supplier evaluation program. Suppliers are evaluated in the areas of product quality, service quality, support services, and pricing. The first three indicate whether or not the supplier is qualified to do business with Graniterock. Only if the supplier is qualified does pricing become an evaluative criterion, and then only when considered concurrently with quality.

All major suppliers are nominated and evaluated for the Golden Chain Award, Graniterock's quality award for suppliers. The quality criteria are communicated through the award evaluation document which is completed by both suppliers and Graniterock. Written feedback is generated for each supplier based on both the evaluation and a continuous supplier quality performance tracking system.

Several more comprehensive supplier partnering relationships have been implemented. Graniterock has partnering arrangements with its major cement supplier, tire service suppliers, several trucking companies, and Southern Pacific Railroad. All of the partnering relationships have resulted in significant benefits to both partners.

Customer Satisfaction

Graniterock measures customer satisfaction levels of both customers (the contractors) and the end user of its products. To deliver high customer satisfaction levels, Graniterock has developed partnering relationships with contractors and supports the contractors with a variety of services.

For example, if a customer is dissatisfied with any product or service, the customer is asked to short-pay the monthly invoice. The customer short-pays an amount that compensates, at the customer's discretion, for whatever the problem may have been. This quickly identifies problems so they can be corrected. It also indicates to the customer that Graniterock is confident of delivering high product and service quality. The annual cost of this short-pay system is .2 percent of sales. Complaints of all types decreased 31 percent from 1988 to 1991.

Graniterock also regularly compares its customer satisfaction levels to those of its direct competitors. Competitive assessments indicate that Graniterock maintains superior performance on virtually all of the 13 attributes measured. The competitive advantages are particularly evident for the most important attributes, to which Graniterock devoted its initial attention and efforts.

Graniterock's construction division, Pavex Construction Company, creates a unique advantage. The division could be viewed as a competitor by some customers. But an important role of Pavex is to allow Graniterock to develop quality improvement processes that can then be shared with contractor partners. Pavex allows Graniterock to develop a better and earlier understanding of trends and new technologies affecting the contractor's business.

The construction industry has generally not adopted total quality management. For example, Graniterock could find no other firms applying statistical process control to processes in its industry and no other cement firms tracking on-time delivery. In spite of little or no industry use of quality management concepts, however, Graniterock has clearly demonstrated that quality improvement concepts can be very successfully applied in its highly variable, project-oriented business. In industries not currently embracing quality concepts, early adoption and use may give a firm a significant competitive advantage, as has happened in the case of Graniterock. If a firm waits and adopts quality improvement only as a necessity for survival, then any hope of creating a competitive advantage will be greatly diminished.

Graniterock's Nine Corporate Objectives

Customer Satisfaction and Service. To earn the respect of our customers by providing them in a timely manner with the products and services that meet their needs and solve their problems.

People. To provide an environment in which each person in the organization gains a sense of satisfaction and accomplishment from personal achievements, to recognize individual and team accomplishments, and to reward individuals based upon their contributions and job performance.

Product Quality Assurance. To provide products which provide lasting value to our customers and conform to state, federal, or local government specifications.

Profit. To provide a profit to fund growth and to provide resources needed to fund achievement of our other objectives.

Management. To foster initiative, creativity, and commitment by allowing the individual greater freedom of action (in deciding how to do a job in attaining well-defined objectives [the goals set by management]).

Community Commitment. To be good citizens in each of the communities in which we operate.

Financial Performance and Growth. Our growth is limited only by our profits and the ability of Graniterock people to creatively develop and implement business growth strategies.

Production Efficiency. To produce and deliver our products at the lowest possible cost consistent with the other objectives.

Safety. To operate all Graniterock facilities with safety as the primary goal. Meeting scheduled or production volume is secondary.

4

The Service Imperative: Creating Value through Service Quality

"The customer doesn't distinguish product quality and service quality."

From the customer's perspective, product quality and service quality are virtually inseparable. Delivering high service quality is now absolutely essential to creating good customer value. Due to the rapidly changing technological environment, service quality now holds more potential for creating a competitive advantage than does product quality. But delivering service quality may be even more difficult than improving product quality.

The previous chapter focused on "product" quality but did not restrict the discussion to purely tangible products. Every aspect of the previous chapter is applicable to firms in service industries as well. Federal Express was the first "service" firm to win a Baldrige National Quality Award, but the company's approach to quality improvement is very similar to that of those firms profiled, all of which produced a tangible product. The ambiguities of service industries do present some unique challenges, which are discussed later in this chapter. But there is also another way of categorizing services.

Every product has some services that supplement the primary product being sold. With tangible products, it is often easy to identify the additional services provided. Computer firms have the services of knowledgeable salespeople who can educate customers about which computer best fits the customers' needs; they also have those follow-up "help" lines. A car purchase involves many additional services; all maintenance and warranty work is a form of service. For virtually every *tangible product*, there is some additional *support service* that accompanies it.

But this idea of support services is not restricted to tangible products only. Virtually every service product also has some support services as well. In the hospitality industry, for instance, the primary "product" may be in the form of a room for the night, but accurate reservations and efficient check-in are important support services. For Federal Express, moving a package from point A to point B is the primary "product," but accurate billing and invoicing and friendly employees are important support services. A doctor's primary product is medical treatment and advice, but keeping a punctual appointment schedule and handling insurance billings are important support services.

So every *product*, be it in a tangible product industry or in a service industry, has some accompanying support services. And this is precisely where many quality problems arise. Customers often don't distinguish between the quality of the primary product or service and the quality of the support service. Customers tend to roll the primary product and the support services together as part of a total package. And if that's the way customers evaluate the "product," then that's also the way a firm should design the product.

This inability of customers to separate product and service quality is a primary cause of the disappointing results of many quality improvement efforts. Many firms have improved their product design and conformance quality from an engineering and production standpoint. Defect rates may be low and reliability may be high. Often, however, these firms may still be looking for the rewards of quality improvement in market share or profitability. And the reason for their lackluster performance is that these firms have not included *support service* quality in their efforts. These firms remain difficult for their customers to do business with and haven't really adopted a customer-driven approach.

For a firm to be customer driven, it must translate customers' wants, needs, desires, and expectations into a product offering—a product offering that includes much more than the tangible product, which is the focus of most quality improvement. The "product" often includes pre-sale service, transaction-related services, and postsale services. Customers collectively rolls up their expectations about these services along with the product to create a bundle of attributes. To that bundle, some value is attached by the customer. If the firm's selling price is consistent with the customer's perception of value, then reasonable equity has probably been achieved. The pricing issue is discussed in the next chapter, so that discussion is deferred until later. For now, our interest is the bundle of attributes that the customer is buying, particularly those services that supplement the tangible product.

It is hard to think of a tangible product that doesn't have a significant support service component. Automobiles certainly have a service element: There are presale services such as education, information, and sales support. There are transaction services such as financing, title transfer, licensing, preparation, and detailing. And there are postsale services such as sales follow-up, maintenance, corrective repair, and problem solving. Yet no one doubts that a car is clearly a tangible product.

Conversely, many, if not most, services have a tangible component. The restaurant business is clearly a service industry, but we all inspect and evaluate the tangible product when dining out. After getting that haircut, styling, or permanent, who among us does not look in the mirror to inspect the product? A consultant is certainly selling a service, but the tangible, written report is typically widely circulated and closely scrutinized by a variety of managers. Frequent grammatical errors, typing mistakes, or misspellings would quickly undermine the consultant's credibility. A doctor's office or examining room that is found to be old, dirty, or unkempt is likely to tarnish one's perception of the doctor's quality.

If we combine the idea that tangible products are usually accompanied by services with the idea that services are usually accompanied by something tangible, most "products" would fall somewhere along the continuum in Figure 4.1. The left side of the figure would include firms whose tangible product characteristics are extremely important to customers. The manufacturer of a space satellite probably wouldn't be too concerned with a supplier's return policy but would be very concerned with design and production specifications and defect rate. Conversely, the right side of the figure would include "pure" service firms. For instance, an airline's getting passengers and their luggage from point A to

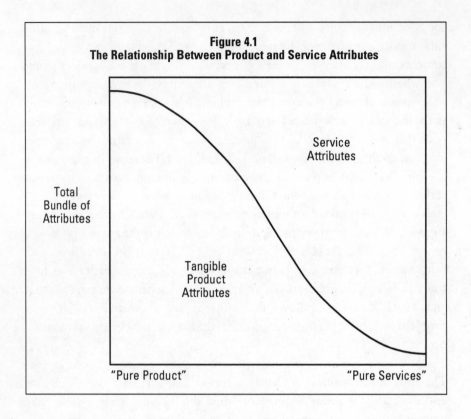

Figure 4.1
The Relationship Between Product and Service Attributes

point B on time in a friendly, courteous fashion would be much more important than the in-flight meal or beverage served. Still, it is very difficult to think of a service product that doesn't have some tangible component.

Although virtually all firms' products fall somewhere on the continuum, most managers cannot empirically validate (not managerially guess) the relative importance to the customer of the tangible versus intangible elements in that bundle of attributes for each product. And if a manager does know the relationship of tangibles to intangibles, most still cannot decompose services into all the subareas and identify which ones are most important to customers. But if a manager can do these things, and good tangible product quality is present, the firm is probably doing pretty well. But if a firm cannot do these things, it is almost certain to experience some quality problems.

If a firm were at the extreme left of the continuum and focused only on tangible product quality, then market and financial performance may be acceptable depending on the competition. Service would probably not be vitally important to customers, within reason. However, the farther to the right that a firm is situated on the continuum, the more severe the penalty for neglecting service quality. Most firms that are disappointed with the results of total quality management effort have neglected the service quality component, which could be significant to customers. After all, tangible product quality is merely a ticket to the dance; it doesn't mean you'll be the queen of the ball. All three aspects of the customer value triad must be consistent: product quality, service quality, and price.

TYPES OF SERVICES

The bundle of attributes that the customer is buying normally includes a variety of support services. For simplicity, let's start with three categories of support services. The first category precedes a purchase transaction, the second category is directly related to the transaction, and the third category follows the transaction and extends throughout the product's life. Certainly, the kinds of services in each category will vary from industry to industry and customer to customer. However, as firms develop closer supplier networks and stress relationship marketing more, the types of support services are likely to increase even more. Also, as competition becomes more intense, consumers will come to expect more and better services as well.

Presale Services

The support services that precede the sale are those that usually furnish the customer with information and assistance in the decision-making process. A firm could offer technical sales seminars in order to educate customers about new product developments. Such seminars could actually be a part of the customer training program, for example. A firm also could provide its customers with a range of managerial and technical assistance. For instance, supplier involvement in quality circles has been commonly used for many years by some firms. Stone Container Company takes the concept of management assistance much further.

Stone Container sells a variety of packaging materials—not stone containers—and provides comprehensive presale service for prospective customers. Stone essentially has a free consulting service that evaluates a customer's packaging needs and comes up with creative solutions. The solutions can range from custom-designed cartons to equipment modifications to changes in material flow to plant layout. Stone Container is so confident of its consulting service that it guarantees customers a cost savings that often runs from $300,000 to $500,000 annually. Stone Container sees its bundle of attributes as including presale consulting services in addition to the more tangible packaging materials.

Some presale services may be as simple as responding to a potential customer's questions in a timely fashion. Texas Instruments (TI) gets about 200,000 inquiries from potential customers each year. Over 95 percent of those inquiries get an answer within 2 hours, and virtually all inquiries get an answer within 24 hours. TI has developed an internal tracking system to ensure that no customer inquiries fall through the cracks. Such a swift response creates a positive service quality image among customers.

The range of presale services is endless. It could include order preparation service or setting up a special safety program for hazardous materials. It could include notice of forthcoming price and inventory changes. It could include consulting and management assistance.

Virtually all customers expect some presale services, but relatively few firms know either precisely what services their customers want or the relative importance of each service. Unfortunately, even when a firm knows the presale support services the customer wants, most firms have neither designed nor put in place a quality process for delivering those services. Instead, the delivery system has usually just gradually evolved over time.

Transaction Services

The second category of support services is directly associated with the exchange transaction between a firm and its customers. Transaction services are as varied as presale services. They may include providing customers with a computer and modem loaded with ordering software to speed order cycle times or be as simple as ordering by fax. Transaction services could include information about inventory surplus or shortage, changes in lot sizes, or order fill rates. They could include commitment to firm delivery dates. They could include financing and credit terms, information on guarantees, or return policies. They may include efficient check-in procedures at a hotel or at an airline.

The Quill Corporation is the nation's largest independent office products mail order dealer, serving over 500,000 customers annually. Every customer gets a copy of the Quill Customer's Bill of Rights, a one-page document that states the rights of customers, such as full value for their money, a guarantee of customer satisfaction, fast delivery, and the like.

If Quill fails in maintaining any of the customer's rights, customers are urged to let the company know. As an indication of commitment to customer satisfaction, every order includes a preauthorized return form if anything is not up to customer expectations. By conveying this information with each transaction, Quill is able to develop an atmosphere of trust with its customers at the time of the transaction.

Very often the transaction services are based on the needs of the selling firm, not on the needs of the customer. The common complaint that results is "you're hard to do business with." What customers are really saying is that a firm hasn't paid attention to transaction-related support services and seems to be ignoring them or treating them impersonally. And personalized service is something we all want, whether in a corporate or an individual transaction.

Postsale Services

The third category of support services consists of those that occur after the transaction. These are the support services that have traditionally attracted the most attention by firms. The initial service is probably delivering on the committed date, which is normally one of the most important criteria for industrial buyers. However, if an order is delayed, then order status, backorder, or shipping delay information becomes important. Customer service and complaint resolution processes also become important in such situations.

Guarantees are often limited to a fixed time period, and service, maintenance, and repair throughout that period are customer expectations. For capital or technical equipment, a variety of training programs are frequently required. When new technological advances occur, older equipment may need to be modified and customers retrained because of changes.

A common postsale service is simply sales follow-up to determine customer satisfaction. Some firms, particularly the more innovative auto dealers, have a specific program for postsale contact that includes cards, letters, and phone calls at various intervals after the transaction.

More and more firms are implementing a formalized customer satisfaction program that solicits quantifiable data on service as well as on product performance. Although customer satisfaction programs are the subject of a subsequent chapter and are discussed in detail there, it should be noted that postsale programs create a very positive image among customers if conducted properly.

Postsale customer contact and service should be initiated by both the firm and the customers. The firm should have a systematic process for postsale service and contact. In addition, the firm should develop a process and create an atmosphere that makes it easy for customers to initiate contact and request desired services. A firm that seldom hears from customers and doesn't contact them except at the time of a sale probably has a customer retention problem.

SERVICES AS A COMPETITIVE ADVANTAGE

With a little time and effort, we could probably come up with a list of 20 or so services in each of the three categories that customers want or expect. For a small percentage of products at the far left of the continuum in Figure 4.1, service may not be important to customers. Realistically, though, it is fairly difficult to think of a situation in which the bundle of services is unimportant. It is far easier to think of situations in which service is vitally important to customers than situations in which it is unimportant. Collectively, these support services may give a firm a competitive advantage, if designed and delivered properly, even in service industries.

With rapid technological changes, adaptations, and modifications occurring in an increasingly competitive environment, maintaining technical product superiority is extremely difficult for most firms. It is simply too easy for competitors to buy the innovative product, reverse-engineer it, and build the new features into their own product offerings, often in a matter of months. Hewlett-Packard, for example, feels that for most new product introductions, the window of technical superiority is difficult to sustain and is less than six months. For other products, the window may be only two or three months. That would seem to place more and more emphasis on support service quality as a competitive tool. If a firm can no longer maintain long-term differentiation based on tangible product characteristics, it is logical that customers may use intangible support service elements as increasingly important decision criteria.

Research has shown that for a variety of reasons, improving tangible product quality is easier for most firms to accomplish than developing service quality. The implication is that while product quality can be copied, service quality is more difficult for competitors to replicate because it flows more closely from a firm's corporate culture. Since virtually all firms provide services in support of products to some degree, service quality may be an overlooked competitive weapon by many firms.

As a quick diagnostic test, how many services in each of the three categories does your firm provide? Are those services the ones that the customers really want? What is the order of importance of the services in each category? (You need this information for resource allocation.) Have all of these services been designed into a bundle of attributes that maximize customer value? Or did the services just gradually evolve based on traditional managerial gut feeling? If you can't answer these questions, don't feel bad; most managers also can't answer all of them, so you're not alone.

TWO-FACTOR MODEL OF SERVICE QUALITY

In the previous chapter, a two-factor model of product quality was introduced that focused predominantly on tangible product attributes or on the primary service product. The same concept can be applied equally well to support service quality. Some support service attributes would be hygiene factors, and others would be satisfiers. The hygiene factors for support services are those that customers expect to be there as part of that bundle of attributes. The customer simply expects some threshold level of performance on certain support service attributes. The absence of hygiene service factors would probably result in customer dissatisfaction, but the presence of those factors wouldn't necessarily contribute to customer satisfaction.

Reliable delivery is probably a hygiene factor. Delivering an order to a customer on time represents a minimum acceptable level of performance. It is simply an expected threshold level of service. Failure to meet that level of expected service will probably result in dissatisfaction. However, consistently delivering orders on time may not contribute much to customer satisfaction.

More broadly, a firm should make sure that hygiene support services meet customer expectations. Beyond that level of performance on hygiene service attributes, additional resources should be devoted to the satisfiers. The support service satisfiers constitute the areas where a firm has the ability to create a unique competitive advantage with customers so as to create customer delight. The satisfiers are typically those support services that go beyond the customers' more basic expectations. Free consulting or problem-solving services typically fall beyond customers' minimum acceptable performance levels. Exceptionally friendly and helpful customer contact personnel would probably be support service satisfiers. These satisfiers may create a distinct competitive advantage and add unexpected customer value to the bundle of attributes.

Combining the concept of hygiene attributes and satisfiers with the concept of the three types of support services discussed earlier results in a six-cell matrix. Examples of support services when buying a car are presented in each of the six cells in Figure 4.2. The types of support services in each cell are intended to be illustrative and not exhaustive. However, it is important to note the minimum level of support service performance that is acceptable to customers. These are the service hygiene attributes that absolutely must be present. The second category of satisfiers provides the opportunity to increase customer satisfaction, customer retention, and profitability. Unfortunately, the ambiguous nature of services makes clarifying customer expectations more difficult than for tangible product characteristics.

When we consider buying a car, we have come to expect some presale services. The test drive is certainly a simple hygiene attribute: all of us expect the opportunity to try a car out before making a large financial sacrifice. How many of us, though, have had a car salesperson deliver a car to our home and suggest a two- or three-day test drive? Probably very few! How many of us have ever received any training in how to use all of the different options? Probably even fewer of us. How many of us have had a dealer provide a free automobile checkup before the warranty expiration date so that any problems could be fixed at the manufacturer's expense? Probably even fewer still.

There is an important message in this categorization of services. If a firm fails to meet the customers' expectations of presale services, then customers will probably simply take their business elsewhere. Failure to deliver transaction-related services at the customers' expected level of performance will lead to some lost sales, but certainly customer dissatisfaction will occur. Failure to deliver postsale support services will certainly cause customer dissatisfaction and result in higher customer turnover.

Though there are certainly some exceptions, most automobile dealers focus on the transaction and postsale hygiene services and pay very little attention to the satisfiers. But the support service satisfiers are the ones that may hold the greatest potential for creating a competitive advan-

Figure 4.2
Types of Services in Buying a Car

	Hygiene Attributes	Satisfier Attributes
Presale Services	• Basic test drive • Availability of knowledgeable salespeople • Friendliness, courteous behavior • Concern for customer's needs	• Delivering car to prospective buyer's door • Extended test drive (several days) • Comparative purchase information • Availability of interactive video
Transaction Services	• Financing • Title transfer & registration • Licensing • Detailing of car • Coffee, refreshments • Specialists to complete paperwork	• Full tank of gas • Car wash coupons • Complimentary service (free oil change) • Debriefing of car's operating features • Child care with activities
Postsale Services	• Basic warranty, guarantee • Some sales force follow-up • Courtesy car (pick-up or delivery) • Quick repair when necessary	• Proactive sales follow-up • Strong dealer support if problems occur • Dealer inspection of car before expiration of warranty • Free loaner car when appropriate • Customer satisfaction measure with customer feedback

tage. The following real-life example illustrates the result of creating customer delight.

Five attorneys from Boise, Idaho, decided not to fly but to drive to a conference in Portland, Oregon—a distance of 500 miles. One of the attorneys owned a late-model Chevrolet Suburban, which he volunteered to drive on the trip because of its roominess. The lawyers were to drive to Portland the afternoon before the conference. Less than 20 miles from Boise the Suburban developed engine problems. The engine quit completely, and the lawyers were stranded alongside the freeway.

Now they were in a real dilemma. Even if they could make flight connections and find empty seats, the airfare would be extremely high due to the same-day purchase of the tickets. So the owner of the Suburban phoned the dealer where he bought the vehicle, and he explained the problem. The lawyer was hoping to rent another Suburban on very short notice.

Instead, the dealer told the attorney to take a brand-new Suburban free of charge. The dealer delivered the new Suburban to the attorneys beside the freeway, the switch was made, and the dealer rode back with the tow truck.

Most of us would consider this uncommonly good service, but the real payoff came later for the dealer. The attorney's Suburban had quit because the engine had seized. The attorney who was driving had been engrossed in conversation and wasn't paying close attention to the gauges. Seems that a technician in one of those fast-lube-and-oil change places had forgotten to tighten the oil drain plug. The plug apparently fell out, the oil drained, and within a few minutes, the engine overheated and seized completely. The dealer had the diagnosis in hand when the attorneys returned several days later.

The group of attorneys was so impressed with the service and the new Suburban they used on their trip that three of them bought new Suburbans from the dealer within two weeks. A fourth, the owner of the original Suburban, instead of returning the loaned Suburban bought the vehicle because he didn't like the idea of a rebuilt engine. The payoff for the dealer was the sale of four Suburbans and an engine rebuild. For readers who aren't familiar with the price of Suburbans, the total sales figure for the four was well over $100,000. The long-term payoff from delighted customers will be even greater.

Virtually all products have a support service component that includes hygiene and satisfier attributes. The inherently ambiguous nature of services of all types makes identification of service hygiene and satisfiers more difficult than for tangible product attributes. This is largely due to the unique characteristics of services, whether they are support services or pure services.

UNIQUE CHARACTERISTICS OF SERVICES

The discussion to this point has concentrated mainly on those support services that accompany either a tangible product or the primary service product. When the primary product is predominantly a service—that is, it would fall on the right side of the continuum in Figure 4.1—some additional challenges emerge. The challenges emanate from the fact that services of all types have unique characteristics. As we shall see, these unique characteristics present problems for the design of the delivery system, measurement of the delivered quality, and measurement of customer expectations.

The four primary unique characteristics identified for services are intangibility, heterogeneity, perishability, and inseparability of production and consumption. Whereas in the literature these characteristics were identified for pure services, the same characteristics are generally appropriate for most support services as well. The primary distinction in applying these characteristics to both pure and support services is that in many cases the firm has the ability to defer demand somewhat more for support services. Though it may be possible to defer the demand for only a few hours or a few days, that is often enough time to adjust the service delivery system. But all services, whether support or pure, suffer from these characteristics.

For example, in a service business such as a restaurant, demand can be deferred very little. Assuming a restaurant does not operate purely on a reservation basis, if a large number of people decide to eat at that restaurant on a Friday evening, customers will likely face a long wait to be seated at a table and perhaps a longer than usual wait to be served after ordering. Due to the heavy demand, waitresses may be rushing so much that personalized service is diminished. Some customers will choose to dine elsewhere and some who stay may be dissatisfied.

Conversely, for some support services such as order processing, returns, or complaint resolution, demand could be spread over, say a 24-hour period. Workers from other areas could be brought in to match supply and demand with no negative customer experiences. Therefore, while some support services may require urgency in response, many others may be delayed slightly. But all services, whether support or pure, suffer from these characteristics.

Intangibility

The characteristic most often mentioned as unique to services is intangibility. A physical product can be touched, examined, and evaluated on its tangible characteristics. This concept is at the heart of statistical process control. The producer of a tangible product can usually determine product quality simply by examining the product. However, a service product is inherently more subjective. A service product is more difficult to define and is subject to alternative perceptions and expectations. For example, if you asked four people in a firm to define high-quality complaint resolution, you would get four different responses due to different perceptions and expectations. If you asked the same question of four customers, you would probably get four additional, and different, responses. As is discussed subsequently, intangibility also causes customers to use different evaluative criteria from the criteria used for tangible products.

Heterogeneity

Because services are inherently labor-intensive and therefore subject to human variability, they tend to vary from situation to situation and from day to day. Because many services inherently require customer involvement, the customer also is often a source of variability, so service delivery can also vary from customer to customer. Indeed, with advancements in computer technology, many customers expect that services should be customized to fit their particular needs. Invoicing and billing procedures, shipping and delivery systems, and quality inspection and documentation are often tailored to fit a specific customer.

Perishability

Many services are perishable: an unsold seat on an airplane, excess capacity in a restaurant, a canceled doctor's appointment. Once a service has been created and delivered, it has no further value. Although support services are not as perishable as pure services, some perishability also inherently exists. For example, order-taking and customer service departments are typically staffed at some expected capacity level. When services such as these are not used, they perish. Training capacity not delivered to customers due to low sales also perishes. For those support services that can be delayed by a few hours or days, perishability becomes less of a concern.

Inseparability of Production and Consumption

Many services, both support services and pure services, are consumed by customers as soon as they are produced. In essence, the do-it-right-the-first-time philosophy is mandatory because there may be no second chance to correct mistakes. The immediacy of consumption also implies that the sellers and buyers are in close contact, interacting with and observing one another. This suggests that service providers must be well prepared and trained before delivering the service. Because of potentially negative customer impact, there is little or no room for "on-the-job training." This means that all service providers become an integral part of the firm's overall marketing effort.

These unique characteristics of services present organizations with equally unique challenges. While a firm may have a very discrete, well-identified product line, for each product there may be 20 or 30 additional potential service attributes or encounters with varying degrees of importance. Managing the service elements may be much more difficult than managing production of the tangible product due to the four unique characteristics of services. However, the design and delivery of service attributes may hold the greatest potential for creating a competitive advantage in this age of rapid technological change and adaptation.

CUSTOMER'S EVALUATIVE CRITERIA FOR SERVICES

With little doubt, the work done by Leonard Berry, A. Parasuraman, and Valarie Zeithaml is at the forefront of research on service quality. Although the group's research focuses predominantly on pure services—those on the right side of the continuum in Figure 4.1—many of the group's ideas and research findings are also generalizable and applicable to support services as well. Their 1990 book, *Delivering Quality Service: Balancing Customer Perceptions and Expectations* (Free Press), provides an excellent summary and the integration of their many articles.

Two aspects of the author's work are particularly appropriate for discussion here. Based on a series of focus group interviews, the authors identified 10 determinants of service quality for relatively pure services (Table 4.1). The 10 criteria are not mutually exclusive or appropriate in all situations, but they do represent a comprehensive summary of the variables that influence the purchase decision process for intangible services.

Information about the 10 criteria is typically acquired in four ways. First, word-of-mouth communications between customers shapes customers' or potential customers' perceptions. As we shall see in a later chapter, negative word-of-mouth communication is often more influential than positive communication. Second, the customer's personal needs

Table 4.1 Determinants of Service Quality

Reliability involves consistency of performance and dependability. It means that the firm performs the service right the first time. It also means that the firm honors its promises. Specifically, it involves:
— accuracy in billing;
— keeping records correctly;
— performing the service at the designated time.

Responsiveness concerns the willingness or readiness of employees to provide service. It involves timeliness of service:
— mailing a transaction slip immediately;
— calling the customer back quickly;
— giving prompt service (e.g., setting up appointments quickly).

Competence means possession of the required skills and knowledge to perform the service. It involves:
— knowledge and skill of the contact personnel;
— knowledge and skill of operational support personnel;
— research capability of the organization (e.g., securities brokerage firm).

Access involves approachability and ease of contact. It means:
— the service is easily accessible by telephone (lines are not busy and they don't put you on hold);
— waiting time to receive service (e.g., at a bank) is not extensive;
— convenient hours of operation;
— convenient location of service facility.

Courtesy involves politeness, respect, consideration, and friendliness of contact personnel (including receptionists, telephone operators, etc.). It includes:
— consideration for the consumer's property (e.g., no muddy shoes on the carpet);
— clean and neat appearance of public contact personnel.

Table 4.1 Determinants of Service Quality (continued)

Communication means keeping customers informed in language they can understand and listening to them. It may mean that the company has to adjust its language for different consumers—increasing the level of sophistication with a well-educated customer and speaking simply and plainly with a novice. It involves:
— explaining the service itself;
— explaining how much the service will cost;
— explaining the trade-offs between service and cost;
— assuring the consumer that a problem will be handled.

Credibility involves trustworthiness, believability, honesty. It involves having the customer's best interests at heart. Contributing to credibility are:
— company name;
— company reputation;
— personal characteristics of the contact personnel;
— the degree of good will involved in interactions with the customer.

Security is freedom from danger, risk, or doubt. It involves:
— physical safety (Will I get mugged at the automatic teller machine?);
— financial security (Does the company know where my stock certificate is?);
— confidentiality (Are my dealings with the company private?).

Understanding/knowing the customer involves making the effort to understand the customer's needs. It involves:
— learning the customer's specific requirements;
— providing individualized attention;
— recognizing the regular customer.

Tangibles include the physical evidence of the service:
— physical facilities;
— appearance of personnel;
— tools or equipment used to provide the service;
— physical representations of the service, such as a plastic credit card or a bank statement;
— other customers in the service facility.

Source: Reprinted with permission from A. Parasuraman, Valarie A. Zeithaml, and Leonard L. Berry, "A Conceptual Model of Service Quality and Its Implications for Future Research," *Journal of Marketing*, 49, 4 (Fall 1985), pp. 41–50, published by the American Marketing Association.

and immediacy of fulfillment influence perceptions of the criteria. A consumer's need for auto repair is quite different when the car breaks down at night on a freeway from the need for a tune-up, which arises gradually. Third, past experience with a company, competitors, or similar types of businesses shapes perceptions of what is possible and acceptable. Fourth, external communications such as advertising, publicity, and general information about a firm shape a customer's perception about suitable service.

The ambiguous nature of services of all types leads to a relatively diverse array of evaluative criteria. Customers tend to use a variety of sources for information acquisition about those criteria. Unfortunately, the relative importance of both the decision criteria and the information source varies from customer to customer and situation to situation. To integrate these concepts, the three aforementioned authors developed a model of service quality.

SERVICE QUALITY MODEL

The service quality model of Parasuraman, Zeithaml, and Berry (Figure 4.3) identifies five key gaps that can cause problems in service delivery. These gaps are created due to the ambiguous nature of services and due to the different perceptions and expectations on the part of producers and customers. When large discrepancies in each gap exist, service quality is low. As the discrepancies are eliminated, service quality increases.

Gap 1

Gap 1 is the gap between customer expectations and management's perception of those expectations. This gap is the result of lack of understanding or a misinterpretation of the customers' wants, needs, and desires. Therefore, this gap could be called the *research* gap. The firm that does little or no marketing or customer satisfaction research is almost certain to experience this gap. The firm that does conduct research but doesn't really integrate the results into the decision-making process probably also has this gap. Managers who assume they know what customers want but who don't have any way of substantiating their position also contribute to this gap.

Of the five gaps in the model, this one is the most serious, simply because discrepancies here will cause problems in each of the other four. If an organization doesn't fully understand the customers' expectations,

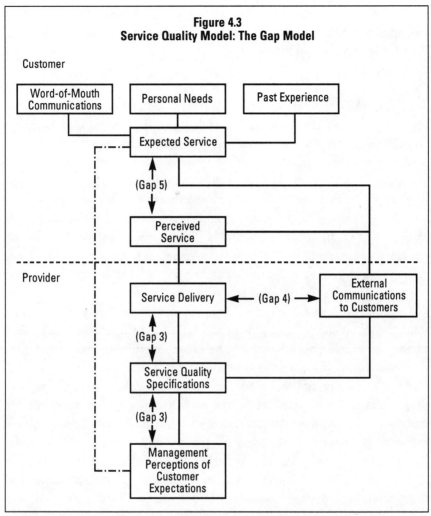

Figure 4.3
Service Quality Model: The Gap Model

Source: Reprinted with permission from A. Parasuraman, Valerie A. Zeithami, and Leonard L. Berry, "A Conceptual Model of Service Quality and its Implications for Future Research," *Journal of Marketing*, 49, 4 (Fall 1985), pp. 41–50, published by the American Marketing Association.

there is no hope of becoming truly customer driven. And unless a firm becomes customer driven, long-term survival will be questionable due to competitive pressure. Surely, some competitor will indeed pay attention to customer needs; and when that happens, a firm with a large discrepancy in gap 1 will experience erosion of its industrial position.

The way to close gap 1 is conceptually simple but pragmatically difficult. Good qualitative and quantitative research is necessary. Qualitatively, customers must be integrated into a firm's decision-making process. Quantitatively, good research is necessary, particularly a good customer satisfaction program. In a general sense, the solution to gap 1 is to become truly customer driven.

Gap 2

This gap is the one between management's perception of what the customer wants and the designed capabilities of the system that management develops to provide the service. Essentially, this gap is the result of management's inability to translate the customer's needs into delivery systems within the firm. Therefore, this could be called the *planning and design* gap. Complacency is a major contributor to this gap as managers adhere to the status quo, traditional way of doing business. When change does occur, it is incremental, and only small modifications of the existing system are made. In a stable environment, low rates of managerial innovation are acceptable, but the rapid rate of environmental change that exists today requires a different response.

Organizations must become flatter, leaner, and more responsive. They must thrive on change and innovation rather than fight them every step of the way as is often the case. The cross-functionally integrated firm that is customer driven is the solution to gap 2.

From a managerial techniques standpoint, quality function deployment (QFD) can be used to overcome this gap. QFD is a system for translating consumer requirements into appropriate company requirements at each stage, from research and product development to engineering and manufacturing to marketing and distribution. Although QFD was developed for application in the area of tangible products, the same concept can easily be applied to services. Once again, QFD is simply a way of ensuring that the voice of the customer is heard and acted upon throughout the firm.

Gap 3

Gap 3 is the gap between what the service system is designed to provide and what it actually provides. Assuming for a moment that both gaps 1 and 2 have been closed, gap 3 then is due to the inability of the management and the employees to do what should be done. Therefore, this could be called the *implementation* gap. When a system is designed properly but is not delivering what it should, the cause of the problem is almost always behavioral.

Poorly trained, poorly motivated, or alienated workers are symptomatic of behavioral problems. The real cause of such symptoms is the inability of management to manage human resources. Too often, management pursues a centralized, autocratic approach, afraid to share its power. Delegation of power and authority is seen as a weakness or the erosion of management's reason for existence.

This unwillingness to unleash the ability of workers has a simple solution: worker empowerment. Again, the solution is conceptually simple but pragmatically difficult. Worker empowerment is the solution to gap 3, but empowerment is not a managerial technique. Worker empowerment is a philosophy that must flow from the corporate culture. As is discussed more fully in the last chapter, empowerment is an organizational characteristic that is essential for long-term success and for becoming responsive. Knowledge does not reside only at the top of organizations. Knowledge is dispersed throughout organizations, and worker empowerment is the only way to harness that knowledge.

Gap 4

This is the gap between what the service system provides and what the customer is told it provides. Discrepancies in this gap have been the source of many of the truth-in-advertising regulations over the years, and the fundamental issue is one of honesty. Therefore, this could be called the *communication* gap.

Misleading promotional campaigns, puffery, and doing whatever it takes to get the business all reflect a very short-term, desperate view on the part of management. The perspective that customers are dumb, illiterate, and easily be duped is an archaic business philosophy. Sure, you might get customers to try your products once, but dissatisfied, disgruntled, angry customers can do a great deal of damage to a firm's reputation and image, as we shall see later.

The solution to this gap is the creation of accurate customer expectations of services provided. This can be done through honest, accurate communication about a firm's service capability and performance. Note that a firm's external communications are only partly responsible for customer expectations.

A customer's expectations are influenced by the customers' knowledge and experience with similar products and by word-of-mouth communication from peers. Competitors' performance capabilities provide customers with a range of alternatives and a frame of reference. Customers have a tendency to believe that if one firm can offer a certain level of service, other firms should be able to offer at least the same level of service as well. Thus, competitors may also have a strong influence on customer expectations.

Gap 5

This gap exists between customers' service expectations and customers' perceptions of that service. Since this gap deals purely with customer expectations and customer perceptions of actual service, it could be called a *reality* gap. Berry, Parasuraman, and Zeithaml contend that if the first four gaps are closed, then this one will automatically cease to exist. Specifically, if all of the previous gaps are closed, then the service delivery system, at the minimum level of performance, meets customer expectations. Conversely, if management feels that all four gaps are closed and gap 5 still exists, then management is wrong. Thus gap 5 is a dose of reality for management, which may be wearing rose-colored glasses.

USING THE SERV-QUAL MODEL

The best application of the service quality model is as a managerial diagnostic tool. By identifying five major sources of possible service quality breakdowns, or gaps, managers may better understand precisely why service quality does, or does not, meet customer expectations. This is quite important because each gap requires a fundamentally different strategy to eliminate it. Gap 1, for example, is caused by a lack of understanding of customer expectations. The managerial strategy to eliminate this gap requires the gathering of both quantitative and qualitative customer-driven data. Gap 3 is caused by the failure of employees to do what they really should be doing. The strategy to eliminate this gap requires motivating and empowering employees.

SUMMARY

The predominant focus for most firms has been on improving *product* quality. Service quality is more ambiguous, more complex, and less understood. Too often service is considered to mean having a good customer service department, a good complaint handling department, and friendly employees. Nothing could be further from the truth.

Service attributes add value to products. But the customer doesn't separate product and service attributes into discrete entities. The customer rolls both types of attributes together, often in an ill-defined, imprecise manner. Since the customer meshes product and service attributes together, the firm should do the same.

Each service attribute is the result of some value-added process that either is carefully designed or just happens. Allowing service quality to just gradually evolve represents exactly the same situation that product quality was in during the 1970s and early 1980s. The best you can hope for is mediocrity. And mediocre service, even when combined with high product quality, does not create high customer value.

Ensuring service quality may be more difficult than ensuring product quality, due to the unique characteristics of services. Intangibility, heterogeneity, perishability, and inseparability of production and consumption lead to ambiguity about service performance and the customer's service expectations. And that ambiguity leads to the five gaps shown in the service quality model.

Further complicating the delivery of service quality is the diversity of services that customers may expect. Some services may need to be delivered before the actual purchase transaction, some during the transaction, and some after the transaction through the life of the product. Some services are hygiene factors that the customer expects to be there. Some services are satisfiers—areas that can create real customer delight.

Closing the gaps in the service quality model and delivering high-quality service are major challenges, requiring an organization-wide commitment. Indeed, it appears that service quality is even more closely related to a firm's corporate culture than is product quality. But in the tumultuous business environment, service quality may become the best way to sustain a competitive advantage or to create an area of distinctive competence.

APPLICATION IDEAS

1. What is the relative importance to your customers of product versus service attributes? Which service attributes are important to your customers, and do you have a system to monitor your performance on those attributes? How does your mix of product and service attributes compare to your competitors'? Where are the competitive strengths or weaknesses?

2. What presale, transaction, and postsale services are expected by your customers? Have you developed explicit quality standards for delivering those

services? Or do they just happen? How do your organization's presale, transaction, and postsale services compare to your competitors'?

3. What are the hygiene services (in each of the three categories) that are expected by your customers? What are the satisfiers that can dazzle your customers? How does your organization's performance on both hygiene factors and satisfiers compare to your competitors'?

4. How large are the five gaps, identified in the service quality model, in your organization? What has been done in your organization to close each of the gaps? Is there any empirical support to validate the size of each gap?

5

Value-based Pricing

"The focus is on finding ways of adding value to a product where the price premium generated by additional value added is greater than the incremental cost to produce the value added."

Understanding the relationships between product quality, service quality, and pricing strategies is essential to delivering good customer value. The product and service quality, relative to competitive alternatives and customer expectations, dictate the appropriate price. Unfortunately, many firms don't understand how product quality and service quality interact to influence price. And value-based pricing is the third essential component of customer value.

There is only one viable approach to pricing for most firms. And that approach has very little to do with the costs that a firm incurs in producing a product or service. This is not to say that controlling cost is unimportant; indeed, reducing cost is vitally important. Clearly, the greater the competitive intensity, the greater the need to reduce costs. Competitors simply will not let production inefficiency go unpunished. However, costs represent only a pricing floor, a level below which prices cannot remain for an extended period of time.

If costs are used as the basis for setting prices, a firm is adopting the old production-oriented mentality of "let's produce the product and add some profit above our costs." The problem with that cost-based approach is that it ignores both the customer and the competition.

Value-based pricing is the approach that should be used by virtually all firms. Value-based pricing starts with the customer first, considers the competition, and then determines the appropriate price. This implies that a customer-driven firm must understand the product and service attributes desired by customers and understand the value of that bundle of attributes to the customer. Since very few firms operate in a pure monopoly, the value, to the customer, of competitive offerings also must be determined. This is necessary because virtually all customers evaluate the value of a product (not just price), relative to other alternatives.

So, essentially, there are two competing forces: (1) Corporate goals for profitability suggest that firms should charge higher prices for their products, thus maximizing long-term shareholder wealth. (2) The competition, however, provides a constraint—a ceiling on prices, which gets lower and lower as global competition intensifies. The competitor who will prevail in this situation is not necessarily the one with the lowest prices; the "winner" will be the firm that maximizes delivered value to the customer. Therefore, developing more detailed understanding of what constitutes delivered value becomes important.

DEFINING CUSTOMER VALUE

Customer value is the ratio of benefits to the sacrifice necessary to obtain those benefits. Since the customer determines the benefits and the sacrifice, the customer's perception of each is important. As indicated in Figure 5.1, the customer's perception of expected benefits flows from the product and service attributes. The sacrifice—or price—that a customer makes typically consists of transaction costs, life cycle costs, and some degree of risk. Yet for most situations, the only factor that is known with reasonable certainty is the transaction cost, and that may be somewhat variable. Each of the other factors is heavily dependent on customer perceptions and expectations.

Expected Benefits

The more experience that a customer has with a type of product or a particular brand, the easier it is for the customer to formulate perceptions and expectations of benefits. In the absence of experience with or knowledge about a product, a customer uses surrogates to form perceptions

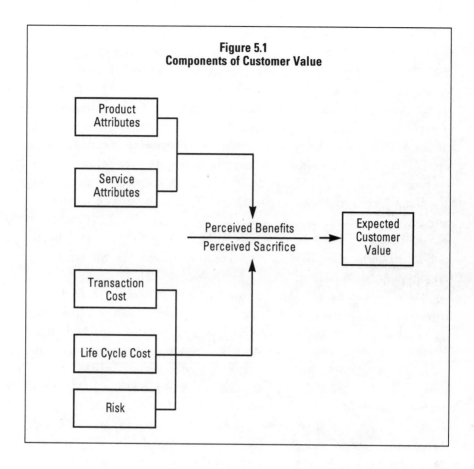

Figure 5.1
Components of Customer Value

and expectations. One dominant surrogate cue is the brand or corporate image.

IBM provides an excellent example of this process. When IBM entered the personal computer (PC) market in the early 1980s, most PC buyers weren't technically knowledgeable about home computers. Most customers at that time knew a little about computers but did not understand the characteristics of computer chip architecture, monitor resolution, processing speed, and so forth. Since customers had difficulty formulating accurate perceptions of product and service quality, they used a surrogate cue—the IBM image. Within a year or so after entering the market, IBM was clearly the market leader. IBM PCs were not technologically superior to competitive alternatives, but since customers couldn't tell the difference, the name IBM conveyed value and justified relatively high prices.

Unfortunately for IBM, the computer buyer of the 1990s is considerably different. PC buyers typically understand the differences between 286, 386, 486, and 586 computer chips. They understand the difference between a 20-megabyte hard drive and an 85-megabyte hard drive and when it's necessary to have the additional memory. They understand the difference between a VGA and an SVGA monitor and the difference between a 25-megahertz and a 33-megahertz processing speed. In short, the PC buyer is able to more accurately formulate perceptions and expectations of product and service attributes and expected benefits. Surrogate cues such as corporate image therefore have become less important to PC customers. Thus, the ability to use the IBM name to differentiate PCs has eroded significantly, leading to the recent highly publicized decision by IBM to begin competing more directly with price as a strategic variable.

IBM does not have to be the lowest-priced PC on the market. The IBM name still conveys added value to customers. However, the value added by the IBM name is far less than just a few years ago. And due to intense competition and increasingly knowledgeable customers, the value-added premium will probably continue to erode for IBM.

But although the value-added premium will erode for IBM, it will probably never disappear completely. Many firms have been able to maintain an image that conveys added value to customers. Kodak, Caterpillar, Coca-Cola, John Deere, Procter and Gamble, Hewlett-Packard, 3M, and Whirlpool are firms that understand the top half of the customer value equation. These firms realize that value is not maximized by delivering an average product at a low price. Value is maximized by delivering high levels of product and service quality at a price that is reasonable and acceptable to customers.

L. L. Bean, for example, doesn't guarantee the lowest price for its merchandise. But L. L. Bean does guarantee customer satisfaction, and L .L. Bean does strive to carry only high-quality products. Customers who do not believe that a product measures up to their individual expectations or who believe that good value has not been delivered are encouraged to return the product for a full refund. The concept of creating and delivering high customer value is the essence of the L. L. Bean corporate philosophy.

There are really three classes of attributes that customers use to evaluate expected benefit; they are related to the earlier discussions about product and service quality.

Search Attributes

Search attributes are those attributes that can be evaluated prior to purchase. Search attributes include all those tangible characteristics of a product that can be examined by a buyer relatively easily before purchase. In the previous IBM example, the search attributes consisted primarily of hardware specifications. However, search attributes can include some services as well. Certainly, Xerox's guarantee of customer satisfaction is an attribute that can be evaluated prior to purchase. It is obviously important for a firm to know which attributes are used by customers in the search process.

Experience-based Attributes

The second category is experience-based attributes. For a customer to evaluate these attributes, the product must be purchased and used. If a customer wanted a fine dining experience, a restaurant's four-star rating might be a search attribute, or a surrogate cue. However, a customer's perceptions and expectations would be inherently vague until a meal had been eaten. After the actual dining experience, the customer could then decide if good value was conveyed. When we get a haircut, it is almost impossible to evaluate the attributes before the "product" is purchased. Many, if not most, service attributes are experience based because the services must be delivered and consumed before a buyer can accurately evaluate service quality. This would apply to both pure services and support services.

Experience-based attributes are not restricted to services, however. To evaluate whether or not a new detergent really gets your clothes cleaner, you must try it. To evaluate the quality of a grocery item, you must first purchase and consume it. In all of these examples of experience-based attributes, at least one item must be purchased or consumed to determine product and service quality. Hence the customer cannot make an accurate assessment of delivered customer value until after the purchase and use of the product.

Credence-based Attributes

Some products are not easily evaluated, even after their purchase. Credence-based attributes are those that must be experienced over an extended period of time. Financial management services, most forms of insurance, consulting services, legal services, and health care must be evaluated over an extended period of time. Before a customer can evaluate the product's attributes, the product must be used or consumed repeatedly. Essentially, the customer must be a brand-loyal user before developing accurate perceptions of the relevant product attributes.

What are the managerial implications of these three categories of product and service attributes? If a firm competes only on search attributes, then competitive alternatives can be easily compared by customers. Assuming that many search attributes can be quickly imitated by competitors since these are often tangible characteristics, then areas of competitive advantage or product differentiation may erode. In such situations, severe price competition is inevitable.

The way to avoid price competition is to stress experience-based and credence-based attributes. These attributes are invariably more difficult for customers to evaluate. Therefore, these attributes hold the greatest potential for creating unique value-added components. What do firms such as Kodak, Caterpillar, John Deere, Hewlett-Packard, 3M, Motorola, Xerox, and Whirlpool have in common? All have created very significant experience-based or credence-based components in their products. The quality of a Kodak print, a Caterpillar bulldozer, a John Deere mower, or a Hewlett-Packard printer must be experienced by the customer to really be appreciated. By doing so, each firm has shielded its products from pure price competition.

EXPECTED SACRIFICE

The bottom half of the equation in Figure 5.1 deals with the sacrifice that a customer must make to obtain expected benefits. Assume for a minute that a customer has formulated perceptions and expectations of the benefits. Simultaneously, the customer compares the benefits to the expected sacrifice. The transaction cost is the immediate financial outlay or commitment that a customer must make. The life cycle costs are the expected additional costs that a customer will incur over the life of the product. And since life cycle costs are inherently based on expectations, there also is some degree of risk involved.

Transaction Costs

For a simple product with a short period of expected use, transaction costs dominate the customer's decision process. There are very few life cycle costs associated with a can of vegetables, a soft drink, or a bottle of wine. There may be some small element of risk such as determining which wine tastes best, but for many products, perceived risk may be minor.

Transaction costs represent a major decision criterion for virtually all undifferentiated products. Since the customer can't distinguish between the attributes of alternative products, the transaction cost, or price, becomes more important. For example, Texaco's current advertising campaign attempts to create a high-quality image for its System 3 gasoline. Most consumers view gasoline as a very generic, undifferentiated product and are sensitive to a price change of even only a few cents per gallon. If Texaco is successful in differentiating its gasoline somewhat, the improved expected benefits will justify a slightly higher price and still convey good value to customers.

Some customers may not place additional value on improved product or service quality. However, for the vast majority of customers, whether individuals or organizations, improved product and service quality does increase the expected benefits. And higher expected benefits justify a higher transaction cost.

Life Cycle Costs

The longer the expected life of the product, the more important life cycle cost becomes. One of the reasons that Caterpillar has been so successful is that, although transaction costs are higher than the competition's, life cycle costs are much lower than competitive products'. Thus the total financial sacrifice is lower. Hewlett-Packard laser printers have a dominant market share in that market. The high transaction cost is offset by a lower life cycle cost.

One of the problems facing the auto industry is changing customer perceptions of financial sacrifice. The high transaction prices of new cars lead customers to keep their older car for a longer period of time. Car buyers see better value in keeping the old car, even with its higher life cycle costs of maintenance and repair.

For virtually all durable products, customers form some perceptions of expected life cycle costs. In the absence of information upon which to base judgments, customer perceptions become much more subjective and often depend on image.

With the numerous strategic alliances in the auto industry, joint ventures abound. In many cases, several different "makes" and "models" are made in the same factory, on the same assembly line, and by the same workers. Essentially, a model by a U.S. manufacturer and a Japanese manufacturer may be identical except for the nameplate. However, in most cases, customers perceive the Japanese model to be of higher quality, more reliable, and more dependable than the same car with an American nameplate. Thus, customers perceive a lower life cycle cost based purely on the image of the "make."

The implication that emerges is that managers must understand the relative importance of life cycle cost in the customer's decision process. When life cycle costs are important, specific information should be conveyed that helps customers to accurately formulate their expectations.

Risk

The longer the expected life of the product, the more important risk also becomes. This is because the customer has more difficulty in accurately evaluating the product before it is used. Hence, financial sacrifice is harder to determine. Let's assume that you need a new set of tires for your car. Your expected benefits might consist of 40,000 miles of tire life, some performance and handling characteristics, and a road hazard warranty.

Your sacrifice would be the transaction cost—say $80 per tire—and the life cycle costs of rotation each year and flat-tire repair. But since tires may last three or four years, there is also an element of risk. If the tires last for only 25,000 or 30,000 or 35,000 miles instead of the 40,000 you expect, what happens to your perception of value? Unfortunately, a tire buyer never knows for sure exactly how long tires will last, so some allowance for risk enters the equation. The tire buyer is concerned not only with transaction costs but with life cycle costs and risk as well.

In the auto industry, late-model used cars are often sold with an additional "maintenance policy." These policies, which typically cost $500–$1,000, are an opportunity for the car buyer to reduce the higher risk of buying a used car. As transaction costs and the expected life of a car have increased, perceived risk also has increased, and in the case of used cars, this has created an opportunity for a new service.

VALUE PROFILES

Buyers do not all value the same attributes equally. An important characteristic to one buyer may be unimportant to another buyer. Likewise, buyers do not all necessarily attach the same value to the sacrifice required to obtain a product. Some may be concerned only with transaction costs; others may add life cycle costs and ignore any risk. To be able to apply value-based pricing, you must be able to segment your market by the customers' value profiles, not just demographic or psychographic or geographic characteristics.

A value profile requires that a firm really understand what attributes are important to each market segment, niche, or customer group. In addition, the value of each attribute must be approximated (this will be discussed shortly). The customer's expected benefits or use of a product will influence the value attached to the product's differentiating attributes. Back to the tire example: the owner of a four-wheel-drive vehicle who uses the 4×4 for off-road excursions may be concerned primarily with traction attributes. Another owner of a 4×4 may be concerned with traction and braking ability on snow or ice. Another owner of a 4×4 may be concerned with the durability of the tires. In each case, a different attribute conveys predominant value to the customer. A firm that doesn't understand the relative value of various attributes to customers would have great difficulty in maximizing customer value.

In order to determine the total delivered value of a product or the incremental value of a specific attribute, several factors must be determined. Virtually all customers, whether individuals or organizations, develop a perception of what constitutes a "fair and reasonable" price for a product. This fair price is typically referred to as a reference point or anchor level. Around this reference price there is a zone of indifference within which a price change, upward or downward, will not influence customers in any significant way. But there is a wider zone of acceptability around the reference price with both an upper and lower threshold. Implementing a value-based pricing strategy requires an understanding of each of these concepts.

Reference Points

Virtually all customers, either implicitly or explicitly, form a perception of a fair price for a product, which serves as a reference point. This reference point is then used as a benchmark for comparison when making a purchase decision. A customer's reference point may or may not correspond to an actual alternative. It may be nothing more than a vague, rough average of comparable products. It may be a vague estimate of the last price paid maybe one, two, or three years ago. The expression "sticker shock" in the auto industry refers to the idea that consumers may have unrealistic, out-of-date reference points based on a previous auto purchase some years ago. But since the customer is making the determination of "fair prices," an understanding of reference points is important.

Two dominant factors seem to influence the formation of a customer's reference point. The factors are the current and past prices for an item. These prices are not restricted to a particular firm, however, and include the competitive alternatives of which the customer is aware.

Current prices of alternatives may be the strongest influence on a reference point. For a consumer purchasing grocery items, the reference point could be the weekly grocery ads in the local newspaper or the competitive alternatives in the store. For industrial products, the reference point could be the current price lists of certain competitors. Depending on the product, the comparison of a product to a reference price may be very brief. The average length to decision on the choice of a grocery item is only a few seconds, for example.

The offering of a "30% off" or "40% off" sale is an attempt to get customers to use the normal price as a reference point. However, frequent use of a sale price can cause a customer to use the lower price as the reference. This is a common problem in the beverage industry. If a brand, say, Coca-Cola, is on sale every few weeks, consumers may use the sale price as a reference point and delay purchase when prices return to their higher, normal level.

Past prices also influence a buyer's reference point. The current retail price for a Hewlett-Packard LaserJet printer is about half of the price charged four years ago. A customer who has seen a sharp drop in price may feel that the current price conveys excellent value. Conversely, past prices, if lower, cause customers to reduce their perceptions of value as current prices rise.

Past prices are particularly significant if the customer actually purchased an item. Research has shown that most customers have reasonably accurate perceptions of the price-last-paid. This implies that, if price increases are necessary, the increases should be phased in gradually so that customers will become used to the higher prices rather than experience the shock of a single, large increase.

The current or past prices may be based on a customer's perception or actual experience with any number of products. Very often, the reference point is a market share leader. The standard reference product and price for jeans is probably the Levi 501. The standard reference for soft drinks is probably Coca-Cola or Pepsi-Cola depending on where you live. The standard reference for beer may be Budweiser, Miller, or Coors, again depending on where you live. If customers use the market share leader as the reference point, then determining the incremental value added by specific attributes will dictate where a competitive product should be priced.

If a product's bundle of attributes convey more value than the reference point, a "superiority premium" is created. That premium could be converted, at least partly, to a price premium. For example, a customer may feel that a package of Perdue chicken is worth one dollar more than a competitor's chicken. If Perdue prices at 80 cents above the competitor, Perdue has captured 80 percent of the superiority premium. The customer feels good value is conveyed since the actual price is 20 percent less than he or she was potentially willing to pay.

If a product's bundle of attributes convey less value than the reference product, an "inferiority premium" is created. If such a product is priced the same as the reference product, the product will sell poorly. The price must be reduced until it is far enough below the inferiority premium so that customers will be induced to buy the product. Once the product is priced below the inferiority premium, it will potentially convey good value if the customer is willing to settle for the lower quality.

Zone of Indifference

Around a perceived reference point, customers often have a pricing zone of indifference. Within this zone, buyers are indifferent to both price increases or price decreases. The price range can be expressed as an absolute change or as a percentage of change, but, as the price of a product increases, buyers typically demonstrate a narrower indifference zone. A price reduction of 5 percent or 10 percent may produce no change in demand because the price is still within the zone of indifference. However, a price reduction of 15 percent may be noticeable to customers and stimulate a significant increase in demand. Conversely, a product could be priced at the upper edge of the zone of indifference with no decrease in demand. Thus, profits could be enhanced considerably.

Zone of Acceptability

Around the reference point, there is also a zone of acceptable prices, which is wider than the zone of indifference. The zone of acceptability has a lower price threshold, below which demand will not increase, and an upper threshold, above which there will be no demand. Research has indicated that as reference prices shift upward or downward, the zone of acceptable prices also moves correspondingly.

The zone of acceptable prices is wide early in a product's life cycle and gradually narrows. The innovations common to new product introductions convey added customer value and justify higher prices, but that uniqueness is subject to dynamic deterioration as competition increases. This being the case, relatively narrow zones of acceptable price variations would be expected as products become more standardized.

Nagle[1] identified a variety of effects that can influence a buyer's perception of price. These factors can widen or narrow a zone of acceptable prices and cause a buyer to be more or less price sensitive.

1. *Unique Value Effect.* The most important effect is the value buyers place on a product's unique attributes. The more unique the product, the less price sensitive buyers tend to be, and the wider the zone of acceptability will be.

2. *Substitute Awareness Effect.* The fewer the number of substitute products of which a buyer is aware, the less price sensitive buyers tend to be, and the wider the zone of acceptability will be.

3. *Difficult Comparison Effect.* Buyers are less price sensitive and have a wider zone of acceptability when comparison of competing products is difficult.

4. *Total Expenditure Effect.* Buyers are more price sensitive and have a narrower zone of acceptability when the expenditure is large, either in absolute terms or as a percentage of income.

5. *End Benefit Effect.* Buyers are more price sensitive and have a narrower zone of acceptability as a product's price accounts for a larger portion of the end benefit. For example, Ford Motor Company's largest single supplier supplies health care coverage, so Ford is very sensitive to that cost.

6. *Price-Quality Effect.* Buyers are less sensitive to a product's price and have a wider zone of acceptability to the extent that a higher price signals higher quality.

7. *Inventory Effect.* Buyers are more sensitive to price when they can hold inventories in anticipation of future price increases or decreases.

From a managerial perspective, the zone of acceptability concept means that firms that continually innovate will have the ability to price their products at the upper end of the zone of acceptability and to enjoy wider profit margins, assuming that costs are under control. Firms that try to milk products for an extended period of time are certain to be subject to intense price competition. Also, outstanding support services can create unique benefits, make comparisons more difficult, and signal higher quality for the product or primary services.

A VALUE-BASED PRICING MODEL

The previous discussions have presented a diverse array of factors related to the development of a value-based pricing strategy. To integrate these concepts, a value-based pricing model is presented in Figure 5.2. The model illustrates how the various concepts interact to contribute to customer value.

Contextual Factors

A variety of contextual factors such as corporate image, store name, or brand name may provide a buyer with cues about a product or service. These extrinsic cues are not necessarily a part of the product but are used by buyers to determine perceptions of product or service quality. The earlier discussion about IBM personal computers illustrated the importance of corporate image, for example.

The corporate images of Caterpillar or Hewlett-Packard or Xerox all provide extrinsic cues to buyers that their products are of high quality or the company wouldn't sell them. The same can be said of brand names. Tide brand products convey a high-quality image to detergent buyers. North Face or Land's End conveys a quality cue to outdoor-clothing buyers. Craftsman brand tools denote high quality. Similarly, the store where an item is purchased serves as an extrinsic cue to buyers. Nordstrom's or Neiman-Marcus or Saks conveys higher-quality cues to many consumers than does K-Mart, Wal-Mart, or JC Penney.

The more difficult it is for a customer to evaluate a specific product before purchase, the more important extrinsic cues become to the customer. Therefore, contextual factors are relatively more important for products with a large service component. Also, if the product that is

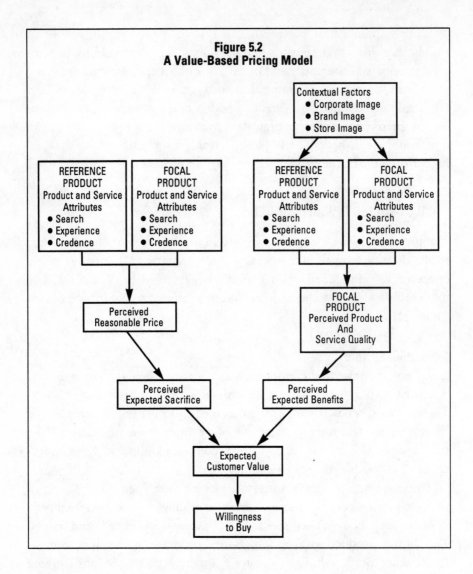

Figure 5.2
A Value-Based Pricing Model

being produced has a large portion of its value derived from experience- or credence-based attributes, then developing strong, positive extrinsic cues becomes very important strategically. It is simply very difficult for buyers to evaluate intangible attributes before the product is actually delivered.

Collectively, these perceptions of contextual factors are often major contributors to customers' perceptions of products. However, those extrinsic cues seldom operate in isolation. Instead, intrinsic, or tangible product, attributes and past experience and familiarity also shape quality perceptions.

Search, Experience, and Credence Attributes

Inevitably, the customer makes some type of comparison with a per-ceived reference product that may or may not be an actual alternative. The reference may be only a vague perception. The focal product under consideration is somehow compared to the buyer's reference product, and some degree of superiority, equivalence, or inferiority is determined. The comparison is normally done through the use of search, experience, and credence attributes.

The search attributes are those tangible, palpable characteristics that can be evaluated in some manner prior to purchase. Often, they are the visible characteristics of a product, for instance, the "fit and finish" of a car. Sometimes, they are technical specifications as with computers. They can be the degree of conformance with specifications or the defect rate.

These intrinsic cues about a product's attributes are somehow meshed with extrinsic contextual factors to create an overall perception of product and service quality. However, more important than intrinsic or extrinsic cues are a customer's actual product familiarity and experience.

The intrinsic and extrinsic cues are important to first-time buyers or "new" customers. For most firms, the preponderance of sales are not to new customers, however. Most sales revenues for most firms are gener-ated by "old" customers, those who have used a product previously. Hence, the experience-based attributes of a product will be far more im-portant in those customers' decision processes. Essentially, the more ex-perience a customer has with a product, the more accurate that cus-tomer's perceptions of expected benefits will be.

Since most purchase criteria consist of some combination of search and experience-based or credence-based attributes, a repeat customer, through experience, can evaluate with some degree of certainty the more intangible attributes. Thus, the perceived risk of buying an unknown product is reduced. The buyer is essentially trading off the known bene-fits of a previously used product against the perceived expected benefit of a competitive alternative. When experience- or credence-based attrib-utes are a large part of the total bundle of attributes, buyers are often un-willing to change and incur the risk of obtaining lesser benefits. For example, most individuals do not change doctors or dentists unless some very significant negative experience occurs.

Product and Service Quality, Expected Benefits

In total, the extrinsic cues, intrinsic cues, and product familiarity and experience lead to the formation of expectations of product and service quality. These expectations allow a customer or a potential customer to develop some perception of expected benefits that constitute the benefit portion of the value-based pricing model. The expected benefits for a particular product can be superior, equivalent, or inferior to the reference product. This difference in expected benefits will then be compared to the difference in expected sacrifice.

Reference, Actual, and Reasonable Prices

In the benefit portion of the model, a reference product and a focal product are compared to determine benefit superiority, equality, or inferiority. The same process occurs in the sacrifice portion of the model when comparing prices. It should first be noted that the term "price" includes transaction costs, expected life cycle costs, and some risk factor. Hence, it is the customer's perception of price that is important and not necessarily some objective, producer-generated price list.

The price of the reference product serves as an anchor point for comparison. However, the comparison process is inherently subjective because customers typically have a zone of indifference and may not be sensitive to some price changes or differences. The perceived reasonable or acceptable price is then formulated. Inherent in this process is the importance of weighting of expected benefits. That is, the benefit superiority, equality, or inferiority of the reference product and the focal product are simultaneously compared to the price superiority, equality, or inferiority to determine what price is reasonable and acceptable.

If the difference in expected benefits is greater than the difference in price, then a buyer has an inducement to buy the product under consideration. If there is no difference, then a buyer would be ambivalent. If the reference product conveyed more benefits for the price, then a buyer would view the focal price as unreasonable.

Brand loyalty becomes important in this comparison process. If you, as a buyer, have familiarity with a product and have used it frequently— that is, you are brand loyal—you have a very low perception of risk.

Switching to another product carries some additional risk in that your perceptions of expected benefits may be wrong or your perceptions of life cycle costs may be inaccurate.

Therefore, in order to get a competitor's brand-loyal customer to switch, a product must offer value inducement that is large enough to offset the increased risk. A slight, say, a 5 percent, difference in transaction cost may result in no change in sales because the perception of increased risk may be 10 percent. This may explain why a zone of indifference usually exists.

For some products, particularly those with few available intrinsic cues, price itself becomes a cue for expected product quality. This is particularly true for products in the over-the-counter health care and cosmetics industries. Since customers have difficulty evaluating the product cues or attributes, extrinsic factors—in this case price itself—help provide signals of quality. After all, if you pay $50 for a bottle of perfume, it must be very good, right?

Perceived Expected Sacrifice

The perceived reasonable and acceptable price is converted to a perceived monetary sacrifice. For a consumer buying a car, the process might go something like this. If a price of $15,000 is reasonable and acceptable to the consumer, then to obtain the expected benefit—a car—the prospective buyer must make a financial sacrifice. Perhaps the buyer might put $5,000 down and pay payments of $300 per month until the car is paid for.

The $300 per month sacrifice may preclude other activities such as a Hawaiian vacation. So the sacrifice is not just a certain amount of money. The sacrifice also includes the forgone opportunity offered by other alternatives.

And price could include numerous life cycle costs. Maintenance may be more, or less, than a competitive alternative. Mileage is variable, and insurance varies from one model to another. Certainly, resale value is a part of life cycle costs and is highly variable from one car to another.

Expected Customer Value

The expected customer value is ultimately determined by the comparison of expected benefits to expected sacrifice. Increasing the benefits while holding the sacrifice constant enhances customer value. Decreasing the sacrifice while holding benefits constant also enhances customer value. Increasing the benefits faster than the sacrifice enhances customer value too. There are many more ways to enhance customer value than to merely cut prices.

Expected customer value is a dynamic concept. What constitutes good value today may be poor value in six months. As suggested throughout the model, the availability of competitive alternatives, whether as reference products or substitutes, exerts a strong influence on perceptions of customer value. As competitive intensity increases, customers may come to expect more and more value from products. Hence the firm that thinks "good enough is good enough" will inevitably have problems.

Willingness to Buy

Willingness to buy is a function of expected value. The greater the expected value, the greater the willingness to buy. In consumer goods, this may be the sale that is just too good to pass up. The consumer may stock up to "save money." How many have heard their spouse say, "Look how much money I saved by buying this"?

CHANNEL ISSUES

The primary focus of the value-based pricing discussion thus far has been on delivering value to the end user of a product. Specifically, the expected benefits to the end user are the major determinants of value and, therefore, price. For some products, particularly consumer goods, channel members play a very influential role. In such instances, the whole channel is a value-creating chain that must be coordinated effectively to maximize value to the end user.

In its simplest form, a channel is a coordinated series of markets. Each channel member possesses unique needs, goals, and objectives. The producer or manufacturer of a product must respond to the needs of the channel intermediaries as attentively as it responds to the needs of the end user. Fortunately, the issue is the same: maximizing customer value. If value is enhanced, satisfaction among channel intermediaries will result. The only major difference is that the needs of the channel intermediaries are significantly different from those of end users. The decision criteria, such as inventory turnover rate, margins, and promotional support, become the customer benefits, ultimately resulting in some expected profit.

To maximize customer value to intermediaries, understanding their needs becomes critical. Ironically, many firms spend virtually all of their market research budget on end users, often neglecting the channel intermediaries. As the distinctions between intermediaries become blurred, the need for a thorough understanding of which channel member can best add value becomes increasingly important.

For industrial products, channel intermediaries generally play a less influential role due to shorter and more direct channels. However, in many situations, close coordination between channel members is vital. If a just-in-time production system is to work properly, then production, warehousing (or a distribution center), and transportation must be integrated efficiently. The most effective integration occurs when the value-added contributions of each intermediary are understood and managed.

Regardless of whether the products are industrial or consumer goods, the entire marketing channel is the unit of competition. A breakdown in any one area limits the ability of the entire channel to maximize delivered customer value. Thus, the entire channel becomes damaged because of the poor performance of any one member. If each channel member is treated as a market and if value is enhanced to that customer, the probability of creating an efficient value-added chain is much more likely.

COMPETITIVE RESPONSE

A key issue with any strategy is the expected competitive response. If a firm operates in a relatively homogeneous market with little product differentiation, then price becomes a dominant competitive variable. This is the situation in which search criteria are dominant in the customer's buying process. If the customer is able to accurately evaluate a product's attributes prior to purchase and if competitive alternatives are very similar, then the sacrifice portion of the value-based pricing model becomes the basis of competition. In these cases, competitors will be sensitive and will respond quickly to price changes.

As experience- and credence-based attributes such as service quality become more important in the buyer's decision process, price becomes less of an issue. This is precisely why value-based pricing is so important. In this case, the focus is not on cost cutting and price reductions. Instead, the focus is on finding ways of adding value to a product so that the price premium generated by additional value added is greater than the incremental cost to produce the value added.

Whereas price changes are easily observable by competitors, changes in delivered customer value are much more difficult to ascertain and respond to, from a competitive standpoint. Accordingly, changes in customer value are likely to provide the basis for a long-term sustainable competitive advantage. Price changes, on the other hand, usually result only in a temporary, short-term advantage that is quickly eroded by competitive response.

SUMMARY

Value-based pricing constitutes the most appropriate pricing strategy for a firm to use in today's business environment. Customers use product and service attributes to formulate perceptions of expected benefits. These expected benefits are weighed against the expected sacrifice to determine expected customer value. The whole process is very complex.

Search, experience, and credence attributes are all used by the customer to formulate perceptions of expected benefits. The customer also uses reference points, prior experience, and competitive offerings to evaluate the benefits that can be derived from a particular product. Clearly, the customer does not rely only on product quality to determine the expected benefits.

The perceived expected benefits, no matter how accurate or inaccurate, are balanced against the financial sacrifice. The sacrifice consists of transaction costs, expected life cycle costs, and risk. The customer also formulates perceptions of a reasonable sacrifice by using reference points, past experience, and competitive offerings.

The formulation of sacrifice is inherently subjective, as a customer typically has a zone of indifference, within which price changes will not influence demand. There is also a wider zone of acceptability, which has both upper and lower thresholds for reasonable prices, however. And price changes within the zone of acceptability will influence demand.

Perhaps arbitrarily, perhaps inaccurately, the customer somehow balances the expected benefits against the expected sacrifice. When the benefits exceed the sacrifice, good customer value is conveyed. And the greater the expected customer value, the greater the customer's willingness to buy. And if the customer's expectations are met or exceeded, high levels of customer satisfaction will result.

APPLICATION IDEAS

1. For the products that your organization sells, what search attributes are used by customers in their decision process? What experience or credence attributes are important to customers, and does your organization provide surrogate cues to help customers evaluate these attributes?
2. How do the customer's expected benefits from your organization's products compare to their expected benefits from competitive products? What attributes or cues help guide the customer?
3. What is the mix of transaction cost, life cycle cost, and risk from the customer's perspective? How consistent are these value profiles across different market segments? Does your organization develop a different pricing strategy for each market segment?
4. What product is the reference point for your industry or market? How does the value of your product compare to the value of the reference product or your closest competitors'?

REFERENCE

1. Thomas Nagle, *The Strategy and Tactics of Pricing: A Guide to Profitable Decision Making*, Englewood Cliffs, NJ: Prentice-Hall, 1987.

6

The High Cost of Low Value

"Providing high value to customers is more profitable than providing low value."

Delivering low customer value dramatically increases customer dissatisfaction and customer turnover. This results in direct and indirect costs that are far greater and far more pervasive than most managers realize. Since high levels of customer satisfaction and customer retention are strongly related to overall profitability, explicit strategies should be developed for both—something few firms are currently doing.

Most managers do not understand the full magnitude of the insidious costs associated with giving customers low value. Giving low value invariably leads to lower levels of customer satisfaction and higher customer turnover. If delivered value is low enough, relative to the competition, the customer will ultimately fire the firm. Customers aren't lost or stolen by competitors. Such an outlook considers the problem from the wrong perspective. Customers are making a conscious decision to fire the firm because better value can be obtained from a competitor. But a firm can incur many costs of dissatisfaction both before and after being fired by the customer.

There are two types of costs incurred due to customer dissatisfaction. The first group of costs consists of those that can be tied directly to dissatisfaction in some way. These costs are normally traceable and show up on cost accounting or financial statements.

The second set of costs are more indirect, intangible, and difficult to trace. These costs can accrue over an extended period of time and are often far greater than the more observable direct costs. However, because these costs are only opportunity costs, they will never show up on accounting or financial statements. Thus, they are hidden and often ignored by most managers.

DIRECT COSTS

The more observable, direct costs of customer dissatisfaction are included in Table 6.1. There are probably other costs that could be included here, but these illustrate the pervasiveness of such costs. The costs of dissatisfaction go far beyond simply replacing defective products.

Customer Service Department

A good portion of the customer service function in many firms can be attributed to dissatisfied customers. In some firms, the role of a customer service department is to handle specific customer complaints, so virtually all of the related costs are due to customer dissatisfaction. In other firms, a customer service department may play a more proactive role, and complaints may constitute only a portion of the total effort.

In the computer hardware and software industries, for example, customer support services are common. Most often, these services offer technical support to customers regarding product usage. In some cases, the customer simply hasn't read the supporting documentation, and although this may indicate something about customer preferences, it probably is not a cost of customer dissatisfaction. However, if the customer support is necessary because the product or documentation lacks user friendliness, then the resultant costs are probably due to dissatisfaction. In some manner, an organization needs to identify the portion of customer service costs that represents normal support service versus the portion that represents customer dissatisfaction.

Hewlett-Packard maintains the primary portion of its LaserJet customer support group in Boise, Idaho. Due to the tremendous success of the product, the customer support group has experienced a significant in-

Table 6.1 The Costs of Customer Dissatisfaction

Direct Costs	Indirect Costs

1. Customer Service
  • Overhead
  • Variable
	1. Lost Sales

2. Recruiting Training	2. Extra Support for New Customers

3. Returns
  • Replacement, Shipping, Handling
	3. Negative Word-of-Mouth
	  • Lost Referrals

4. Warranties, Guarantees	4. Lost Innovations
5. Customer Acquisition	5. Reduced Managerial Productivity due to Putting Out Fires

crease in demand for its services. This expansion has resulted in a variety of costs.

New facilities had to be leased and remodeled. Offices had to be designed and furnished. Computer hardware and software and new phone systems had to be installed. All of these costs are purely overhead costs.

Additional customer support personnel had to be hired, so all of the recruiting and selection costs are relevant. Training was necessary, not only for new employees but for existing employees as well, as new products were continually introduced. The additional costs of salaries, heat, electricity, phones, and insurance also were relevant. These variable or operating costs need to be aggregated and combined with the overhead costs to get a true overall estimate of the cost of customer service for a firm such as Hewlett-Packard.

The same type of overhead and variable costs are relevant to virtually every firm that has a customer service department. While not all of these costs should be attributed to the cost of customer dissatisfaction, certainly a portion should be. It is up to the individual firm to determine the proper percentage.

Returns

The return and replacement of defective products are obvious costs of dissatisfaction. The related costs of shipping, handling, and labor also are relevant. More difficult to determine and implement is a logical policy for handling the return of partially used items. Because of the difficulty of coordinating a variety of channel members, many firms are finding that an unconditional, no-questions-asked return policy conveys a strong message to customers. Interestingly, most firms that adopt such a policy find that very little abuse by customers occurs.

Warranties and Guarantees

Warranties and guarantees typically appear as a liability charge on accounting or financial statements. Estimates of defective rates are projected throughout a product's expected life. These estimates could be charged to a particular production run or time period or amortized over an extended period of time. Regardless of how they are handled, charges for warranties or guarantees are often in addition to the actual return of defective merchandise.

Acquisition Costs

The acquisition of new customers often carries significant direct costs. The majority of advertising and promotion and sales representative time is usually attributable to customer acquisition. For each new customer, credit checks, data processing, and other administrative tasks are necessary. While these are sunk costs, they can represent a significant investment. It is fairly common for a firm to lose 15 percent of its customers each year. If a firm has, say, a total customer base of 1,000, it could lose 150 customers annually.

An average sales call in the field of industrial products costs about $250. Let's assume that a sales representative has to make three sales calls to a customer before finally getting an order, a fairly common situation. Let's also assume that each new account requires another $250 worth of costs attributable to catalogs, credit checks, samples, telemarketing, and so forth. The total acquisition cost for one customer would therefore be $1,000, and that figure does not include any allocation for other promotional activities such as advertising. Therefore, if a firm is losing 150 customers each year, it is also losing at least $150,000 in acquisition costs.

There are probably many other costs that are direct and traceable to customer dissatisfaction. However, those illustrated here indicate the magnitude of the problem. Research has indicated that only about 4–5 percent of dissatisfied customers actually complain. Thus, it is a relatively small portion of total customers who are generating most of these direct costs. The irony is that the direct costs, such as these, are usually dwarfed by the indirect, opportunity costs.

INDIRECT COSTS

The following example illustrates the pervasiveness of the indirect costs of customer dissatisfaction. Gem Processing (GP) is a small specialty chemicals company with annual sales in the $10-million range generated from a customer base of about 1,000 firms. GP has typically generated about 80 percent of its sales from existing customers that have been with the firm for more than one year, and the firm has grown at the rate of about 10 percent per year for the past several years. GP's management acknowledged that about 20 percent of the customer accounts go dormant in a year, but the steady growth rate has compensated for the lost customers. Management figured the loss of customers was about normal in a highly competitive industry like specialty chemicals. Because of GP's profitability and steady growth, management never worried much about the impact of losing customers, nor had it previously attempted to calculate the resulting costs. However, when GP finally did examine the cost of customer turnover, it was shocked.

Since about 20 percent of customers quit buying from GP each year, that figure was used as an estimate of customer turnover. Although some of the lost customers could have gone out of business or been bought by another firm, GP lacked data on this and just decided to use the 20 percent as an estimate. Based on an annual customer turnover rate of 20 percent, GP could expect to turn its total customer base over every five years. Hence, a customer had a life expectancy of five years. Since an average customer does $10,000 annually in business with GP, the expected lifetime sales value of each customer is approximately $50,000 (5 years × $10,000/annual purchase). At the current rate of customer loss, GP will lose $2 million in sales per year, or $10 million over the expected customer life.

As staggering as the indirect costs are when measured in sales dollars, the figures probably understate the total indirect dissatisfaction cost by a substantial amount. Satisfied customers buy more and stay longer.

If, over time, GP improved customer satisfaction, the customer turnover rate would probably decline. If the annual customer turnover rate declined from 20 percent to 15 percent, a relatively small decline, the life expectancy of a customer would increase from five years to seven years. Also, the annual purchase amount would likely increase if GP becomes the favorite supplier of its customers. If annual sales increase by 10 percent—$11,000 per customer—a very conservative estimate, the expected sales value of the customer would increase from $50,000 to $77,000 (assuming a seven-year life expectancy). This represents an opportunity cost to the firm of $27,000 per customer in lost sales revenue by not improving customer satisfaction. If the customer base remains steady—at 1,000—the opportunity cost over the seven-year life would be $27 million, but since the firm is growing, that figure is probably an understatement. And many firms are able to achieve customer retention rates of over 90 percent.

Even the higher sales figure for satisfied customers may understate the profit impact of customer retention. The cost of acquiring new customers in most firms is five to six times the cost of retaining an existing one. To achieve a 10 percent annual growth rate, GP's sales force must generate about 300 new customers each year: About 200 new customers are needed to replace lost customers, and another 100 new customers are needed to allow for growth. In fact, GP found that it had to generate more than 300 new customers, because the average first-year purchases of these new accounts was less than the overall $10,000 average. However, attracting 300 new customers was not an easy task in the specialty chemicals industry. The sales manager figured the sales representatives spent about 60 percent of their time cultivating new accounts and only 40 percent servicing old accounts. It isn't hard to understand why customers leave, when the firm's primary contact with the customer spends so little time servicing the customer. When these costs are attributed to the acquisition of new accounts, each new account becomes an expensive proposition. In many cases, due to the high acquisition costs, new accounts don't really become profitable until after a year of their doing business with GP.

Not only did the new accounts require a significant, up-front investment in acquisition costs, but many were a real pain until they were "trained." Due to the specialized, and often customized, nature of its products, GP works closely with customers. The firm has found that many new customers require a good deal of training by GP's chemical engineers to educate them about what was or was not possible. The management at GP estimated that about 60–70 percent of all support services, such as technical consulting, was devoted to customers who represented accounts less than two or three years old. The "old" customers needed very little in the way of support services.

The situation faced by Gem Processing is not unique. However, until recently, GP's management personnel had never attempted to translate the direct or indirect costs of dissatisfaction into the language of managers: money. When they finally did this, GP found that its direct costs accounted for about 2 percent of sales, or $200,000 per year. However, the indirect costs of dissatisfaction in lost sales were over 10 times greater, at about $2 million annually. With a profit margin of approximately 20 percent, the indirect costs of lost sales resulted in a loss of $400,000 in profits, twice the total for direct costs. The opportunity cost of $27 million in lost sales over the seven-year customer life expectancy was even larger! This of course ignores the fact that by not moving to a customer focus, GP's customer loss rate is likely to increase beyond the 20 percent rate over time as the quality of the competition improves.

Word-of-Mouth Referrals

Firms like Gem Processing that have focused on acquiring new customers tend to forget that the effort to retain existing customers does not preclude attracting new customers. In fact, satisfied existing customers are a vital resource in acquiring new customers. Eismann, a German frozen foods firm, has determined that nearly 30 percent of new customers were attracted as a result of referrals by existing satisfied customers. Thus, when customer satisfaction is increased, a firm's reputation will be enhanced through informal communication networks. The acquisition cost of gaining a new customer by way of a referral is only a faction of the normal acquisition cost.

Conversely, negative word of mouth can also have a ripple effect. Studies show that, on average, a dissatisfied customer will tell seven or eight other individuals about his or her experiences. If a firm has 100 dissatisfied customers, about four or five will actually complain. If the other 96 dissatisfied customers each tell seven people, a total of 672 current or potential customers will be exposed to the negative experiences. The old adage that "bad news travels fast" is very applicable among customers. As Jan Carlzon, CEO of Scandinavian Airlines says, one negative offsets five or six positives. Hence, negative word of mouth carries some implicit, though ambiguous, cost of dissatisfaction.

Lost Innovations

Another cost for firms that have not adopted a customer orientation is the opportunity cost associated with the failure to recognize customer-driven product innovations. Such innovations usually represent incremental improvements to existing products. If customers are a good source of innovations, then those innovative ideas have some value. The customers most likely to share ideas for product improvement are those who are most satisfied with a supplier. Thus, a firm with a high customer turnover rate is likely to have less satisfied customers and is less likely to benefit from customer suggestions for improvement. That loss of innovative ideas represents an opportunity that is likely to be difficult to quantify, but it is real nonetheless.

For firms that operate in an industry characterized by rapid technological change, those lead, innovative customers can generate between 30 and 80 percent of the ideas for product improvement. While many factors influence a customer's willingness and ability to try to improve products, few producers try to capture customers' innovative ideas. Instead, most are lost or, worse yet, captured by competitors. It certainly appears that an important part of any customer database would be the identification of those lead users who are constantly trying to improve your products.

The point this discussion makes is that the indirect costs of customer dissatisfaction are diverse. Those few firms that do attempt to calculate the cost of dissatisfaction usually concentrate on clearly identifiable direct costs. Calculating the indirect costs of lost sales, opportunity costs, negative word-of-mouth communication, or lost sources of innovation is much more difficult. However, the indirect costs of dissatisfaction are usually far greater than most firms realize and are usually greater than the direct costs. Once managers begin to measure these costs, they will more clearly see the advantages associated with increased customer satisfaction.

CUSTOMER RETENTION

Some of the direct and most of the indirect costs of customer dissatisfaction can be traced either to the loss of valued customers or to customer turnover. While some loss of customers is normal due to mergers, acquisitions, going out of business, and so forth, most customer turnover is dysfunctional. Most firms only speculate about the reason they lose customers, however; they often do not really know the specific causes. The reasons that a customer fires a firm are often not simply the inverse of why customers are highly satisfied.

Back in Chapters 3 and 4, the concept of a two-factor theory of product and service quality was developed. Some attributes—hygiene factors—were those that the customer simply expected as part of doing business. Exceptional performance in these areas contributed very little to customer satisfaction. High levels of customer satisfaction resulted from the exceptional delivery of satisfiers—the second factor. To really delight customers, a firm's performance on hygiene factors must be adequate, accompanied by high performance on the satisfiers.

If we now broaden the concept further to include simultaneously *all* attributes deemed important by customers—both product and services— we can gain insight into why valued customers leave. We also can develop more effective strategies to reduce customer turnover.

Figure 6.1 presents such a broadened concept. On the vertical axis are the hygiene attributes that customers expect to be delivered. These attributes could be product characteristics or service elements. They could be the delivery of a product on time, accuracy on a billing statement, or getting some expected use from a product. On the horizontal axis are the satisfiers. These factors are often the above-and-beyond things that a firm provides for customers. They could be exceptional product quality, outstanding follow up customer care, or presale consulting and advice.

The four corners of the matrix represent radically different situations. Regardless of the industry or type of business, a firm in the lower left corner will be in a crisis. Customer satisfaction will be low and customer turnover will be high. Although the firm may muddle along here for a short while, the long-term outlook is bleak. Unless a firm in this corner becomes strongly committed to radical changes to get closer to the customer, it will soon be out of business.

The firm in the upper left corner has a much greater chance for survival. This firm is performing very well on the basic attributes demanded by customers. Unfortunately, however, it has neglected other attributes. The firm may be, for example, a restaurant that serves good food but has a poor atmosphere and poorly trained waiters or waitresses. The degree of competitive intensity will largely determine the survival of this firm. If the restaurant's competitors also haven't achieved high cus-

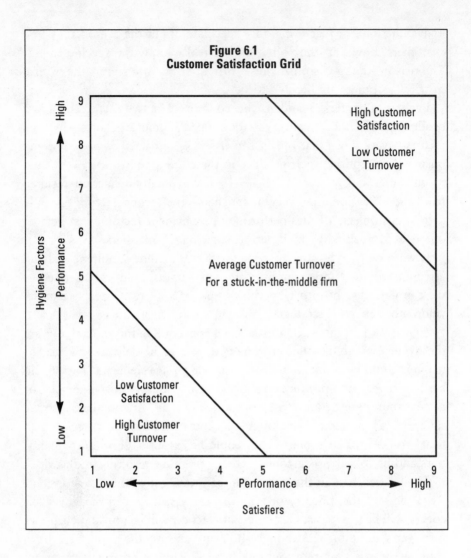

Figure 6.1
Customer Satisfaction Grid

tomer satisfaction levels, then this firm has a chance to maintain its status quo. However, as its competitors begin to perform at a high level and deliver better value to customers, this firm's market position will quickly erode.

Firms in the bottom right corner of the matrix are in a puzzling situation. Their performance is high on some or all satisfiers, but hygiene factors remain deficient. Firms that have been disappointed with the market results of their total quality management efforts are probably in this condition. Tangible products may have considerably higher quality levels, but low performance on hygiene service factors may be a constraint to improving market position. These firms are simply not delivering good value across all product or services attributes. Since firms in this corner are performing well on satisfiers, they have a good deal of potential. These firms simply need to be more thorough and comprehensive in their identification and delivery of hygiene attributes.

The top right corner is where the innovative, industry leaders are located. These firms have a good grasp of all customer expectations and have developed and implemented effective value-added delivery systems. These firms have goals of 100 percent customer satisfaction, creating customer delight, and six sigma product and service quality. Firms in the top right corner that compete with firms that lie elsewhere in the matrix leave little doubt about who the winners will be. Such innovative firms have developed a sustainable, competitive advantage.

Implicit in this model is the idea that the causes of a customer's firing a firm are found in the lower left portion of the customer satisfaction grid. Generally, the cause is low performance on attributes deemed important by the customer. To determine which attributes contribute to customer turnover, root cause analysis must be conducted. This simply means that firms must track the root causes of customer turnover, primarily through exit interviews with lost customers. The pattern of causes will quickly become evident in most cases.

The causes of customer turnover are not always uniform across market segments. What may be extremely important to one customer group may be unimportant to another customer group. Therefore, root cause studies should also be segmented by market segments or customer groupings.

Regardless of the industry, studies have indicated there is a strong, positive correlation between customer retention rates and profitability. The most profitable firms typically are those that have the lowest customer turnover rates. The greater the customer satisfaction, the lower the customer turnover, and, therefore, the fewer the direct and indirect costs of customer dissatisfaction. Essentially, these studies indicate that the conveying of good customer value, which increases customer satisfaction and reduces customer turnover, will show up as benefits directly in the bottom line. The question that then arises is, How can a firm afford not to try to maximize customer value and increase customer satisfaction?

SUMMARY

The costs of delivering low customer value are quite high and often overlooked. When attempts are made to calculate the costs associated with customer dissatisfaction, the attention is invariably on direct costs, which translates into issues such as returns, replacement, shipping, and handling or on warranties and guarantees. Less frequently, the costs are calculated for overhead and variable customer service and customer acquisition. Even when all of these costs are examined, they are usually much smaller than the indirect costs.

The indirect costs of customer dissatisfaction include lost sales and the associated profits. Lost innovations, lost referrals, and negative word of mouth can be significant. New customers nearly always use more customer support services of all types than do "old" customers. In total, these costs are usually two or three times greater than the more obvious direct costs.

A wide variety of studies indicate that overall profitability and customer retention are strongly and positively related to each other. Firms that have low customer turnover are consistently more profitable than firms with high customer turnover, regardless of the industry.

The implication is quite clear. The causes of customer turnover and customer dissatisfaction must be determined, tracked, and corrected. Despite the ease of conducting such research, few firms conduct exit interviews with customers who have fired the firm as a supplier.

When such research is conducted, construction of a customer satisfaction grid becomes a simple task. The delivery performance of the attributes in the lower left corner of the grid are well-known to disgruntled customers. When asked, these customers often tell much more than many managers really want to hear. Despite getting an earful of what is being done wrong, every firm should have an explicit customer retention program in place that quickly identifies the causes of customer turnover.

APPLICATION IDEAS

1. What is the total of all the direct costs of customer dissatisfaction in your organization? What percentage of your customer base is generating these costs?
2. What is your organization's customer turnover rate? What is the life expectancy of the average customer? What is the annual value of the lost

sales? How does your organization's customer turnover rate compare to your key competitors'?

3. Does your organization have a system for capturing the ideas for innovation that are generated by customers? Does your organization have a customer database that can help identify the most profitable and innovative customers?

4. Where is your organization on the customer satisfaction grid? Where are your competitors? What areas of improvement are necessary to move to the upper right-hand corner? Do you have any empirical data to support your assumptions?

7

A Customer Satisfaction Program: The Scorecard that Measures Delivered Customer Value

"Satisfy your customers or your competitors will."

A customer satisfaction measurement program is quite simply the most important type of marketing research a firm can conduct. Ironically, about 80 percent of all such programs are superficial and virtually worthless. To be valuable, a customer satisfaction program must flow from and be embedded in a firm's culture. It is essential for long-term survival that a firm design, implement, and improve a good customer satisfaction program.

If maximizing customer value is the ultimate business goal, customer satisfaction is the scorecard that tells you how you're doing. If carried out correctly, a customer satisfaction program will point out your firm's strengths and weaknesses relative to the competition's. If carried out incorrectly, a customer satisfaction program will yield vague, positive responses that will be virtually worthless. Unfortunately, most customer satisfaction programs fall into the latter category. The purpose of this chapter is to provide you with enough discussion about customer satisfaction programs so that either you can evaluate your company's program if it has one or you can begin to design one.

A firm that has no customer satisfaction program and no interest in starting one should be the delight of the firm's competitors. After all, a customer satisfaction program is at the heart of being customer driven. And if a firm doesn't become customer driven in the 1990s, it probably won't have to worry about the era after 2000.

In a recent Price Waterhouse survey of executives, customer satisfaction was viewed as one of the top strategic issues for the 1990s. Therefore, it is not surprising that many firms, perhaps as many as 50 percent of all companies, solicit customer comments in some way. What *is* surprising is that most programs, around 80 percent, are worthless or worse. A poor customer satisfaction program not only yields vague data but also raises customer expectations. And if customer expectations increase and a firm's performance does not, customer satisfaction will decrease.

A large regional utility company gathered customer satisfaction data annually, as it was required to do by the public utility commission. The utility had outsourced the customer satisfaction program to an independent research firm that surveyed customers, analyzed the data, and reported the results to the firm.

The customer satisfaction committee in the utility met each year to discuss the results of the survey. The data were gathered from an annual survey of all customers, with all market segments lumped together. The aggregated results demonstrated a very consistent pattern—a continual decline in customer satisfaction levels. During the first year of the survey, 95 percent of the customers were satisfied. In the most recent survey year, only 85 percent of the customers were satisfied. The firm was trying to improve its services but was dismayed at the deteriorating results.

The firm wasn't getting worse, but the customers' expectations were getting higher and higher. Since the firm wasn't improving as fast as expectations were increasing, customer satisfaction was consistently declining. Although the firm was gathering customer satisfaction data, the data were not being used to improve the firm's value-added processes. At best, the customer satisfaction program served only as a warning that something was wrong. Unfortunately, the situation experienced by this company is very common.

Customer satisfaction research is probably the most important type of marketing research that a firm can conduct. It provides valuable and useful information about what needs to be improved. But unlike much other research, customer satisfaction research cannot be just a one-shot study. If a business is considered as representing a series of processes designed to deliver value to customers, then a customer satisfaction program must be a continuous process as well. The customer satisfaction program should detect variation in those value creation processes. Since a customer satisfaction program should be a permanent, ongoing process that translates the voice of the customer into usable data, getting the process started properly is important.

THE TEN BASIC RULES OF CUSTOMER SATISFACTION

The basic rules that are necessary in a good customer satisfaction program are presented in Table 7.1. The rules are roughly in the order required for implementation, but all of the elements are important. The absence of any one ingredient could greatly reduce the value of the whole program.

Rule 1: Involve Top Management

As with product quality and service quality, top management's actual involvement, not just its lip service, is important to successful implementation. In most organizations, employees realize that top management personnel are serious when they "walk their talk." A few memos or top management appearances won't have much impact, but when top management gathers customer satisfaction data, sits in on cross-functional team meetings, and asks, "What is being done to improve?" the importance of customer satisfaction will become immediately apparent. Managers will soon quit making excuses such as claims that short-term budget constraints limit their ability to make changes. Sales managers will quit professing that they know what customers want, based purely on gut feeling.

John Fery, CEO of Boise Cascade Corporation, recently revamped the firm's executive performance evaluation process. Previously, bottom line financial performance had been the dominant evaluation criterion. Now the top three criteria are employee satisfaction, continuous improvement, and customer satisfaction. When evaluative criteria change, the importance of the customer becomes evident throughout an organization. Further, Fery recently estimated that he had had more conversations with customers during 1992 than during the previous 10 years combined.

Table 7.1 The Ten Basic Rules of Customer Satisfaction

1. Involve top management.
2. Know the customers.
3. Let the customers define what attributes are important.
4. Know the customers' requirements, expectations, wants.
5. Know the relative importance of customers' decision criteria.
6. Gather and trust the data.
7. Benchmark the data against the competitors', and identify the competitive strengths and weaknesses.
8. Develop cross-functional action plans that enhance strengths and correct weaknesses.
9. Measure performance continually, and spread the data throughout the firm.
10. Be committed to getting better and better and better.

By contrast, the vice president of sales at a consumer products firm had been trying to improve the sales force's performance, particularly that among retail buyers at large chains. So the vice president hired an external consultant to interview the buyers and gather information on how well the recent effort had improved perceived sales representative performance. Obviously, the vice president was expecting some positive feedback. The consultant reported, however, that the buyers thought the firm's sales reps were terrible, their delivery was poor, and the pricing structure and price points were illogical and inconsistent with the industry. While there are many flaws in this type of customer satisfaction program, there was no real commitment by top management to use the data anyway. In fact, it is highly probable that the consultant's report was never seen by anyone other than the vice president of sales.

Examples abound of functional area managers' resisting customer satisfaction programs on the theory "If you don't ask the questions, you don't have to hear the answer." Unfortunately, too many managers are afraid to hear what customers think of them, and that fear indicates a weakness in the corporate culture.

The primary reason that top management involvement is so necessary for customer satisfaction is that responsibility for creating customer satisfaction cuts across functional boundaries. For instance, a customer service department alone will have little impact on customer attitudes. Depending on the specific attribute, three, four, or five departments may be directly involved in creating customer satisfaction. Since customer satisfaction is the result of a pervasive, organization-wide effort, top management must create cascading sponsorship: each level in an organization must make customer satisfaction a visible, tangible goal for everyone. It is top management's responsibility to make sure that everyone knows the importance of focusing on the customer. Cascading sponsorship implies that responsibility cannot simply be delegated to one department; it must be adopted at the top and flow from there.

Rule 2: Know the Customers

For much of the time during the 1980s, a good deal of business literature touted the virtues of being market driven. Identifying various segments, tracking market growth, competitive intensity, and milking cash cows were all important to being market driven. Sadly, after 10 or 15 years of being market driven, many firms still know very little about their customers. They may know a good deal about markets in general, but they know very little about customers specifically, and that is the key difference between being market driven and being customer driven. The customer-driven firm views each customer as a valuable asset and constantly tries to increase its asset base.

There are two broad categories of customers—internal and external. Internal customers are an important part of the total quality effort as discussed earlier. In some companies or divisions, intracompany transfers may constitute a large portion of sales. Generating satisfaction among these internal customers is important, but since the same concepts could apply internally, this discussion focuses on external customers. After all, the external customers are the ones who represent the justification for customer focus.

The category of external customers can be divided into two parts: channel intermediaries and ultimate consumers. Channel intermediaries are, however, often neglected in customer satisfaction programs. As power has shifted more clearly to consumers, channel members, particularly those close to the consumer, have gained in power. Because of the diversity of brands competing for shelf space, retailers play more of a gatekeeper role than ever before. Grocery stores such as Albertson's, Safeway, and Alpha Beta carry a couple of private labels and a few additional independent brands that can generate a good inventory turnover rate. Ensuring that these gatekeepers are satisfied is obviously important.

However, channels also often include brokers, wholesalers, and distribution centers, for example, each of whom may have different decision criteria. A good customer satisfaction program will include, at the least, the most important of these types of channel customers.

In most customer firms, the power to make purchase decisions is dispersed. In high-tech industries such as electronics, the functional areas of engineering, production, purchasing, quality assurance, and research and development all may be involved in the purchase decision process, each applying different evaluative criteria. A good customer satisfaction program will track the multiple views normally found among channel intermediaries and industrial consumers. Specifically, multiple respondents within a particular firm will be identified and included, rather than including only one respondent per firm. The one-respondent-only approach can be very unreliable.

A firm that knows its customers is able to identify the major consumer groups for each of its major product lines. For industrial customers, it means knowing who is involved in purchase decisions and knowing which of those individuals is most influential. For channel members, it means identifying the key players who add value to your products before they reach the ultimate consumer. For each of these groups, a firm must identify what is important in that group's decision processes.

Rule 3: Let the Customers Define What Attributes Are Important

For those of you who were raised in a family with at least three or four members, do you know what each person likes or dislikes and why? For those of you who have a family, do you know what each son or daughter or your spouse likes regarding food or music or clothes? Among your fellow employees whom you work with each day, do you know their values or their motivational patterns? Despite the fact that we may see and interact with family members or fellow employees on a daily basis, few of us really know what motivates each of them. The same situation applies to customers. Just because a firm may deal with customers doesn't mean the firm really understands the customers. Unfortunately, the assumption is often made that the sales representative or the sales manager does know what the customer wants.

Managers who believe they know based on gut feel or experience what attributes are most important to their customers are probably wrong. Most managers can identify some of the attributes, but few managers can identify all of the attributes expected by customers. Therefore, this stage of the customer satisfaction program is referred to as "discovery," because companies for the first time discover what their customers really want. And it is important to define in customers' own words what customers want. If those wants are quickly translated into the language of the firm, such as "technical specifications," something may be lost in the translation.

Most firms have acquired and therefore already possess various types of customer information. So the first step in determining customer attitudes is to systematically assess internally available data. This step often includes gathering new information from customer contact personnel. Though such internally generated data may be somewhat biased, the information helps define the general issues and directions for further study. That is precisely what happened at Motorola.

Motorola, unlike other firms such as Xerox or Cadillac, was not facing a crisis situation when it initially embarked on its total quality program. In 1979, during an executive-level strategic planning session, the vice president of sales interrupted the meeting by pointing out that the issue of most importance to customers—product quality—was not even on the agenda. That initial discussion about the customers' quality expectations led to Motorola's first five-year plan and subsequently to its current six sigma goal. Feedback from customers, which had gone unnoticed or was ignored for years, finally was heard, leading to outstanding improvement. It is likely that most customers will provide early warning of trends and issues if their opinions are solicited formally.

Once the internal information has been exhausted and the general issues defined, the second step is to talk to customers. The goal of this step is to discover everything that is important to customers. In particular, discovery should include not only product quality issues but service quality and price perceptions as well. In addition, customer views should cover the product's entire life, not just the purchase transaction. The customer's purchase decision processes and decision alternatives should be determined to the extent possible.

The process at this point should consist only of soft, or subjective, research. Primarily through one-on-one depth interviews and focus groups of some type, the intent is to dredge up as many ideas and attributes as possible. Sorting, combining, and synthesizing the ideas into a customer satisfaction questionnaire will come later.

The most common weakness at this point is to include only current customers in the process. Ideally, lost customers and potential customers should be included as well. Normally, the lost customers will provide a detailed statement about the strengths and weaknesses of a particular firm, whereas potential customers are a good source of overall industry perceptions and trends. Thus, a goal of this process is to gain an initial view of appropriate benchmark criteria. That is, a firm should try to identify all of the attributes that are used by customers when they select a product from a set of competitive alternatives. A firm that solicits information only from current customers, although they can provide very specific comments, increases the chances of getting a somewhat biased set of attributes.

Rule 4: Know the Customers' Requirements, Expectations, Wants

For collection of customer information, it is often helpful to categorize the responses into three categories: requirements, expectations, and wants.

Requirements are those product and service attributes that the customer must have—the hygiene factors. When diners go to a restaurant, most will absolutely require cleanliness, for example. When a firm guarantees an order will be delivered within five days, that becomes a requirement.

Expectations are product or service quality standards that the customer should be able to expect. When one orders a steak medium rare, one has some expectation about what medium rare should be. It can be a little too well-done or a little too rare and still meet requirements but not meet expectations.

Finally, there are wants, those things that customers would really like to have but don't really expect. Sometimes these are referred to as delighters or exciters, but essentially, they are those above and beyond things such as truly outstanding service at a restaurant. They are usually the satisfier items discussed previously.

A word of caution should be noted about distinguishing between requirements, expectations, and wants. Though it is often possible to distinguish between these at any one point in time, the customer's views move upward dynamically. An expectation this year may be a requirement next year. The rate of change between these categories is determined largely by buying alternatives—the product or service offered by the competition. The customer's expectations are not static so company performance must also increase.

Rule 5: Know the Relative Importance of Customers' Decision Criteria

Determining the relative importance of each attribute to customers is a critical part of the discovery process. Obviously, the most important of the attributes will receive the initial attention. There are a number of ways to determine the relative importance of various criteria.

During the soft research, customers can be asked to define a critical incident, a situation when they were very satisfied or very dissatisfied. Then it's up to management to sift through these responses and identify the common threads that yield satisfaction. Other ways of determining relative importance are to have the customer use a rating scale, a rank ordering, or a forced allocation technique to determine the relative importance of each attribute. The importance of each attribute also can be determined by statistically analyzing the data generated from such an approach.

The point of this is that relative importance can be determined in a variety of ways. Unfortunately, a common weakness in customer satisfaction research is to devote most of the effort to measuring performance on attributes and not enough to determining the relative importance of each attribute from the customer's perspective. The end result of this weakness is that a firm may expend a lot of effort trying to improve in an unimportant area.

Rule 6: Gather and Trust the Data

Assuming that the discovery process has identified the issues, a pretested questionnaire must then be developed. The process implies that the attributes that are relevant to customers must be measured in some objective fashion. Typically, three types of data are gathered: First, the questionnaire must measure the customer's perception of the firm's ability to deliver that attribute, or, its performance. Second, the questionnaire must gather data indicating the importance of each attribute. Third, the questionnaire must also measure how a firm's performance compares to the competitor's performance. Once the questionnaire is developed, the next step is to gather the data. Because of the complexity of this process, it may be necessary to design several different questionnaires and then aggregate the data. Often, there are just too many questions for a single questionnaire.

A number of research design issues must be resolved. These issues are concerned primarily with bias and cost. The earlier discussion on familiarity with the firm's customers outlined some of the difficulties in identifying various segments. If a firm has a relatively small customer base, a census of all customers is appropriate. Solectron, a 1991 Baldrige award winner, includes all of its 60–70 customers in its customer satisfaction program. Since there are only a little over 200 airlines in the world, the commercial aircraft division of Boeing can survey all customers. When a company, like Xerox, has 2.2 million customers, the task becomes more formidable.

If the customer base is quite large, most firms resort to a sample. The sample could be a randomly generated cross section of customers or it could be transaction based. The transaction-based approach consists of a follow-up contact with every 10th or 15th or 30th customer contact. Most firms embarking on customer satisfaction research do so by initially gathering a large sample and then tracking with smaller samples or a transaction sample. The large initial sample yields a reliable base of comparison against which subsequent performance can be measured. The sample size is normally constrained by cost considerations.

The majority of customer satisfaction research identifies the sponsor, particularly when a firm surveys its own customers. The act of surveying customers creates goodwill, and response rates are typically high when sponsorship is known. However, there is some risk of bias since some customers may not want to be too harsh in their statements. Also, asking customers about their satisfaction levels normally ratchets customer expectations upward. Customers develop an expectation that the company should improve. When a company is developing external benchmarks based on responses from potential customers or competitors' customers, sponsorship is usually not provided to remove potential bias.

The most common methods of gathering data are by telephone, by mail, in person, or some combination. Telephone surveys usually yield high response rates, provide good control, and can be done quickly but are more costly than mail. Mail surveys are typically the least expensive and least intrusive, but they yield low response rates. In-person interviews yield more detail and create more goodwill, but they are far more expensive and are usually more subjective.

Every survey instrument has weaknesses. Every research design has some limitations. However, if care is taken in the discovery phase, if instruments are developed based on that information and pretested, and if research design issues are carefully thought out, then reasonably good data will result. Since no research is perfect, the goal is usually to reduce potential weakness to an acceptable level.

Rule 7: Benchmark Against Competitors

Benchmarking is the process of comparing a firm's performance to some standard, and there are three types of standards. The first benchmark is typically based on some internal performance base. Motorola's initial quality benchmark was its 1980 quality level. Xerox's initial customer satisfaction benchmark was 1984. The reason for exerting a good deal of effort in the initial customer satisfaction survey is to create a reliable baseline for future comparison. Starting out with a poor benchmark renders subsequent comparisons useless.

A second type of benchmark is based on industry-wide comparison. There are two types of industry standards: One type occurs when a firm such as J. D. Power and Associates gathers information about the various competitors in an industry. J. D. Power gathers information about the auto industry, for example, that measures customer satisfaction on a variety of attributes. Elrick and Lavidge Inc., a marketing research firm, gathers customer satisfaction information about the utility industry by surveying 14,000 respondents nationwide. An individual firm may buy such databases to get relatively unbiased data. However, the data are seldom in a form that is consistent with internal customer satisfaction historical data, so comparisons are more difficult. Such surveys do provide a good rough comparison and can raise issues that may have been overlooked in internal surveys.

The second type of industry standard is measured when a number of competitors jointly fund a study that compares the performance of each with an industry average. The cost to each firm is usually much lower because more firms are defraying the cost. The specific company data are proprietary, while the overall averages are shared among participants. The specific questions can be modified somewhat to fit a participating firm's needs, so this type of industry standard is normally more detailed and useful than the more generic type.

The third, most useful and strategically important, type of benchmarking is against key competitors. A firm needs to simply identify the number of key competitors in its industry and then gather information from those competitors' customers as well as its own customers. What quickly emerges is a detailed profile of competitive strengths and weaknesses that can be combined with relative importance ratings. Such information enables a firm to pinpoint critical deficiencies and to develop detailed action plans to correct any shortcomings.

Some firms have taken this benchmarking concept a step further. Instead of developing a benchmark only on competitors, some firms identify the firm that is best at a particular activity or process in any specific industry. It may be L. L. Bean, for telephone order processing or customer service. It may be American Express, for billing and payment transactions. And then the firm steals shamelessly from those acknowledged experts so as to improve its own processes. This is now commonly referred to as best-in-class benchmarking.

Regardless of how the external benchmarking is conducted, it provides a measure of reality. For years, Cadillac surveyed its own customers and thought satisfaction was pretty good. It wasn't until Cadillac conducted external benchmarking that it realized the competition was getting better much faster. Though Cadillac was improving, it was getting further and further behind.

Internal data are often tracked on a monthly basis; external benchmarking often annually or, in some dynamic industries, semiannually. Normally, competitive perceptions are fairly stable so that annual or semiannual tracking provides a reasonably accurate competitive profile.

Rule 8: Develop Cross-Functional Action Plans

The purpose of customer satisfaction programs is to generate detailed action plans. If continual improvement does not result and if a firm does not make internal changes to increase customer satisfaction based on good data, then management has given only superficial support. When the results of a customer satisfaction program lead to changes within the firm, then the process is worthwhile. The real litmus test of such research is that it provides direction for organizational change and improvement. Action plans should logically flow from the data. The issue is discussed in detail in the example that follows shortly.

Rule 9: Measure Continually, and Spread the Data

This rule stresses the fact that a firm's customer satisfaction effort must be continuous and ongoing. There are three reasons for this. First, very few firms will achieve 100 percent customer satisfaction quickly, although it is possible and has been done. But by striving for the goal, the organization will improve on a continuous basis. By a firm's constantly striving for improvement, employee morale is usually much higher due to the empowerment of workers.

Anyone who has ever engaged in mountain climbing may identify with the following analogy. On a clear day, when the summit is in full view, the morale of a climbing party is almost always high. The climbers can see their goal and monitor their progress toward the peak. The climbing may be arduous, but the mood is often jovial and spirits are high. On a cloudy, rainy, or snowy day, the peak and the intermediate goals are obscured. Climbers plod on with no clear target in mind. Morale is almost always lower, climbers are more irritable, and the probability of ailments such as altitude sickness increases.

The same situation applies in organizations. If all of an organization's employees can focus on a clearly defined goal of 100 percent customer satisfaction and can participate in the intermediate steps of getting there through employee empowerment, employee morale and satisfaction will improve.

A second reason for making the process continuous has been mentioned previously. Customers' needs are continually changing, evolving. If a firm's customer satisfaction program presents only one-shot glimpses of customers' views, customers may evolve away. If the customers are dynamic and the firm is static, gaps will quickly emerge.

The third reason for continual customer satisfaction measurement is the competition. While some competitors may be static, many will not. Competition in virtually every industry is increasing. If a firm is not engaging in competitive benchmarking on a continual basis, the competition may also evolve away from it. A firm may be improving but at a slower rate than the competitors. The result will be competitive vulnerability followed by reduced financial performance.

Rule 10: Be Committed to Getting Better and Better and Better

Finally, no customer satisfaction program is perfect. Over time, every program can be improved and enhanced. The decision criteria may change, and the relative importance of individual criteria may change. Whereas large changes may make comparisons with benchmarks difficult, most changes consist of small refinements, such as the fine-tuning of an instrument. If care is taken during the discovery phase of developing a customer satisfaction program, subsequent changes should be minor. But the question should always be asked, "Is there a better way to do this?" and if the answer is yes, is that better way worth the marginal cost?

THE WONDER CORPORATION

For integration of the ten basic rules, an example may be useful along with some of the graphics commonly used. The example is based on an actual firm. Some of the steps and actual data have been modified to facilitate clarity of discussion. And for obvious reasons, a fictitious name is used—the Wonder Corporation.

Let's assume that the Wonder Corporation has six different, relatively distinct product groupings, one of which is product A. To keep matters simple, product A will have only one large customer group. Product A is the most important product for Wonder Corporation—accounting for 30 percent of sales—so top management has decided to initiate a customer satisfaction program in that division first, because the competition is getting tougher and the product is very important to overall profitability. Top management realizes that, if successful, the customer satisfaction program will need to be extended to the other five product divisions. But for now, product A is the priority.

Consistent with common practice, depth interviews and focus groups were conducted using current customer contact employees, current customers, previous customers, and even some competitors' customers. From these sources, a list of over 40 attributes that contribute to customer satisfaction was generated. Realizing that it might take three or four questions to accurately measure a specific attribute, management viewed the list of over 40 attributes as too long and pared it down to a list of 22 "critically important" attributes. This was accomplished through statistical techniques (primarily factor analysis) and several focus group interactions. The list of 22 attributes is shown in Table 7.2.

Although the attributes certainly hadn't started that way, management grouped them, after numerous iterations, into seven general categories (Figure 7.1). This grouping process was chosen to facilitate the development of cross-functional teams, a subject to be discussed later. The basic rationale behind the grouping was that attributes that have common value-added processes should be grouped together because a solution to one issue may impact other attributes. Although the argument could be made that each attribute is somehow related to every other attribute, the most dominant relationships drove the grouping process.

In this stage, the most shocking finding to top management was the number of variables that influenced customer satisfaction. The Wonder Corporation had started a quality improvement program several years earlier and had made significant strides in increasing product quality. But

Table 7.2   Reduced List of Specific Attributes

Specific Attributes	
Durability	Technical quality
Appearance	Complaint resolution
Reliability	Telephone response
Shipment timeliness	Information accuracy
Shipment damage	Invoice accuracy
Driver courtesy	Invoice timeliness
Rep's accessibility	Inquiry responsiveness
Rep's knowledge	Total cost of use
Rep's reliability, follow-up	Market price
Structural designs	Supply costs
Sample timeliness	Productivity

the company was a bit chagrined to learn that product quality was only one of seven broad characteristics with which the customer was concerned. In retrospect, management realized it had fallen into a common quality trap, focusing on conformance to specifications developed by management rather than on conformance to customer expectations. At least top management was about to correct that flaw, something the competitors had not yet done.

The customer satisfaction model for product A, is presented in Figure 7.2, captured most of the cause and effect relationships for product A, although some attributes could be further decomposed, as we shall see later. At this point, a questionnaire was developed for a telephone survey. Since product A is a component subassembly sold to about 150 customers, all customer firms were included in the research. However, in each of the firms, three or four functional areas were involved in the purchase decision and the postpurchase use of product A, so each of those functional areas was included for a sample of 500 current customers. Also surveyed was a sample of about 200 past customers and 150 competitors' customers. Thus, about 850 respondents were contacted. The current customers seemed pleasantly surprised that the Wonder Corporation was concerned enough about customer satisfaction to contact them, and they were very open in their comments.

The questionnaire development and design was pretty straightforward. The questionnaire had three portions. The first portion consisted

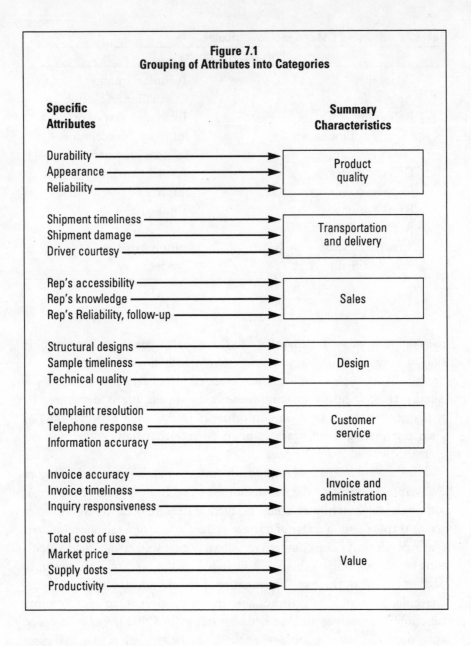

Figure 7.1
Grouping of Attributes into Categories

Specific Attributes	Summary Characteristics
Durability Appearance Reliability	Product quality
Shipment timeliness Shipment damage Driver courtesy	Transportation and delivery
Rep's accessibility Rep's knowledge Rep's Reliability, follow-up	Sales
Structural designs Sample timeliness Technical quality	Design
Complaint resolution Telephone response Information accuracy	Customer service
Invoice accuracy Invoice timeliness Inquiry responsiveness	Invoice and administration
Total cost of use Market price Supply dosts Productivity	Value

of the typical screening data that categorized respondents on a number of important variables. The second portion of the questionnaire was designed to determine the relative importance of each of the attributes to customers. The third portion measured Wonder Corporation's performance on each attribute. For present and past customers, respondents were asked to rate Wonder's actual performance.

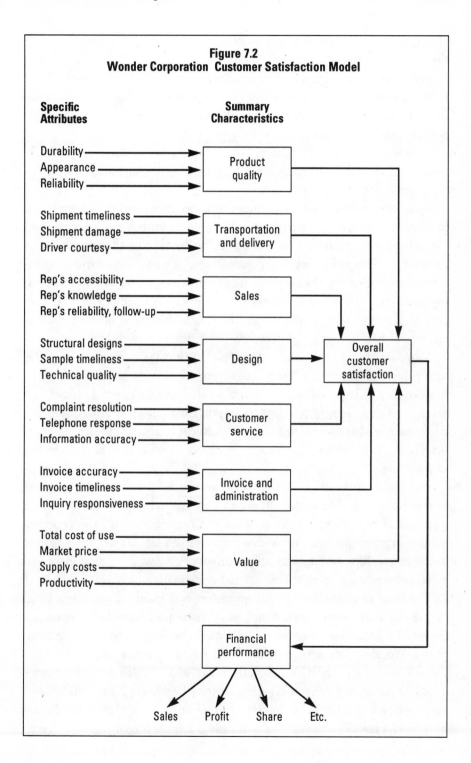

**Figure 7.2
Wonder Corporation Customer Satisfaction Model**

The technique used to rate importance was a 100-point forced allocation. Initially, respondents were asked to allocate the 100 points based on the relative importance of each of the seven broad categories. Then, for each category, respondents were asked to rate the relative importance of each attribute, again allocating 100 points based on the relative importance of each of the three or four attributes.

Wonder Corporation's performance was measured using a simple 7-point rating scale. A 1 represented very poor performance, and a 7 represented very good performance.

Once the executives had gathered the performance evaluations and importance ratings from current and previous customers, they plotted the overall mean value of each category by combining the results into a performance/importance grid (Figure 7.3). Wonder Corporation executives were glad to see that their quality improvement efforts had not been misdirected. Both product quality and design were important to customers, and product A was viewed as reasonably good in both characteristics although there was certainly room for improvement.

More troubling to Wonder Corporation management were the sales and value characteristics. Both areas were reasonably important to customers, but performance was much weaker than expected. Customer service was apparently a little less important than sales and value, but performance was subpar on this characteristic also. These three characteristics held some very clear potential for improving customer satisfaction.

Since transportation was contracted out to a trucking firm, problems in the areas of shipment timeliness and transit damage would require a joint effort to resolve. Perhaps Wonder Corporation and the trucking firm together could come up with some improvement strategies. The new automated billing system was apparently working well, as customers had rated performance on that characteristic fairly high.

The next step for Wonder Corporation was external benchmarking. While the data from current and past customers provided a good internal benchmark against which subsequent performance could be compared, Wonder Corporation really needed to know its competitive position. Wonder Corporation executives realized that their performance could be compared to each key competitor (there were three others), and they decided initially to compare their own performance with the industry average. The average was simply a composite of the three com-

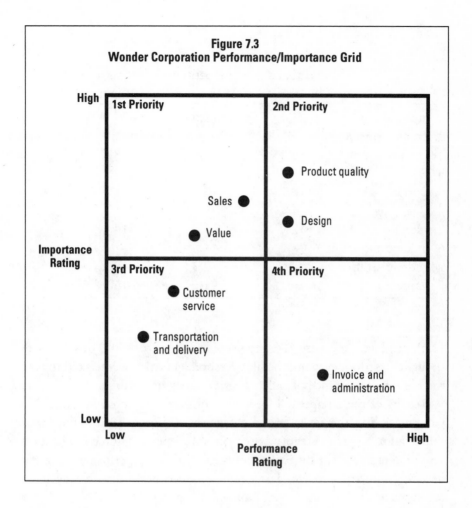

Figure 7.3
Wonder Corporation Performance/Importance Grid

petitors and Wonder Corporation. To the 150 responses from competitors' customers, the management at Wonder Corporation randomly added 50 current Wonder Corporation customers. The 200 responses constituted the industry average or the external benchmark. Although the use of 50 customers per firm constituted a relatively small sample, management felt that in aggregate, the sample of 200 would be fairly valid.

The 200 customers were administered a disguised questionnaire. The identity of the sponsoring firm was not made known to the customers, because each customer was evaluating the performance of all four key competitors. If the respondents had no experience with a particular

Table 7.3 Competitive Benchmarking

Characteristic	Mean Importance Weight	Mean Competitive Difference	Strategic Weight	Priority
1. Product quality	25	+1.0	+25.0	7
2. Transportation and delivery	6	−1.4	−8.4	4
3. Sales	19	−.5	-9.5	3
4. Design	18	+1.2	+21.6	6
5. Customer service	12	−1.2	−14.4	2
6. Invoice and administration	4	+2.3	+9.2	5
7. Value	16	−1.0	−16.0	1

firm's product, they were asked to provide their perceptions of what they thought the product would be like. Respondents also were asked to rate the relative importance of each major category of attributes.

Results of the competitive benchmarking are presented in Table 7.3. Column 1 lists the seven broad categories. Column 2 gives the mean importance of each category based on a 100 percent forced allocation scale. Column 3 is the difference between product A's performance rating and the industry average. For example, since performance was measured using a 7-point scale, Wonder Corporation's rating of 5 for product quality was 1 higher than the average of 4. A positive sign means product A was better than the industry average; a negative sign means product A was below the industry average. Column 4, the strategic weight, is obtained by multiplying the importance value times the competitive difference. The idea here is that the importance and performance data must be combined to yield managerially actionable data. The larger the positive number, the more that characteristic is a competitive strength. The more negative the number, the more that characteristic is a competitive weakness, relative to the industry. Column 5 establishes the priority for action; the most negative numbers are the highest priorities because they are the greatest strategic weaknesses. The higher the strategic weight, the more likely it is viewed as an area of competitive strength.

Figure 7.4
Product Quality Characteristics

Appearance	1. Durability	2. Appearance	3. Reliability
Production Function	★	■	■
Engineering Function	●	★	■
Quality Assurance		■	★
Supplier A	■	●	
Supplier B			●
Importance Weight	30	20	50
Competitive Difference	1.1	−1.1	−0.3
Strategic Weight	+33	−22	−15
Priority	3	1	2

★ High Involvement: The Champion
● Moderate Involvement: Team Member
■ Low Involvement: Team Member

For each of the categories, cross-functional teams were established to develop and implement action plans. When resources were necessary, they were allocated on the basis of the priorities established in Table 7.3. However, since importance ratings and competitive position were also gathered for each of the 22 attributes, each cross-functional team further decomposed the data. Figure 7.4 shows how the product quality team categorized the data even further.

The most important product quality attribute, as indicated by the mean portion of the 100-point allocation, was reliability followed by

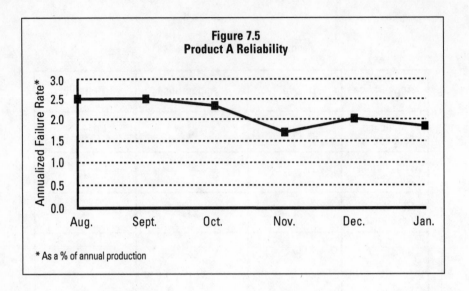

Figure 7.5
Product A Reliability

* As a % of annual production

durability and appearance. Improvement of each of these attributes was the responsibility of a separate cross-functional team. However, a weak competitive position made appearance a priority issue.

Appearance had the largest negative strategic weight, and therefore it was the top priority within the product quality group. Since product A contained components purchased from supplier A and supplier B, outside suppliers were important to improving appearance, particularly supplier A. Internally at Wonder Corporation, engineering was most involved with appearance and was designated as the team champion responsible for coordinating the efforts of production, quality assurance, and supplier A. Though development of the action plan to improve appearance was a team effort, final responsibility for leadership rested with the team champion.

The product reliability team, consisting of production, engineering, quality assurance, and supplier B, met and began tracking the annualized failure rate (AFR) for product A. The team gathered data and plotted it on a process control chart (Figure 7.5) to determine the trends. Fortunately, the AFR was declining. To be of more value, the root causes of failure were tabulated by the team, and specific strategies were developed to reduce each cause of product failure. The reduction of failure

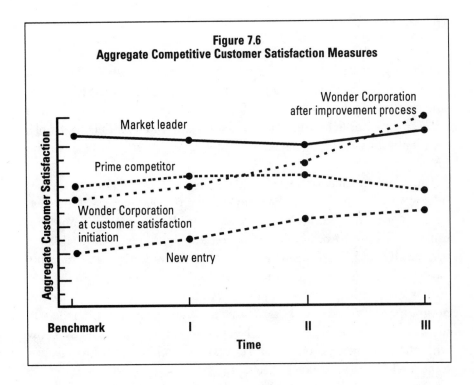

Figure 7.6
Aggregate Competitive Customer Satisfaction Measures

rates by nearly a full percentage point resulted in a very significant cost savings.

Top management at Wonder Corporation was now a year into its customer satisfaction program for product A. The process had been trying at times, but employees were becoming believers. There were 22 cross-functional teams and progress had been made in every attribute, although successes were harder to attain in some areas than others. Whereas the aggregate customer satisfaction score, composed of three overall measures, was a relatively crude measure, current external benchmark data (Figure 7.6) showed that Wonder Corporation had passed the market leader in overall customer satisfaction. The top management at Wonder Corporation decided to embark on the challenge of extending its customer satisfaction program to its five other product divisions. Implementation in the other divisions would certainly be easier, since the customer satisfaction program for product A had resulted in visible, tangible improvements.

SUMMARY

The customer satisfaction measurement program of the Wonder Corporation was not perfect; several flaws and weaknesses existed. However, there is probably no such thing as a perfect customer satisfaction measurement program. The key issue for the Wonder Corporation is that a program was designed and implemented and was producing visible, tangible results. Wonder Corporation's program is certain to evolve and improve.

Customer satisfaction research is clearly the most important type of research that a firm can conduct. It produces the real scorecard for measuring delivered customer value. It is the feedback loop from the customer to the firm. And it allows the voice of the customer to evaluate a firm's value-added processes. After all, the customer is really the only true evaluator of delivered customer value.

It is ironic, then, that so many firms have no customer satisfaction program at all or have only a superficial, token program. Managers in those firms must be operating on the assumption that they already know what the customer wants. Or worse yet, they could be afraid to ask customers what customers really feel.

Unlike much marketing research, good customer satisfaction measurement data can be used widely throughout a firm to improve value-added processes. The ten basic rules for a good program are simply a set of prerequisites that must be in place to ensure widespread use. If customer satisfaction data are gathered and used only by marketing, then the organization is only superficially committed to the customer.

The rapid increase in the use of customer satisfaction programs by innovative firms attests to their value. In virtually all these firms, such a program is intimately linked to a continuous improvement effort. The real purpose of the program is to create a formalized system for becoming customer driven.

APPLICATION IDEAS

1. Is the CEO or COO in your organization strongly committed to improving customer satisfaction? Has this commitment been reflected in action programs and resource allocations? Is the CEO or COO actively involved in implementing customer satisfaction as a strategic goal?
2. What are your organization's key customer groups? What channel intermediaries are important value-added partners? Which individuals in customer

organizations are important to the purchase decision for your products? Are all of these groups represented in your customer satisfaction program?

3. Were the attributes measured in your customer satisfaction questionnaire generated from customers? Do the questions differentiate between requirements, expectations, and wants? Is the relative importance of each attribute combined with competitor performance to determine strategic strengths and weaknesses?

4. Are the customer satisfaction data used to drive continuous improvement, particularly by cross-functional teams? Or are the data used only by a few functional areas?

5. Is the customer satisfaction program itself subject to continuous improvement? Or has the program remained unchanged since its inception?

8

Getting Close to the Customer: The Human Touch

"Every customer contact is an opportunity to learn and improve."

Customers are not targets! Customers are probably a firm's most valuable asset, and they should be nurtured, developed, and treated accordingly. Each and every customer should be the objective of proactive, bonding relationships. And customers, in person, should be integrated into the firm's decision-making processes. To be truly customer driven, a firm must spread throughout the firm the human touch of its customers.

For years, the virtues of "getting close to customers" and understanding their needs have been touted. This goal of focusing on the customer has led many organizations to design a high-powered marketing research engine capable of spewing out mountains of data. The output of sophisticated statistical models got analyzed in minute detail, and the marketers tried to mold the "statistically significant" relationships into a model that depicted a customer's behavior. Sadly, their reliance on "the numbers" led many managers to become detached from their customers. For many organizations, the primary contact with customers was through the sales force. And that is now a fatal flaw.

Perhaps, during a time when customers had fewer choices and more stable expectations, a sales force could be counted on to sell products that reflected the findings of market research studies. The current environment of proliferating customer choice, due to increasing global competition and rapidly changing customer expectations, however, requires a different approach.

This newer approach is called customer integration. Customer integration requires that customers become embedded into a firm's decision-making and value-added processes. The previous chapter examined how customer satisfaction measurement can be empirically used to drive continuous improvement. And using the "hard" data generated by a good customer satisfaction program is necessary, but it is insufficient to accomplish customer integration.

This chapter addresses how customers can be used to drive continuous improvement in a soft, nonempirical fashion. There is probably no faster way to become customer driven than to establish many points of direct customer contact at all organizational levels and across various functions. And there is nothing more valuable than the human touch of customers.

There are two basic types of customer contact: The first is a "reactive" approach whereby contact is initiated by the customer. The second type is a "proactive" approach whereby contact is initiated by the organization. Ironically, most firms see the importance of reactive contact but far fewer see the importance of proactive contact with customers.

REACTIVE CUSTOMER CONTACT

Getting reactive feedback from customers normally results in highly biased information for several reasons. First, the vast majority of customers—90–95 percent—never bother to initiate contact with the firm. Therefore, those that do initiate contact are not representative of the whole customer base. Instead, most of the customers that contact a firm have a stronger emotional response than the average customer. This brings us to the second reason for biased information.

The majority of customer-initiated response is due to a negative experience; that is, they have an axe to grind. While there certainly is merit in analyzing customer complaints, basing major organization changes or responses on complaint data is a poor strategic rationale. Such a response is like closing the gate after all the cows have escaped. As we shall see, a proactive approach ensures that the gate is never left open in the first place. However, we need to discuss first the reactive approaches to customer contact.

Customer Service Department

One of the first steps in organizational evolution to customer integration is the creation of a customer service department. The name of such a department is really a misnomer; a better name would be "customer complaint catch-all" for many firms. The department doesn't really provide service; it serves as a repository of customer complaints, a sort of lightning rod for the wrath of customers so that others in the organization don't have to feel the heat. While the customer service department in some firms may be different, most firms fit this model.

Many firms in the computer industry have customer support lines to provide service for customers when customers have a problem. However, a significant portion of those support lines do not have a toll-free number. The most common organizational justification is that it is too costly. The following reconstructs a recent situation that I experienced.

Assume that you buy a new personal computer (PC) by mail from a mail order house. When you open the boxes containing the PC, you find an apologetic note saying, "Sorry, we were out of stock of the supporting documentation when your PC was packaged. Please complete and mail the attached card and we'll send you the documentation." You do as requested, but two weeks later no documentation has arrived yet. So you phone the mail order house where you bought the PC to get a phone number for the manufacturer since none was included. You are given the manufacturer's 800 number for "customer service." When you call the toll-free number, you find that it doesn't work from your area code. To get the regular number, you must call information.

When you finally reach the company, your call is routed twice so that it finally goes into the "customer service" queue. Fifteen minutes later you get a real person, who assures you that the documentation will be "in the mail today." A week later it arrives and is so poor that it doesn't answer your questions.

So you phone the company again. You've had your PC for almost a month now. The PC had come preloaded with a variety of software, and after waiting on hold again, you are told by a customer service representative that your problem is not with the computer but with the software and that you should really call the software manufacturer. The customer service representative gives you the phone number for the software manufacturer's customer service department. Ultimately the problem was finally resolved. Did this "support service" create customer satisfaction? Of course not. In fact, the support service itself was an irritant and almost led to the return of the PC.

Unfortunately, such a situation is not the exception for customer-initiated contact. Instead, the situation represented a typical customer contact and a typical organizational response.

800 Hotlines

The number of toll-free 800 customer hotlines has grown extensively over the past few years, and justifiably so. A toll-free number removes the cost constraint for customers. But the 800 number must still be managed properly.

When I tried phoning a relatively new, rapidly growing discount airline, using its toll-free reservation line, I never got an answer. The implicit message that I got was that the airline wasn't really concerned about customers. The firm's failure to deliver a presale, hygiene factor resulted in the loss of a sale. And I certainly never bothered to complain; I simply took my business elsewhere.

Another common 800 experience is to get put on hold automatically and have a recording tell you, "Your call is important and will be answered in the order in which it was received." Twenty minutes later you're still holding, and somehow, you don't feel your call is quite so important.

A worse version of this is to phone a toll-free number, get put on hold, and then have to access a voice mail system instead of getting a real person. And even then you may not be sure which category of response fits your situation. I recently phoned the Australian consul general's office in San Francisco three times, trying different subdirectories, before I realized that none of the voice mail categories offered fit my question. I am still waiting for a response to the message I left on the voice mail.

When a toll-free customer access system is designed, it should be designed from the perspective of the customer. Unfortunately, many organizations design a "customer service" system to reduce costs or fit the organization's needs. A poorly designed toll-free system is like throwing salt into the wounds of customer discontent.

Sales Contact

A sales force can also be an avenue for reactive customer contact. Customers may complain or offer ideas for improvement to salespeople. Ironically, studies have shown that most of this information is filtered out or ignored by salespeople.

There are several reasons for this. First, most compensation systems are designed to encourage salespeople to increase sales volume. All other activities therefore become tangential to and may actually detract from sales efforts. Therefore, many salespeople feel it isn't their job to be a conduit of complaints from customers.

Another reason that salespeople are not a good upward conduit of information is that they may not want to be the bearer of bad tidings. If management hears lots of complaints from a particular salesperson, the messenger may be shot (figuratively speaking, of course!). Management may conclude that the complaints are due to a salesperson's low performance, so a new person may "solve" the problem.

For the vast majority of firms, the salesperson is the primary point of customer contact. The sales force is indeed a necessary contact point, but it is clearly insufficient in many respects in today's highly competitive business environment. A far more proactive approach is needed.

PROACTIVE CUSTOMER CONTACT

A proactive approach means that the organization initiates contact with the customer for the purpose of getting advice and input that may not show up on customer satisfaction surveys. A proactive approach means that a firm contacts some of the 90–95 percent of customers that will never voice complaints or initiate contact. It means that the human touch of customer contact must be integrated throughout a firm's decision-making processes.

The term "customer" is used broadly here and means much more than only the consumers or end users of a product. The term "customer" also includes channel intermediaries such as wholesalers, distributors, and retailers. In many cases, facilitating organizations such as marketing research firms or shipping companies or advertising agencies also need to be integrated into a firm's decision-making processes. The philosophy that underlies every aspect of customer integration is that all types of customers are valuable assets or portions of the value-added chain, and they need to be treated accordingly. Customers are not targets; they are assets that must be nurtured and developed.

Table 8.1 Proactive Approaches to Customer Contact

1. *Executive contact*—regular interaction with customers by top management.
2. *Customer visits*—managerial and team visits to customer sites
3. *New product development*—getting customers involved early in the design process
4. *Beta sites*—providing prototypes for key customers before full production
5. *Customer panels*—samples of customers that openly discuss their changing needs
6. *Customer representatives on internal teams*—having customers involved in quality improvement teams to ensure the voice of the customer is heard

Some of the types of proactive customer contact are listed in Table 8.1. The type of contact is limited only by the creativity of a particular organization, but the ones shown provide a good sampling of proactive activities.

Executive Contact

The president of Pepsi-Cola North America, Craig Weatherup, runs a corporation with $5 billion in sales annually. Yet he takes time to proactively talk to at least four customers each day. After certain recent product tampering problems, he has probably talked to many more than four customers a day. Executives at Procter and Gamble conduct consumer intercepts in grocery stores to interview customers and get their opinions about P&G products. Even P&G executives answer customer service phone lines periodically. At Hewlett-Packard, executives are assigned to key clients in order to maintain regular, open, high-level contact.

The message that cascades through these organizations is that customers are vitally important. If top management is concerned enough to contact customers, then that activity is probably in the best interest of other managers and employees as well. Liberty Mutual Insurance has a program in which every customer has been adopted by an employee. *Every* customer is regularly contacted by the employee, and personal relationships are built. Not only do customers feel important, but also every employee recognizes the importance of each customer.

Customer Visits

At Motorola and 3M, managers from the CEO on down make visits to customers' facilities. The visits are often conducted by a team of managers that meets with the actual users of their company's products, not just the executives of the customer firm. Afterward, written reports result that are broadly shared throughout Motorola or 3M. The primary reason for such visits is to get direct feedback about products and ideas for improvement from customers who would never see a customer satisfaction survey or initiate direct contact. Many firms are finding that these customer visits should include more than just the upper-level managers. In some firms, cross-functional teams are making customer visits, with impressive results.

New Product Development

When Boeing was considering the development of a more fuel efficient aircraft, representatives of eight major customer airlines were involved in the initial concept discussions. Areas of common concern and unique differences were identified early in the design process. Major suppliers also were involved in the initial concept discussions to provide ideas and suggestions as well as to learn about the ultimate customer's evolving needs.

When Hewlett-Packard begins development of a new laser printer, key customers are involved from the start. H-P views early customer integration as an important part of cycle time reduction and of improving speed to market. By obtaining customer feedback early in the product design stage, the firm reduces its need for test marketing. Design changes are made early in the development process, not after production begins. Currently, customers are helping design the product that will replace the next generation of laser printers that will replace the just introduced LaserJet 4. The customers are providing input for products two generations ahead of the current innovations!

The line between customers and suppliers often becomes hazy in new product development. General Motors and General Electric often have researchers working at each other's research facilities in a joint commitment to continuous improvement, for example. This type of supplier-customer relationship will become the norm in the future.

Beta Sites

For some firms, prototypes are furnished to key customers for trial and feedback. These beta sites are a type of user lab that facilitates early customer input. Xerox and other high-tech firms use this technique to test new products and identify necessary changes before full production begins.

A beta site doesn't have to be highly technical. Some computer firms have customers simply go through the process of uncrating and installing a computer just to find out what the customer really does do and whether or not the directions are actually read. As might be expected, many customers never bother to read the directions. Ironically, some supposedly customer-driven firms have never monitored how customers really use their products.

Customer Panels
Bank of America has customer panels that meet regularly at corporate headquarters to advise the company on how to improve. The customer group sits onstage in an auditorium, and the managers in the audience ask the customers questions. After these lengthy sessions, the managers develop action plans based on customer preferences.

Some firms have found that data from customer satisfaction measurement programs provide an excellent starting point for these discussions. The empirical data often identify issues that need more detailed analysis and discussion. Both Humana Corporation and Marriott Hotels-Resorts use survey data as a starting point for more detailed root cause analysis discussions with customers.

Customer Representatives on Internal Teams
IBM invited customers from around the world to join in a top-level strategic planning conference. The customers were asked to tell what IBM was doing right, was doing wrong, or was not doing at all. Such top-level face-to-face contact with customers was designed to ensure that the "voice of the customer" was heard at the top of IBM.

However, customers should not be restricted only to executive-level contact. Customers could be involved in a variety of cross-functional teams at all organizational levels. The previous chapter demonstrated how customers could be integrated into process improvement teams acting on customer satisfaction data. The next chapter examines how joint action teams help to clarify supplier-customer alliances.

A CUSTOMER INTEGRATION CULTURE
Use of reactive or proactive techniques to achieve customer integration is a reflection of the orientation of a firm's cultural values. A highly pro-

duction oriented firm is far more likely to be reactive, whereas a truly customer driven firm is very proactive.

The Malcolm Baldrige National Quality Award has a decidedly proactive, customer-driven orientation. The most important single criterion in the evaluation process is customer satisfaction, and customer input drives most of the evaluative categories. Examining how Solectron, a 1991 award winner, achieves customer integration is enlightening.

SOLECTRON

Solectron, located in the San Francisco Bay area, is a manufacturer of computer-related component products. Solectron has a very team oriented approach to customer relationships. Joint Solectron-customer teams clarify and design virtually all aspects of the interaction. The teams begin with identification of a customer's needs and flow through a design, manufacturing, testing, delivery, and postpurchase evaluation process. Solectron's Partnership Development Roadmap is presented in Figure 8.1. Every step in this process is jointly discussed and designed by both Solectron and the customer. All goals are continually monitored to determine progress.

Customer satisfaction data are gathered weekly and diffused throughout Solectron in a few days. Any customer concerns are acted upon immediately and the customer receives feedback regarding corrective action within one week. All customers and potential customers are invited to attend the weekly customer satisfaction meetings that go over the data and design immediate solutions.

In addition to customer involvement in team problem solving and frequent customer satisfaction feedback, Solectron also has implemented an impressive array of customer integration activities.

The communication channels designed in the roadmap are very detailed (Figure 8.2). Because of a just-in-time production relationship, much of the communication is on a daily basis. Thus, a wide variety of Solectron managers and employees get direct, immediate feedback from customers. Within Solectron, the project managers, engineers, quality assurance personnel, customer service representatives, and sales representatives all have daily contact with *all* Solectron customers. The primary issues for discussion are quality performance, delivery schedules, and technical matters.

On a weekly basis, the production manager maintains contact with all customers. Customers, and prospective customers, are invited to partic-

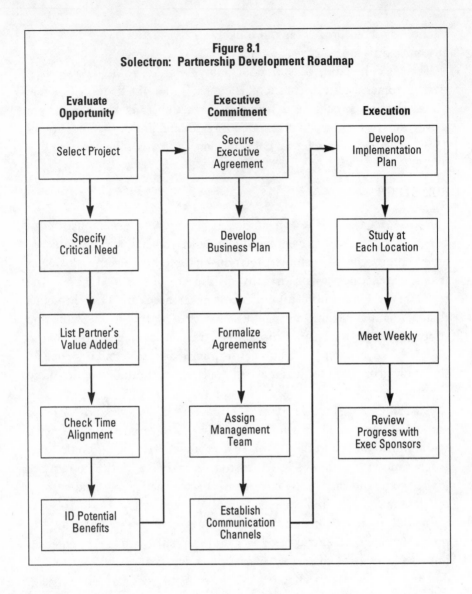

Figure 8.1
Solectron: Partnership Development Roadmap

Evaluate Opportunity	Executive Commitment	Execution
Select Project	Secure Executive Agreement	Develop Implementation Plan
Specify Critical Need	Develop Business Plan	Study at Each Location
List Partner's Value Added	Formalize Agreements	Meet Weekly
Check Time Alignment	Assign Management Team	Review Progress with Exec Sponsors
ID Potential Benefits	Establish Communication Channels	

ipate in Solectron's weekly customer satisfaction meetings. The joint action teams that designed the details of Figure 8.1 have a weekly conference call to discuss implementation and ideas for improvement.

On a monthly basis, a management review of each Solectron-customer relationship is conducted. This requires management and team visits to the customer's site to discuss and improve tactical issues.

On a quarterly basis, executive-level customer reviews are conducted. Solectron executives visit customer sites to align long-term strategic

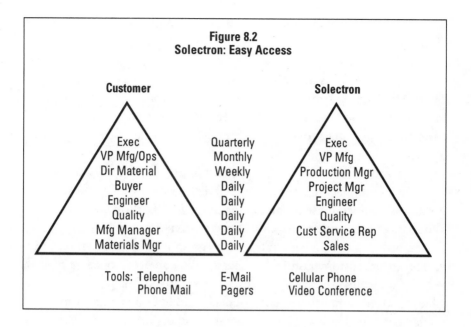

Figure 8.2
Solectron: Easy Access

Customer		Solectron
Exec	Quarterly	Exec
VP Mfg/Ops	Monthly	VP Mfg
Dir Material	Weekly	Production Mgr
Buyer	Daily	Project Mgr
Engineer	Daily	Engineer
Quality	Daily	Quality
Mfg Manager	Daily	Cust Service Rep
Materials Mgr	Daily	Sales

Tools: Telephone	E-Mail	Cellular Phone
Phone Mail	Pagers	Video Conference

goals. If a customer anticipates using a new technology or process, Solectron will begin training its own workforce so that when the time for change comes, the necessary skills are present. As an indication of this commitment to continually improving the knowledge base of its employees, Solectron's average annual hours of training per employee are expected to increase from 85 in 1991 to 150 in 1995. The primary driver of the training needs are the *future* needs of customers. Without complete customer integration, Solectron would never be able to identify the long-term strategic needs of customers. Relying only on the reactive approach or on customer satisfaction survey results would be inadequate.

Solectron's approach to proactive customer contact is very comprehensive from top to bottom in the company. Solectron's goal is the continual improvement of every aspect of the customer relationship. To achieve it, the management at Solectron attempts to harness the knowledge and skills of every employee. Delegation of the management of the customer relationship to a few individuals would represent an overwhelming task destined for mediocrity.

SUMMARY

A customer is an asset that must be nurtured, developed, and cherished. A customer is not just a target for a high-powered marketing machine.

Relying only on quantitative data to understand customers is a major weakness that does nothing to develop bonding relationships *with* customers.

Far too many firms utilize the reactive approach for customer contact. These firms simply sit back and wait for the customer to initiate contact in some way. Unfortunately, only a very small percentage of dissatisfied customers will bother to contact a firm. Most will simply fire the firm as a supplier.

Firms should develop and implement a proactive approach to customer contact whereby the firm regularly contacts customers. Every proactive contact presents an opportunity for the firm to learn more about customers and improve delivered customer value.

The proactive customer contact strategy should be frequent and pervasive. *Every* customer should be personally contacted once or twice a year by someone other than a sales representative. This may not be feasible for a very large consumer products firm, but almost all firms could implement this. Even a large consumer products firm could proactively contact all of its channel customers.

Customer contact should not be restricted to CEO or top management site visits. Customer contact could include consumer panels, continuous improvement teams, or adopt-a-customer programs. There are many types of proactive customer contact and the specific ones chosen are not what is critical. What is critical is that the majority of employees be exposed in some way to the direct voice of the customer. When the customer becomes human and is no longer a target, firms become much more customer driven.

Proactive contact works best when accompanied by training and support systems. British Telecom put its entire 230,000-person workforce through quality training that was designed to make all employees aware of the need to respond to the voice of the customer. Every job was linked directly to delivered customer value. Being proactively customer driven is why Solectron's 1995 training goal is 150 hours per employee when the average for U.S. firms is 40 hours.

The best way to become customer driven is to develop a proactive system of customer contact. When the human touch of direct customer contact is spread pervasively throughout a firm, the customer will be treated as a valuable asset.

APPLICATION IDEAS

1. What are the points of direct customer contact in your organization? What percentage of the various departments or the workforce has the opportunity to have customer contact?
2. Aside from contact by the sales force, is the preponderance of customer contact in your organization reactive or proactive? Does the reward system for the sales force encourage and reinforce an upward flow of ideas for improvement from customers?
3. For each level in your organization's hierarchy, identify the frequency and nature of customer contact. Is an organized system in place? Or does customer contact just happen naturally?
4. Does your organization anticipate the future needs of customers and use that information to drive the training and development of the workforce? Has your organization's training budget increased in response to a more rapidly changing environment?

9

Supplier Partnering: Optimizing Value Added in the Channel

"The goal of partnering is to reduce the total cost of ownership and cycle time while simultaneously improving quality."

Virtually every firm is dependent upon suppliers or downstream channel intermediaries to create and deliver good customer value. The whole value-added chain is the unit of competition, and the success of each firm depends heavily on others. The emerging trend is toward much more tightly integrated business relationships between the channel members. This trend has extremely important implications for business strategies.

The discussions to this point have focused on value-added processes within an individual firm. Occasionally, channel issues have been mentioned briefly, but the focus has been on downstream channel members—those between producers and the consumers. Overall, discussion of upstream channel coordination with suppliers has been deferred to this chapter for a more detailed treatment.

The reason for the separate treatment is the critical importance of the topic. Maximization of customer value cannot occur unless it is the common goal of an entire chain of organizations. Relatively few organizations are fully integrated from the source of supply to the delivery of a product to the end user. Thus, the delivery of customer value will be no better than the weakest link in the value-added chain.

Total quality management (TQM), when applied properly, improves the performance of an individual firm. However, TQM typically does not address the idea of channel coordination. Only when TQM is combined with supplier partnering will delivered customer value be maximized.

The oil industry provides a good example of this. The price of a barrel of oil is uncontrollable by any single firm, and the long-term price outlook is not attractive, from the oil industry's perspective. The only potential area for profit improvement is control of the cost structure. Logically, some of the larger oil companies have adopted a TQM philosophy. Competitive intensity is expected to remain high indefinitely, so using TQM should make those firms more efficient.

While the degree of vertical integration is highly variable across companies, it is not unusual for 30–40 percent of an oil firm's cost structure to be internal to the firm, with 60–70 percent of the cost going to suppliers or support service. If an individual firm were trying to achieve a 30 percent cost reduction through its TQM efforts, the savings would be only 9–12 percent of total costs. The only way for an oil company to achieve significant total cost reduction is to get all members of its supplier chain mobilized toward the common goal. Most likely, this would occur by first getting all the suppliers to individually endorse and implement TQM and then developing partnering relationships.

In manufacturing industries, 50 percent of total costs are often attributable to suppliers. In service industries, 30–40 percent of total costs are often attributable to suppliers. Thus, supplier quality improvement should be important to virtually every industry. The ultimate goal of supplier partnering is to convey the total cost of ownership to the end user.

While cost and value are quite different from each other, costs do provide a rough measure of the value added by each intermediary. Therefore, as costs are reduced—typically through product quality and service quality improvements—delivered customer value is simultaneously increased. Understanding what supplier partnering is and how to implement the concept are the subject of the remainder of this chapter.

SUPPLIER PARTNERING

In its broadest form, partnering is a business philosophy that recognizes the mutual dependencies between and within organizations. Within-organization partnering is simply the recognition that the needs of internal customers must be addressed by TQM efforts. Between-organization partnering is the integration of organizations into a tightly meshed supply chain. This also implies that most organizations simultaneously are customers to their suppliers and are suppliers to downstream channel organizations.

Supplier partnering is the development of a long-term, joint problem-solving relationship based on high levels of communication, trust, and sharing of information and resources. A common goal of partnering is the continuous improvement of the value-added processes in a channel. The distinctions between organizations blur as the us-versus-them, adversarial relationship disappears.

With the rapidly changing business environment, supplier partnership also leads to a coherent response to changes in technology or competitive intensity. Continuous improvement in technologies, skills, quality, delivery, administration, and responsiveness are common goals shared throughout the partnering organizations. Since the ultimate goal of supplier partnering is to reduce the total cost of ownership in a channel, cost savings also are shared throughout the channel.

In a time of organizational downsizing, particularly at the managerial level, supplier partnering can identify firms' areas for potential savings as well as firms' weaknesses. Activities that are duplicated among partners hold the potential for cost savings. Conversely, partnering also identifies strategic weaknesses that may be in need of additional resources.

BENEFITS OF SUPPLIER PARTNERSHIP

Partnering typically has a variety of direct and indirect benefits. The primary benefit is improvement in delivered customer value in a channel. This in turn results in much higher levels of customer satisfaction and a significant reduction in costs. However, a variety of additional benefits emerge from partnering efforts.

Goal Clarity

One significant benefit is the improved clarity of organizational goals. As goals are shared between supplier partners, a higher level of goal congruity occurs throughout the channel. This requires that customers and their needs be clearly identified and used as the driver for designing value-added processes throughout the channel.

As goals between organizations come into closer alignment, the concept of continuous improvement nearly always emerges. Such improvement in product and service quality typically leads to more responsiveness, flexibility, and adaptability among partners. Individual partners are usually willing to improve the channel performance because it is in their best interest to do so. The long-term relationship moves suppliers away from the mode of worrying about the next bid or losing a customer.

Improved Communication

Alignment of goals leads to improved communication within and between organizations. Within organizations, the TQM process that accompanies supplier partnering breaks down functional boundaries by way of the cross-functional sharing of information. Since continuous improvement is a common goal, the joint problem-solving mechanisms destroy the not-invented-here mentality.

Between organizations, suppliers have access to customers' forecasts and performance data. This allows suppliers to play an active role in joint problem solving and proactive planning. This can only be accomplished by interface between multiple organizational functions. The traditional sales-to-purchasing interaction is simply inadequate.

Because supplier partners are aware of and participate in the long-term product development of customers, suppliers can more effectively align their resources and productive processes with their customers. This improved efficiency can be accomplished only by continual, open, two-way communication and feedback.

Production Efficiency

As goals are aligned and open communication established, suppliers are better able to manage production and capacity planning. This typically results in more responsiveness, cycle time reduction, and reduced unit costs.

As stability in partner relationships increases, suppliers can more effectively implement continuous improvement in the productive systems. Performance expectations are clarified and performance measurement processes are mutually defined among partners.

Initial partnering may focus on joint problem solving to reduce or eliminate problem areas. However, longer-term partnering leads to a more proactive identification of opportunities for improvement. The continual goal becomes one of how to make a good process even better.

Improved Competitiveness

As the partner's goals, communication, and productive systems become more closely aligned, overall competitiveness is enhanced. The channel, as a whole, becomes much more proactive and responsive to the end user and the external environment. This is evident particularly in cycle time reduction and improved service quality.

As continuous quality improvement becomes a shared philosophy among partners, the cost of quality drops. This results in lower operating costs for each partner and a lower total cost of ownership throughout the channel, in addition to higher customer and supplier loyalty within the channel and among end users.

WHY HASN'T PARTNERING BEEN USED MORE?

The use of partnering in the United States has been very uneven across industries. The most successful uses have been in rapidly changing, intensely competitive industries such as computers and electronics. In the computer industry, an increasing portion of costs go to the specialized, technologically advanced suppliers that stay abreast of the cutting-edge technologies. The larger customers simply are not able to sustain the rate of technological change necessary purely on an internal basis. Therefore, the large customers have become increasingly reliant on supplier partners to contribute to the continuous improvement process.

Probably the best examples of supplier partnering are the Japanese *keiretsu* and the South Korean *chaebol*. These large families of companies have grown through the explicit goal of mutual cooperation. Interlocking boards of directors, shared technology, shared research and development, and stock ownership intertwine these groups of companies.

Mitsubishi's *keiretsu* provides a good example of such partnering. There are 3 core companies and an additional 25 closely related firms (Table 9.1). The percentage figures in Table 9.1 indicate the portion of each firm's stock owned by other members of the *keiretsu*. Below this core of 28 firms is another layer of hundreds of suppliers that are linked to the Mitsubishi group. The headquarters of 19 of the 28 core firms are located within a four- or five-block area in downtown Tokyo. The physical proximity also is reflected in operational proximity, as various combinations of Mitsubishi companies have jointly purchased numerous firms around the world. The close cooperation and integration within individual *keiretsus* are generally viewed as the significant contributors to

Table 9.1 Mitsubishi *Keiretsu*

Core Companies	% Joint Stock Ownership
1. Mitsubishi Corporation (trading company)	32
2. Mitsubishi Heavy Industries	20
3. Mitsubishi Bank	26
Key *Keiretsu* Members (not in order of importance)	
4. Mitsubishi Paper Mills	32
5. Mitsubishi Kasei	23
6. Mitsubishi Plastics Industries	57
7. Mitsubishi Petrochemical	37
8. Mitsubishi Gas and Chemical	24
9. Mitsubishi Oil	41
10. Mitsubishi Steel and Manufacturing	38
11. Mitsubishi Cable Industries	48
12. Mitsubishi Estate	25
13. Mitsubishi Warehouse and Transportation	40
14. Mitsubishi Metal	21
15. Mitsubishi Construction	100
16. Mitsubishi Rayon	25
17. Mitsubishi Electric	17
18. Mitsubishi Kakoki	37
19. Mitsubishi Motors	55
20. Mitsubishi Aluminum	100
21. Mitsubishi Mining and Cement	37
22. Mitsubishi Trust and Banking	28
23. Kirin Brewery	19
24. Nikon Corporation	27
25. Asahi Glass	28
26. Tokyo Marine and Fire Insurance	24
27. Meiji Mutual Life Insurance	0
28. Nippon Yusen	25

the economic success of Japan. The other major Japanese *keiretsus* (Table 9.2) along with Mitsubishi have controlled a good portion of Japan's economic growth.

In South Korea, the *chaebols*, which are organizations similar to the *keiretsus*, have controlled an even larger portion of economic growth.

Table 9.2
Japanese *Keiretsus*

Keiretsu	Number of Firms
1. Dai-Ichi Kangin	47
• Seibu Department Stores	
• Shimizu	
• Yokohama Rubber	
2. Sanwa	44
• Teijin	
• Ohbayashi	
• Kobe Steel	
3. Fuyo	29
• Marubeni	
• Nissan Motors	
• Canon	
4. Mitsui Group	24
• Toyota Motor	
• Toshiba	
• Toray Industries	
5. Sumitomo	20
• NEC	
• Sumitomo Chemical	
• Sumitomo Metal Industries	

While supplier partnering in the United States will probably never reach the magnitude found in the Japanese *keiretsu* or Korean *chaebol*, certain major benefits should accrue to U.S. firms that fully embrace the concept. The status quo complacency evidenced by the not-invented-here syndrome must be overcome by way of innovative interorganizational linkages.

IMPLEMENTING SUPPLIER PARTNERING

Implementation of supplier partnering requires a long-term, organization-wide effort. It is not a simple set of techniques or activities that can be superimposed over traditional management practices. Since it represents a philosophical approach to business relationships, a number of prerequisites must be present before any attempt to implement partnering.

Prerequisites

First, there must be strong top management support at both of the partnering organizations that indicates a willingness to change traditional relationships and commit resources when necessary. It requires cross-functional integration between the organizations. Partnering requires human resources to make training programs available to suppliers so that common knowledge and skill development result. It requires the sharing of new product development, production, long-term goals and strategies, cost structures, and lots of other information. This could not happen if partnering is the responsibility of only one function, such as purchasing.

Second, it is hard to conceive of partnering's occurring unless both supplier and customer firms are committed to TQM. The cross-functional teams that coordinate many partnering activities must be empowered to implement their recommendations, or else behavioral support will quickly be lost. A key TQM belief is that the knowledge of all workers must be harnessed to drive continuous improvement. The knowledge in an organization does not all reside in the executive suites. Nor does all knowledge rest in only one organization. Therefore, partnering tries to use the knowledge base of the entire channel to drive continuous improvement.

Third, partnering is not a short-term quick fix. Clarifying common goals, developing open communication networks, and aligning production systems take a good deal of time: it normally takes several years for significant financial results to emerge.

TWO LEVELS OF PARTNERING

Supplier partnering can be applied to all suppliers, though the degree of involvement is variable. For large organizations, with hundreds or thousands of suppliers of varying size, developing a detailed, fully integrated relationship with every supplier would be an overwhelming task. Therefore, suppliers are often segmented by use of the old 80/20 rule.

The vast majority of suppliers are partnered at a lower level of involvement. However, the few important suppliers are the focus of a comprehensive partnering effort. The critical few suppliers that do a large volume of business hold the greatest potential for increasing value and reducing the total cost of ownership.

Therefore, the nature of the supplier partnership program for the majority will be quite different from the program for the critical few. Some organizations have developed a three-tier approach to partnering, but for simplicity, two types of partnering programs are presented here. The first, a level I program, is directed at the majority of suppliers. The second, a level II program, is directed at the critically important, but relatively few suppliers.

Both levels of supplier partnering require a supplier reduction effort. Xerox, for example, reduced its supplier base for manufacturing from 5,000 to only 500 firms. Harris Corporation reduced its vital supplier base from 2,500 to 283 firms. Motorola reduced its supplier base from 6,000 to 1,000 firms. For companies that are strongly committed to the concept of supplier partnering, a reduction of 80–90 percent in the number of their suppliers is common. It is with this smaller, reduced supplier base that both levels of partnering are implemented.

An example of the Harris Corporation's supplier reduction process is given at the end of the chapter. Unfortunately, limitations of focus and space do not permit a detailed discussion here. However, a book on supplier partnerships is in process by the author.

Level I

This level assumes that the three major prerequisites have been met. A strong, long-term, visible top management commitment must be evident. Also, the organization must be committed to the implementation of TQM, and continuous improvement, in one fashion or another. If these are in place, then the following steps must be implemented (Table 9.3).

Step 1

Management must engender organizational commitment to the partnering process. Some members of top management must express explicit support for partnering and clearly communicate that support throughout the organization. Some organizations have written a position paper to clarify the concept. In order to generate significant commitment, management must institute progress on partnering as one of the performance evaluation criteria. And since the supplier reduction effort must come first, top management should have played a visible role in initiating and implementing those efforts.

Step 2

Management must develop and distribute internally and to all suppliers explicit documents that describe the partnering principles. Often these documents set out the criteria for supplier certification programs. Car-

Table 9.3 Steps to level I Partnering

1. Top management commitment
2. Partnering policies and procedures distributed internally and externally
3. Goal of long-term, mutually profitable relationships instilled
4. Symbiotic, nonadversarial relationship with suppliers developed
5. Needs and expectations of partners jointly clarified
6. Customer satisfaction program implemented to monitor performance
7. Continual improvement striven for in all areas of business
8. Workers empowered
9. Employee training and development invested in
10. Quality assurance processes jointly developed and shared with partners
11. Open communication and sharing of information established between partners

rier Corporation uses 31 criteria to group suppliers into six classifications: (1) unacceptable vendor, (2) normal supplier, (3) annual renewal supplier, (4) long-term contract supplier, (5) Project 120 alliance, and (6) Project 120 partner. The first four categories require level I partnering; the last two are analogous to level II partnering. Other firms use classifications of unacceptable, acceptable, certified, and preferred suppliers. Regardless of the number of categories used, the process, criteria, and consequences of certification programs should be clear both internally in an organization and to outside suppliers.

Step 3
Management must stress that long-term, mutually profitable relationships are the goal of the partnering process. Since a reduced supplier base clearly requires heavier dependence on the remaining suppliers, long-term success is in everyone's best interest. Supplier reduction and subsequent partnering are not simply a strategy to gain additional leverage over suppliers so that margins can be shaved. Cost reduction should come from improved efficiencies, not reduced profit margins.

Step 4
Management must stress that the mutual dependencies require a symbiotic, nonadversarial relationship between the partners. Level I partnering

with a reduced supplier base assures suppliers of a larger revenue stream for a longer time period. In return, suppliers must be willing to harmonize their own business processes to mesh with those of their partners. This requires the more open sharing of planning information, training goals, technical support, and information systems. Suppliers may need to change or modify their computer systems to facilitate electronic data interchange with their partners—an issue that becomes particularly important in level II partnering.

Step 5

Management must mutually clarify the needs and expectations of partners and engage in joint problem solving. As needs and expectations become clarified, areas of difference of opinion quickly emerge. Most commonly, those areas involve quality issues. Product quality issues include both design and conformance characteristics. Support service quality issues that typically emerge are scheduling, delivery, and invoicing. Techniques and trade-offs in cost reduction in the partnership are a third major area for joint problem solving. Less frequent, but potentially important, areas are the rate and nature of technological change and compatibility, product design changes and modification, and financial support for areas of joint concern. Though the possible areas for joint problem solving are endless, these six general issues are probably the most common.

Step 6

A customer satisfaction program should be implemented to monitor suppliers' performance and provide feedback. Since customer satisfaction measurement was discussed in detail in an earlier chapter, the topic will not be discussed further here in any detail. However, the use of customer satisfaction programs indicates a strong commitment by suppliers to become customer driven.

Step 7

Both of the partners must demonstrate strong commitment to continuous improvement in all aspects of business. In the rapidly changing business environment, state-of-the-art business practices become obsolete very quickly. Establishing rigid performance standards will likely lead to stagnation and mediocrity. Therefore, continuous improvement must be a key element of all supplier-customer relationships. As discussed earlier, a customer satisfaction program plays an important role in using the voice of the customer to drive continuous improvement.

Step 8

Both partners must be committed to the concept of worker empowerment to reduce cycle time and increase responsiveness. For joint problem solving and continuous improvement to be meaningful, employee empowerment and involvement must be present so that employees at the lowest levels of the organization have the ability to improve processes. Without empowerment and involvement, bureaucratic structures and processes lengthen decision-making cycle times and hinder responsiveness. The effective implementation of TQM essentially requires that empowerment be a characteristic of corporate culture. This is a major justification for the use of a TQM diagnostic as one of the supplier evaluation criteria. It will be discussed in detail shortly.

Step 9

Both of the partners must be committed to employee training and must invest in the knowledge base of employees. The skills for success are constantly changing, evolving, and the old standard of one week of training per employee annually is antiquated and abysmally deficient. Such a small amount of training support makes it virtually impossible to maintain a leading-edge skill base among employees. Therefore, all organizations strongly committed to continuous organizational improvement must be equally committed to increased training that improves both skills and knowledge.

Step 10

Quality assurance criteria, methods, processes, and results are shared with suppliers. Common metrics and processes must be developed so that all suppliers know how quality is evaluated. Training in statistical process control, tools of quality, process capability, and quality is often required for suppliers. In many cases, suppliers and customers jointly defray these costs. The real goal at this level of partnering is to reduce or eliminate incoming quality inspections, meaning that the responsibility for conformance compliance and documentation rests with the supplier.

Step 11

Open communication between the partners is designed to share performance data, forecasts, quality data, and other information necessary for evaluating the total cost of quality. Even with level I partnering, a much more comprehensive and open flow of communication between partners is necessary. This is often accomplished through electronic data interchange, although certain security and confidentiality problems arise with this technological link. One of the thorniest issues is the degree to which cost data are exchanged between partners. The trend is toward increased levels of joint disclosure, but this obviously requires concomitantly high levels of interorganizational trust.

The theme that underlies all eleven steps is that the continuous improvement process should result in a long-term, mutually profitably partner relationship. Firms unwilling to continually improve, normally evidenced by their lack of TQM effort, will eventually atrophy and lose their role as a supplier.

Level II

For most organizations, the majority of external costs are attributable to relatively few suppliers. Normally, the performance of those suppliers has a very significant impact on a customer firm's cost structure and, ultimately, its competitiveness. Therefore, ensuring the success and continual improvement of a customer firm's key suppliers is critical to the long-term survival of the customer firm.

Due to this mutual dependency between key suppliers and customer firms, level II supplier partnering is much more comprehensive and detailed than a level I program. Realistically, few firms have the time and resources to commit to level II relationships with all of their suppliers, and, even if they did, it probably wouldn't be worthwhile to do so. The many smaller, less important suppliers simply don't hold the economic potential of the larger, critically important ones. The critical few should receive a good deal of attention and effort when a firm implements supplier partnering.

As with level I partnering, a series of steps are necessary to implement a level II program (Table 9.4). To get to level II, the assumption is made that the level I steps are in place. Although some of the 11 level I steps are more important than others, the absence of any of the steps could make the achievement of level II difficult, if not impossible.

Step 1

Depending on the structure of the organization, the CEO or COO must be visibly involved in the initiation and maintenance of the partnering effort. This implies that performance in implementing partnering be evaluated at the highest levels of management. If partnering is a visible component of performance evaluation at the top, then cascading sponsorship

Table 9.4 Steps to Level II Partnering

1. Top management involvement
2. Partnering advisory council formulated
3. Critical suppliers or commodities identified
4. Internal diagnostic test conducted
5. Action teams formed
6. Supplier diagnostic test administered (and supplier evaluation and site visit conducted, if necessary)
7. Desired partner (if relevant) selected
8. Joint negotiation of the partner relationship
9. Partner agreement approval from PAC obtained
10. Management of the partnership

will likely result. If partnering is not evaluated at the highest levels, the message will be sent through the organization that partnering is not really important.

Expecting high levels of continual CEO or COO involvement in the partnering effort is unrealistic due to competing time demands. Therefore, a senior-level, executive partnering champion is normally selected to implement and improve the partnering program. The champion must be at a sufficiently high organizational level to give credibility to the partnering program and to control adequate resources.

The champion would have the internal role of generating support for supplier partnering, spearheading training, and working with action teams (discussed later). In addition, the champion would have the external responsibilities of interacting with senior management in supplier firms and acting as the lightning rod if problems arise. The champion also would be directly involved in the customer/supplier team meetings (also discussed later).

Step 2

The partnering champion could not be expected to have specialized expertise in all aspects of the business. Therefore, a cross-functional advisory council is typically formed in order to provide advice on various issues. This partnering advisory council (PAC) would consist of senior managers from areas such as purchasing, materials, engineering, quality, marketing, human resources, finance, and law.

The PAC would allow a responsive, short decision-making cycle for quick resolution of partnering issues. The PAC is not directly involved in detailed partnering negotiations with suppliers, however. The role of the PAC is to address design and implementation issues primarily, but it also can play the role of ombudsman when necessary.

One of the most significant benefits of a PAC is to increase cross-functional buy-in to the partnering process. Because the PAC is composed of senior managers, the cascading sponsorship will spill over into the key functional areas. The PAC members would help sell the idea to their functional areas.

Step 3
One of the initial tasks of the PAC is to identify the suppliers that are likely candidates for level II partnering. In some organizations there may be only 5 or 10 candidates for initial inclusion, but in other organizations there could easily be 50 or more. There are typically two ways of identifying potential supplier partners.

The first method identifies the commodities or services most critical to a firm's value-added processes. In many cases this could be done by evaluating the total cost attributable to each commodity. The highest dollar-volume commodities would receive the initial attention due to their potential profit impact. However, dollar volume alone makes for an inadequate criterion. Often there may be critically important products purchased that constitute a minor or a moderate expenditure level. Thus, the PAC should identify the products most critical to the firm's value-added processes.

The second method to identifying candidates for supplier partnering concentrates on supplier characteristics. As with commodities, an initial ranking of suppliers is often done by ranking dollar-volume expenditure patterns. But here too, dollar volume is inadequate as the sole criterion. Some smaller suppliers may be very important to the value-added processes. Also, some smaller suppliers may be very innovative or have valuable partnering experiences. These suppliers could help to move the customer firm farther along the partnering learning curve.

Regardless of the selection criteria used by the PAC to select the initial candidate suppliers, this is only the beginning of the partnering process—the starting point. Additional commodities or suppliers will naturally emerge as candidates for level II partnering as the concept becomes adopted organization wide.

Step 4
Before beginning discussions and negotiations with supplier firms, a customer firm's clear self-image is normally helpful. Most firms that have

implemented TQM come to the realization that improving quality internally makes for a good start. But only by partnering will major quality improvement be achieved. Since both TQM and partnering are evolutionary developments in organizations, two types of diagnostic tests are necessary.

One diagnostic test determines where an organization is in its evolution toward TQM. The farther it is along the evolutionary process, the easier will be implementation of partnering. Meshing the activities of a traditional, bureaucratic management style with those of a flat, highly participatory, TQM management style can be challenging at best.

By identifying the stage of TQM evolution early on, a firm can develop specific strategies to overcome anticipated problems in the harmonization of partnering activities. Primary among the potential constraints is the behavioral skepticism that accompanies a radical change in business philosophies. The strategies to overcome such resistance include training, participation in the change process, empowerment, and a reward system—both financial and nonfinancial—that rewards the new behavior.

A TQM self-diagnostic test that uses the Baldrige National Quality Award as a template appears in Appendix A. Typically, such a test is completed independently by individuals who then meet jointly to discuss the results and reach some consensus view of the organization. It is important that this self-test be administered to a cross-functional sample as well as a representative vertical slice of organization levels.

The second internal diagnostic test identifies where an organization is in its evolution toward supplier partnering. Over the past 10 years, the trend in organizational purchasing has been toward a closer relationship with fewer suppliers. However, in many organizations this has been a haphazard process lacking strategic guidance. Therefore, identifying the current status of partnering development is essential to formulating an effective partnering implementation strategy.

Some firms may have naturally evolved to such a detailed relationship with a few suppliers but still lack integration with other important suppliers. Those divergent situations would each require a significantly different implementation strategy.

A partnering self-diagnostic test is included in Appendix B. The test should be administered in much the same way as a TQM self-evaluation: to a cross-functional, vertical sample of individuals.

Step 5

The PAC described in step 2 was composed of senior-level managers charged with guiding internal implementation of the supplier partnering process organization wide. Action teams (ATs) are cross-functional teams that deal directly with suppliers in formulating the specific interorganizational linkages. The AT normally consists of 6–10 members, who have some type of direct involvement with a value-added process. The team composition could range from hourly laborers to upper managers, but it normally includes members from purchasing, quality, engineering, and various user groups. ATs are normally larger for the first six months or so and then reduce in size once a partnering relationship is established.

Each AT typically selects a team leader, who is responsible for organizing and facilitating meetings, is the contact point for suppliers, and also communicates with the partnering champion and the PAC. Since partnering relationships are complex, individual team members may manage a particular aspect of partnering development. However, all activities are ultimately discussed and coordinated by the complete AT.

There are two types of ATs that are formed, depending on how step 3 was done. If the critical suppliers were identified, then the AT will concentrate on the ongoing relationship already established. If the critical commodities were identified, then the AT must go through a more complex supplier identification and reduction process. In both cases, one of the typical starting points is assessing where the relevant suppliers are in their TQM evolution.

Step 6

The purpose of the supplier diagnostic test is much the same as that of the internal diagnostic test: to assess where the suppliers or potential suppliers are in their TQM and partnering evolutions. Therefore, the questionnaires in Appendix A and Appendix B can be used for this purpose also. Some companies, particularly in the computer industry, require that suppliers be strongly committed to TQM. Those that cannot demonstrate such a commitment are often immediately screened out as potential suppliers. The reason for this is that the evolution to a fully integrated TQM culture may take four, five, or six years. A supplier that hasn't made significant progress down the quality path would constitute a competitive weakness to the customer firm for quite some time.

The diagnostic test for suppliers is one of the preliminary evaluative criteria for formulating the supplier partnership. The supplier's self-test results are evaluated by the customer prior to a site visit by the AT. This allows the AT to identify areas for analysis and evaluation. All AT members develop a list of relevant evaluative criteria, which they individually assess. After the site visit, a comprehensive summary profile of each potential supplier is developed. Occasionally, this may require the gathering of additional supportive documentation or material.

Step 7
This step may have been completed earlier if key suppliers were previously identified. However, if potential suppliers were evaluated in step 6, then step 7 is the ultimate supplier selection decision. A significant portion of the selection process is the supplier's willingness to blur the traditional organizational boundaries so that value-added processes can be synchronized.

Step 8
For a supplier firm, a partnering champion and AT must be identified. These individuals meet with the customer firm's partnering champion and AT at a joint kickoff meeting. Behaviorally, the kickoff meeting demonstrates both organizations' strong organizational commitment to the partnering process. The meeting also facilitates the initiation of interpersonal communication between the joint AT members.

The initial meeting also typically results in the clarification of partnering goals. The ultimate partnering goals are both continual improvement in all aspects of the value-added linkage and reduction in the total cost of ownership. Beyond these goals, the joint AT establishes goals relevant to the supplier and commodity. The purpose of the AT is to design improved, value-added processes in the whole value-added chain.

Eventually, the joint AT will develop a specific set of goals, expectations, and means of attaining those goals. This constitutes the initial partner agreement. Due to the goal of continual improvement, this relationship will most certainly evolve over time.

Step 9
The joint AT has responsibility for developing the specific partner agreement. The AT normally makes a presentation to the PAC, describing the issues and explaining the partner arrangements. Normally, the PAC will approve such agreements, but in some cases, additional information may be requested or changes recommended.

The role of the PAC is not one of censorship or maintaining managerial power. Rather, the PAC often is more familiar with long-term strategic issues that may impact specific partner relationships. The PAC therefore is a conduit for strategic information. Since the partnering champion should maintain close contact with each AT, long-term strategic issues should be integrated continually into AT activities.

Step 10

Once the partnering relationship has been developed, approved, and implemented, a reduced AT monitors ongoing improvement and progress. This AT is a joint team, consisting of only two or three individuals from each organization. In the supplier firm, production and quality assurance are normally involved; in the customer firm, purchasing and user groups. The joint AT compares progress to the goals established by the larger AT.

For the larger supplier-customer relationships typical of level II partnering, executive partners often are identified. Such executives can be part of or in addition to the joint AT. The role of executive partners is to maintain regular personal contact and allow for direct contact should a problem arise. This normally shortens the cycle time both for resolution of problems and for decision making.

To maintain personal relationships, the joint AT and executive partners should meet at least quarterly. The individuals jointly could attend seminars and quality training sessions.

Either the joint AT or the executive partner should furnish progress reports to the partnering champion. This allows a centralized system for monitoring partnering progress and tabulating the results of partnering programs.

HARRIS CORPORATION'S PARTNERING SUCCESS

Harris Corporation (HC) is a Melbourne, Florida, aerospace and defense contractor that began its supplier partnering effort in 1988. Since that time, HC has achieved significant results from its supplier partnerships as they were phased in.

The partnering process began with HC's Electronic Systems Sector, which consisted of eight divisions that concentrated on government contracting. A PAC was created by drawing together senior managers in procurement, engineering, and product assurance from five divisions. As described earlier, the role of the PAC was to formulate the partnering strategy.

The PAC decided that the first step in the partnering process had to be a major reduction in the supplier base. At that time, 5,000 suppliers were providing over a million parts. The total procurement volume was in excess of $200 million, through the use of about 300,000 separate purchase transactions. Implementing partnering with all suppliers would have been an overwhelming obstacle.

Therefore, HC developed four categories of suppliers and proceeded to place each of the 5,000 suppliers into one of them. Group one was the "tactical few." These were primarily subcontractors that were involved in specific projects. Although the dollar volume was significant, these suppliers had a sporadic relationship with HC, because their skills were needed on a project basis and several years could pass before they again became a subcontractor. Also, these suppliers tended to be involved with only one division rather than the whole corporation. As a result, the "tactical few" were not good candidates for level II strategic partnering.

Group two was the "trivial many." Although many suppliers fell into this category, the dollar volume, individually and collectively, was relatively small compared to the other categories. Because of that smaller dollar volume, the impact of partnering efforts did not hold a great deal of profit potential.

In total, the first two categories consisted of 2,500 suppliers—approximately half of the supply base—but achieving partnering benefits with them would still be difficult because of their diversity. Therefore, these categories were the lowest priorities, whereas the last two categories held the greatest potential.

Group three was the "vital few." As with many firms, this was the 20 percent of suppliers that account for the majority of procurement dollars—although not 80 percent of costs in HC's situation. Primarily, these suppliers provided high-volume commodities that were essential to most of the divisions. The relationship with most of these suppliers was continuous and had extended over many years.

Group four was the "vital commodities." Though their dollar volume was not necessarily large, the products they provided were of critical importance to HC. Therefore, the criticality of the products justified inclusion of those suppliers in this category. The relationship with those suppliers tended to be long term and very close. And procurement of products in this category required a good deal of interaction and negotiation between HC and the supplier, with much joint problem solving.

Table 9.5 Harris Corporation Supplier Capability Evaluation

1. Financial strength, strategy, and experience
2. Management commitment to excellence
3. Design/technology strength
4. Quality capability, including statistical process control
5. Cost competitiveness
6. Service/flexibility
7. Manufacturing skills
8. Cycle time concentration
9. Partnership extension to subsuppliers
10. Employee participation climate

Collectively, the 2,500 suppliers in the third and fourth categories were a diverse lot as well, ranging from large, multinational corporations to very small businesses. However, the common trait shared by all was a long-term, significant contribution to the strategic success of HC. Because of the strategic importance and profit potential, these firms were subject to a supplier reduction effort.

To facilitate the supplier reduction, the PAC at HC developed four new rating categories of supplier performance based on a variety of criteria. The broad categories of evaluation are presented in Table 9.5 but each individual category consisted of 10 subareas.

The rating categories were candidate-preferred suppliers, preferred suppliers, best-in-class suppliers, and approved socially disadvantaged businesses. The first category included the suppliers that were expected to demonstrate acceptable performance within a reasonably short length of time. The second category consisted of firms that performed at a high level: 95 percent performance rating on HC's evaluative criteria. The third category consisted of suppliers that demonstrated excellence: a 98 percent performance rating. The fourth category consisted predominantly of small businesses that earned at least a 90 percent performance rating but were committed to improving and needed time and in some cases, support from HC.

Rather than the PAC's performing the exhausting task of evaluating 2,500 suppliers, HC created 15 commodity action teams (CATs) to perform the evaluations. The cross-functional CATs were empowered to make the supplier reduction themselves.

Beginning in early to mid-1989, the CATs had reduced the supplier base from 2,500 to 283 by January 1990—an 88 percent reduction. Any supplier not meeting the minimum criteria for candidate preferred was eliminated. All remaining suppliers were in the candidate-preferred category or higher.

The CEOs of all 283 suppliers were invited in April 1990 to HC's corporate offices in Florida for a kickoff meeting. The purpose of the meeting was to inform the suppliers about HC's goals and plans for partnering. The CEOs also were able to meet the members of the CATs, who would be responsible for phasing in the partnering program.

During the later part of 1990 and throughout 1991, the partnering process was phased in. Most suppliers have advanced to the preferred or best-in-class category and have become involved in HC's strategic planning process.

The benefits to HC have been significant: The percentage of HC's procurement expenditures going to supplier partners has doubled. The reject rate for incoming materials has dropped by 70 percent. And HC's delivery performance to its customers has improved by 50 percent. Small businesses still constitute about 50 percent of the HC supplier base, and the number of socially disadvantaged suppliers has doubled. Overall, HC has experienced cost reduction while simultaneously improving product and service for both inbound materials and outbound products.

SUMMARY

Supplier partnering is a business philosophy based on recognition of the mutual dependencies in a value-added chain of organizations. For many organizations, the majority of the cost structure, as well as value added, is external to an individual firm. In today's intensely competitive environment, therefore, the activities of both suppliers and customers must be harmonized and synchronized in order to optimize the efficiency of the entire value-added chain. No longer can an individual firm expect to maintain or improve its competitive position by only improving its internal activities. Only when TQM and supplier partnering are intertwined intimately will major improvements in competitiveness result.

The current adversarial relationship that typifies most supplier-customer linkages must give way to a different, new culture. The new culture must be based on open communication, mutual trust, and cooperation between organizations. The goal of partnering must be continual improvement in all aspects of the value-added chain, not in just one activity or one firm. This continuous improvement should result in a reduced total cost of ownership, thus enhancing delivered customer value at the end of the channel.

The ability of a channel to deliver good customer value to the end user is the ultimate determinant of survival for any individual firm. And partnering is an essential part of delivering good customer value.

APPLICATION IDEAS

1. How many suppliers does your organization have? What has been the rate of supplier reduction? How much multiple sourcing still occurs?
2. To what extent does your organization monitor its suppliers' commitment to TQM and continuous improvement as an evaluative criteria? (This is not the same as monitoring incoming quality level!)
3. How has your organization addressed the 11 steps for a level I partnering relationship? Are all suppliers informed of the basic partnering principles?
4. How extensive is the partnering relationship with your organization's key suppliers? How does your partnering program compare to the level II relationship described in this chapter?

10

Cooking Frogs, Charles Darwin, and Kaizen

"One of the greatest reasons people cannot mobilize themselves is that they try to accomplish great things. Most worthwhile achievements are the result of many little things done in a single direction."
—Nido Qubein

The cure for complacency is continuous improvement in every aspect of business. The increasing rate of change virtually ensures that complacency will quickly lead to obsolescence, especially in the area of knowledge. Continuous learning must be integrated into every aspect of corporate culture and permeate every corner of the business. Increased customer expectations of delivered value absolutely, positively guarantee that "good enough" never is.

There is an old parable about cooking frogs that is rich with managerial wisdom: If you bring a pot of water to a boil and then drop a frog in, the reaction is immediate. The frog reacts vigorously—thrashing about and splashing water—and usually then leaps out. The cook is frustrated, the kitchen or at least the stove is a mess, and the frog is injured and insulted. However, if you place a frog in a pot of cold water and gradually turn the heat up, the frog succumbs peacefully, offering no resistance. By stressing gradual changes, the cook has accomplished the objective—a cooked frog—but the process is more palatable.

When managers attempt organizational change, it is often like cooking frogs in hot water. Most organizations seem to sail along unscathed for periods of time, rewarding the status quo, rewarding those who "do things right." With near certainty, such organizations slip slowly but surely toward mediocrity. They keep reinforcing the behaviors that made them successful in the past, gradually losing their competitive edge. But such complacency does not go unpunished forever. Recent examples in the business press are abundant; IBM and GM are highly visible, but many others are in the same position.

The environment continues to change and to evolve. Both consumers and customers begin to change their preferences, decision criteria, and buying processes. Technology contributes to new products and newer production processes. More and more competitors emerge, stealing customers away. Suddenly, management is rattled from its asleep-at-the-wheel mentality. And sadly it often finds itself in the proverbial hot water.

At this point there is often floundering about, much splashing, and a good deal of noise. Some managers leap out, others are booted out. New CEOs and new top management teams are commonplace. Crash programs are the rage: reduce costs, increase sales this month, cut R&D expenditures, cut labor costs, reduce training and development, delay purchases, and, more recently, reduce managerial intensity. Perhaps the firm rushes to improve product quality and even jumps on the TQM bandwagon as a road to recovery. Unfortunately, as in Shakespeare's parlance, there is often much ado about nothing. The success of such crash programs is often minimal.

Because the fundamental corporate culture often remains unchanged, old behaviors gradually emerge. Those managerial layoffs that were supposed to create significant salary savings often don't. Service levels decline, and the do-more-with-less mentality creates resistance and skepticism among the survivors. Such knee-jerk reactions generate a lot of attention because management knows it has to do something, but the long-term result is either an organizational death spiral or a return to mediocrity.

Rather than slip into hot water and be forced into crash survival programs, a firm should institute gradual warming of the water as a far better approach. Indeed, the best-managed firms of the 1980s and the 1990s are those that developed the ability to be creative, flexible, and innovative, such as Motorola, GE, and Microsoft. Continually, they made small adjustments to fit the changing environment, constantly trying to improve and to get better at whatever they do. The well-managed firms hate complacency, and they develop processes to fight it every step of the way. They do all in their power to avoid the shock of that hot water, much preferring gradual changing and adaptation.

CHARLES DARWIN, BUSINESS STRATEGIST

The best-managed firms on Fortune's Most Admired list are those that manage change effectively. With a business environment as turbulent and chaotic as the remainder of the 1990s and beyond are expected to be, flexibility, creativity, and innovation appear to be not only valuable organizational characteristics but also key success factors. Yet, an examination of the business literature of the past 20 or 30 years shows that these characteristics have only recently been recognized as important. Strategic planning, bureaucratic structures, span of control, leadership styles, and control systems are discussed at length, for example, but discussions about organizational flexibility, creativity, and innovation are only recently, and rarely, discussed. In short, the characteristics for success—those key success factors—continually change and evolve over time.

In virtually every endeavor, humanity has an innate desire to improve. In sports, there are more world records each year as athletes become bigger, stronger, faster, and more skilled than ever before. In space, scientists are continually pushing the boundaries of knowledge, even if missions to Mars malfunction. In medicine, there are continual searches for new treatments and new drugs, and some procedures that were innovative 10 years ago are now commonplace. But this trend toward continual improvement is not new.

One of the first to identify a pattern of continual change, improvement, and adaptation was Charles Darwin in the 1860s. Although the time horizons are certainly much shorter, the evolutionary pattern of today's organizations is strikingly similar to the evolutionary patterns that Darwin identified in nature.

In fact, if Darwin were alive today, he probably wouldn't be a naturalist. With his keen insight, he'd probably be the CEO of a large, multinational corporation in a highly competitive global industry. He'd be a very successful CEO, too, since his theories of evolution provide an excellent strategic framework for businesses in the 1990s.

Although reducing the various versions of *Origin of Species* to a few pages requires the condensing of many detailed ideas, several themes very relevant to business are recurrent in Darwin's writings. Probably best known are his ideas about variation in nature, about natural selection, and about survival of the fittest. But each of those ideas has a variety of related and supporting concepts that enrich the core ideas. In total, Darwin's theories, or Darwinism, contended that these concepts interacted to form a continual, dynamic pattern of evolution. Those concepts appear to have important strategic implications for business.

Variation in Nature

Darwin suggested that variation in the characteristics of plants and animals is a natural phenomenon. Even though a population is normally distributed around a mean, still, significant variation exists and is necessary for evolution. This normally distributed variation implies that some organisms possesses beneficial variations and others possess detrimental variations. The organisms possessing the beneficial variations will be more successful as the environment changes. Their beneficial characteristics will be inherited by their descendants and gradually, over a lengthy period of time, the mean for the whole population will shift toward the beneficial characteristics. Those possessing the detrimental characteristics will be less well suited for the environment and therefore less successful in transmitting their characteristics to descendants.

The rigid, bureaucratic organization structures of the 1960s and 1970s are giving way to the flatter, leaner, more responsive organization structures of the 1990s. While bureaucracy was suited for a very stable business environment, bureaucracy in the current environment is definitely a detrimental variation in nature, one that will become largely extinct. The flatter, leaner, more responsive structure is not the ultimate structure for the future. The flatter, leaner, more responsive organization is just a transitory step in the long-term evolution of business. The ideal structure 20 years from now is sure to be different in many ways. The visionary leaders in business are those who possess a clearer, more accurate perception of the future and who anticipate the new success factors.

Darwin also noted the existence of what he called "monstrosities." These were variations that were radically different from the normal population in some way. Darwin contended that such discontinuous variations were often traumatic and rarely advantageous. Further, these discontinuous variations were unable to reproduce their unusual characteristics in their offspring.

Organizationally, monstrosities might be radically different structures, business relationships, or management styles. These radical differences are often seen in entrepreneurship when the influence of the owner's charisma is pervasive and makes unusual practices successful. But without the entrepreneur, the unusual practices are not self-sustaining, and the organization withers and becomes extinct. The organization is simply unable to reproduce its success.

Darwin's views of continuous and discontinuous change are much like cooking frogs. Gradual changes are more successful in changing a population than are sudden, traumatic changes. In fact, Darwin's word choice, monstrosities," might be very appropriate for many managerial crash programs. Many crash programs are just an intermediate step to organizational extinction.

The idea of normally distributed variation almost implies that organisms are passive participants in the evolutionary process. Darwin was careful to point out that creatures can play an active role in evolution. The use of behaviors can become habits, which can be transmitted to offspring as learned behaviors. Detrimental behaviors can be extinguished in the same manner.

Organizationally, behaviors can be learned, ingrained, and passed on through the context of organizational culture, but are most effective when acquired and implemented gradually. Thus, the concept of continuous learning and improvement appears to be a very important success factor, whether one is evaluating survival in nature or survival by organizations. Conversely, the absence of continuous learning is increasingly becoming a detrimental variation.

Isolation

Another Darwinian idea associated with variation in nature is isolation. Populations that are geographically isolated tend to evolve somewhat differently due to different environments, which may reward slightly different variations in the population's characteristics. Populations that have open access to other populations tend to intermingle and the distinctions between the two populations gradually erode.

When countries, and their economies, are isolated and they do not interact with other countries, unique characteristics will be maintained. The East European countries, China, and most communist countries isolated themselves from Western economies. As a result, their economies evolved as very different entities from capitalistic economies. Ultimately, their isolation also led to the deterioration of their economies. At one point, Japan was relatively isolated economically, so Japanese business practices evolved differently from other countries'. But differences are eroding as economies internationally become more intermingled and mutually dependent.

Taking this idea a step further, eventually there will be no Japanese, or German, or U.S. business practices or managerial styles. National distinctions will evolve toward generally recognized forms of managerial excellence. Currently, capital has no nationality, and in the future, good business practices will have no nationality either.

Overpopulation

Darwin contended that there is a natural tendency in any population to overproduce. As a population expands, more pressure is placed on the resource base that supports the population. Those creatures that possess, or learn, beneficial variations are better able to compete for the increasingly scarce resources. Those with competitive weaknesses will do worse and worse, eventually becoming extinct.

Accompanying the concepts of overpopulation is the concept of emigration. As competition for the resource base increases due to overpopulation, some emigration to new areas occurs. Extending the boundaries of a population is a normal tendency. But as that emigration occurs, the creatures are exposed to new environments. The beneficial characteristics developed in the original environment may prove extremely beneficial in the new environments. Or, conversely, the characteristics that were beneficial in the original environment may become detrimental variations in the new environments, leading to rapid adaptation or extinction.

In an organizational context, when a domestic firm in the United States or Japan or Germany is successful, its production capability is expanded. As a firm achieves domestic success, it often continues to expand internationally or it expands into new domestic markets. Although firms don't necessarily overpopulate, they certainly overproduce or create overcapacity. Virtually all major industries are plagued by chronic overcapacity in virtually all of the industrialized, Western economies. This tendency toward multinational overcapacity is simply an evolutionary characteristic and not just a passing occurrence. Overcapacity will plague all major industries in all industrial economies, leading to more intense competitive pressure globally. Competition never decreases naturally. However, increased international competition does increase the probability of extinction for firms possessing detrimental variation.

As firms emigrate to new opportunities internationally, the new environment changes the rules of the game somewhat. Some firms may be very competitive in the new situation, whereas others may be spectacularly unsuccessful. The success or failure is due largely to the next Darwinian concept.

Natural Selection

Another major concept in Darwin's theories of evolution is natural selection. As an environment gradually changes, the organisms possessing the more beneficial characteristics are better suited for the newer environment. The environmental changes are the major causal factors. However, each major factor tends also to spawn a variety of indirect environmental actions. An organism cannot adapt to only one major change; adaptation to all of the direct and indirect environmental changes must occur.

Global warming is an obvious direct action, an environmental shift that could influence an ecosystem in many ways. The winter of 1991–92 was the warmest on record. The direct effect was a warmer, less stressful winter. The indirect effects are many and complex.

Because of a warm winter and a light snowpack, rivers and aquifers have lower water levels by late summer. Low water levels usually result in higher water temperatures, which may change aquatic life patterns. Grasses that normally grow all summer may dry out and die by midsummer. A mild winter may stimulate animal populations to overpopulate compared to normal levels. Thus global warming may result in a whole series of direct and indirect actions. In total, these changes contribute to the emergence of a different set of survival characteristics, or key success factors.

If we make the assumption that technological innovation is a direct environmental action, such changes could alter the success factors for business directly and indirectly. Technology certainly influences in a very direct way how we communicate, how we manage, and how we produce things. Indirectly, technological innovations have facilitated globalization through telecommunications, transportation, and computer advances of all types. Quite simply, technology has helped to shrink the world. But technology also indirectly changed business by influencing product assortment, customer expectations, and, most certainly, competitive intensity.

The overall result is that the rapidly changing business environment has led to the emergence of a whole new set of business characteristics that are necessary for survival—necessary for adaptation to the new environment. The characteristics and behaviors that led to success 5, 10, or 15 years ago may have little relevance today. Natural selection is not based on just one characteristic; natural selection is based on the complex interaction of responses to both direct and indirect environmental changes.

Some firms have downsized their workforce as a knee-jerk reaction to the increasingly competitive environment. Many of those firms have been very disappointed by the results of such efforts. The reason is that other factors, most notably becoming truly customer driven, were probably ignored. These firms thought that success would flow from making one major change. Clearly, it didn't.

Survival of the Fittest

This brings us to the last major concept of Darwinism—survival of the fittest—a concept that integrates the earlier ideas. In naturally diverse populations, there is a good deal of variation, a tendency to overpopulate, and emigration. This all takes place within the context of a changing environment that is constantly altering the rules of the game ever so subtly. The fittest species are those that develop the ability to change and evolve at least as fast as the environment changes. Those that lack the ability to keep pace with the changing environment drift toward extinction, their existence marked only by their archaeological record. Is the rapidly changing global business environment really any different?

To summarize the application of Darwinism to business in the 1990s, there are continuous variations—some good, some mediocre—and some bad management practices. Geographic isolation is disappearing into a rapidly evolving business environment that is changing faster than ever before. Traumatic, crash programs probably won't result in any beneficial variation in behavior that will lead to long-term success and survival. The key survival characteristics will more likely be flexibility, creativity, innovativeness, and continuous learning. This sets a premium on the organizational process for implementing gradual adaptation and improvement rather than on crash programs. And a process for continuous improvement is precisely what *kaizen* is all about.

KAIZEN: INSTITUTIONALIZING CONTINUOUS IMPROVEMENT

The concept of *kaizen* (pronounced *"kai-zan"*) has been referred to as the single most important idea in Japanese management. It is the real key to competitiveness in almost any activity or business. Yet the concept of *kaizen* is shockingly simple. It is not embedded within a huge array of theories and techniques. It really doesn't take long to understand and accept, although its organizational implementation may be difficult. Quite simply, *kaizen* means improvement, continuous improvement. *Kaizen* is the road or race with no end; it is a career-long journey based on the idea that good enough never is. It is the antithesis of if it ain't broke, don't fix it. It is diametrically opposite to status quo complacency.

While toiling through various academic programs—bachelor's, master's, and doctoral—I supported my educational habit by working in the forest products industry. Over the years, I worked in various positions in logging or in lumber mills. As a result, I gained rather wide exposure to a broad cross section of the industry.

Recently, I had the opportunity to reexamine the industry while studying its international competitiveness. This is an industry battered continually by environmentalists seeking to save old growth forests, roadless areas, and the infamous spotted owl. This is an industry battered by declining demand for new houses due to an aging population. This is an industry subject to technological changes in manufacturing and in residential construction.

In spite of such environmental turbulence, what is most striking about the industry is its lack of change. Certainly, some firms have been progressive and have changed markedly, but most firms have changed very little in the past 20 years. Logging techniques have remained almost identical. Some lumber mills and plywood plants have made technological improvements but most have not. The technology of 20 years ago remains much the same.

The result of this economic complacency is a declining industry. Mills throughout the Northwest are closing and not just because of the spotted owl. Many are closing because for years management failed to modernize and improve operations. Many are simply no longer competitive.

Unfortunately, this situation is all too common in many other businesses and industries as well. Management felt that the status quo was good enough. In short, management in many businesses abrogated its fundamental responsibility of managing change.

Manage Change or Change Management

Complacency, the real root of evil in business, was discussed earlier, so it won't be rehashed in detail here. But the reason for complacency's evil is the relentless advance of competition. You may feel your firm is doing a good job. You may not feel the need to change things. But some competitor out there somewhere will feel the need to get better. If it does get better and you don't, you'll wake up in that hot water.

Every firm's market position is subject to dynamic deterioration by competitive forces. Areas of distinctive competencies or advantage will always erode. And market requirements—those customer expectations—will continue to increase to higher and higher levels.

Every aspect of the customer value triad must be continually attacked. Product quality must improve. Service quality must improve. Price should decrease. And each of these areas must reflect continuous improvement, not a one-shot fix. For example, the CEO of a computer chip manufacturer stated the corporate goals quite clearly: "We must make our chips 20 percent smaller, produce them 20 percent faster, improve capability by 20 percent, and reduce costs by 20 percent *annually*. If we fail to do so, we'll be out of business in a few years."

Thus the fundamental responsibility of management is to manage change, to manage the improvement process. Any organization that doesn't manage the continuous improvement process is, by default, managing its way to economic decline, gradually evolving toward extinction.

Comprehensive Change

The key foundation of *kaizen* is a corporate culture that cherishes change. The responsibility for improvement does not reside solely either in the executive suites or at the departmental level or on the shop floor. The responsibility resides in all aspects of the firm. It is the responsibility of each and every employee to be part of the continuous improvement effort, continually trying to improve the organization as a whole or, at the least, to improve the task they perform. The responsibility to be part of the continous improvement effort cannot be delegated to subordinates either. What does change at different organizational levels are the type of improvement and the time horizon.

At the highest levels of the organization, the primary focus of managers should be on long-term improvement. This often involves conducting best-in-class benchmarking studies for process improvement. Making major changes to processes often requires significant managerial and financial commitment and support. But once the processes are in place, the responsibility of middle- and lower-level employees should be one of continual improvement.

The reason most crash programs fail is that they are inconsistent with the corporate culture. In management's haste to implement some type of program, supporting systems are seldom changed. The same people, with little or no additional training, are asked to change their behavior or performance in some way. But the old organizational structure, the old information systems, the old performance evaluation and reward systems are seldom changed significantly. As a result, these supporting elements all reinforce the *old* way of doing things, not the new. Just like Pavlov's dogs, behavior that is rewarded will be reinforced and become stronger, and behavior that is not supported will be extinguished.

What is necessary to create a *kaizen* organization? What does the organization look like? McKinsey and Company uses a 7-S framework as a cultural diagnostic tool that provides a concise overview of corporate culture. In a *kaizen* organization, the profile would have the following characteristics for each of the S's.

Strategy

The concept of *kaizen*, or continuous improvement, must be explicitly built into a firm's corporate strategies. This essentially requires recognition by top management that problems exist throughout the organization at all levels. At the highest levels, strategies must include both innovation and continuous improvement.

The difference between innovation and continuous improvement is significant. Innovation consists of the radical new idea, the technological breakthrough, the totally new product. Innovation normally occurs as part of a planned strategy or a research and development effort. When Burroughs-Wellcome developed the AIDS drug AZT, it was the result of planned efforts at innovation in the research labs. When 3M developed Post-it notes, it was the result of an individual developing an idea in an organizational environment that sought out and encouraged innovation and radical ideas. For innovation to occur, strategies must reflect the fact that innovation is important in terms of policies, procedures, resource allocation, and so forth. Accordingly, innovation is predominantly the responsibility of the top levels of management.

Kaizen, on the other hand, consists of the gradual improvement of every aspect of an organization. It is a teacher developing a new teaching technique for class. It is an accountant offering a better way to track product costs. It is a salesperson creating a more efficient way to serve customers. Thus, *kaizen* is the goal of everyone, every day, in all parts of the organization. It can occur with or without innovation.

When innovation yields a new product, *kaizen* improves the product and improves the product's production process. Organizations normally need both innovation and continous improvement. It is therefore top management's responsibility to make sure both innovation and *kaizen* are explicit strategic elements within the firm. If they aren't strategic issues, then neither will spontaneously occur.

Structure

If strategies are intended to foster creativity and flexibility, then worker empowerment is almost mandatory. That is, workers must be empowered to make more decisions and have more direct control over their jobs. Logically, then, flatter organization structures will follow. This flattening of organizational structures means both fewer layers of management as well as fewer managers at all levels. In short, the ratio of managers to laborers, or administrative intensity, must be reduced.

During the lingering recession of 1991 and 1992, corporate downsizing was the rage, as is normally the case in a recession. But what was unique about that most recent wave of downsizing was that the proportion of managers being laid off or fired was the highest ever. And few of those vacant positions were refilled as the economy picked up. A major factor enabling managerial downsizing, or lean management, is the trend toward empowerment. Once workers have been really empowered, the there is simply less need for managers to make decisions and, hence, less need for managers.

In addition to organizational structures' flattening and leaning facilitated by empowerment, the distinctions between functional areas are blurring. *Kaizen* is inherently built upon the concept of cross-functional problem-solving teams that attempt to improve value-added processes. If a problem resides in only one functional area, it can be solved fairly quickly and simply in most cases. However, the thornier, more difficult problems nearly always cut across functional boundaries. The solution, then, must also cut across functional boundaries. And the only way to get different functional areas to buy in to the solutions is to involve them in the problem-solving process. As workers coordinate problem resolution across functional boundaries, the need for bureaucratic controls is lessened. If *kaizen* is truly being adopted, the cross-functional teams are continually trying to improve all aspects of the organization and are not waiting to be told by management to do something.

Systems
"Systems" is a somewhat generic term intended to capture the processes that get things done in organizations. Included would be information systems, quality control processes, budgeting and accounting systems, performance evaluation, and reward systems.

Solectron, one of the 1991 Baldrige National Quality Award winners, has a comprehensive customer satisfaction system, for example. Customer satisfaction data are gathered weekly and fed back into the organization through formal reporting systems. Customer satisfaction scores are shared throughout the firm, and weekly customer satisfaction meetings are held that are not only cross-functional but include also current customers and prospective customers. By having such systems in place, a firm quickly conveys the message that customer satisfaction is vitally important to everyone.

Important to *kaizen* is the idea that useful information is generated and shared throughout an organization. If workers are empowered to improve the organization, then they must also have the data on which to base decisions. The old managerial belief was that information was the base of power. If a manager tightly controlled information, the power base would be maintained. Such beliefs are antiquated! Now the approach should be to make information widely available so that empowered workers can make better decisions at lower organizational levels. And the performance evaluation systems should reward them for doing so. All the systems in the organization must be oriented toward helping employees to continually improve themselves and the processes.

Style
The management style necessary to *kaizen* is that of facilitator, coach, enabler. The not-invented-here mentality that contends that all good ideas flow from management is clearly unacceptable. Accompanying the flatter structures, the empowered workers, and the open sharing of information is the need for highly participatory managerial styles.

Flexibility, creativity, and good interpersonal and communication skills will continue to become more important. Managers will need to walk their talk. That means top management's lip service or superficial support will be readily exposed: managers will need to lead by example and be actively involved in the improvement process and in the cross-functional teams. And it means top to bottom managerial involvement, not just delegation to lower organizational levels.

Staff

In McKinsey's parlance, staff is the human element. Lots of CEOs say, "Our people are our most important asset," but relatively few organizations really treat employees accordingly. Cost-cutting programs almost always include layoffs or firings. Ironically, many of the individuals are hired back a short while later, with a significant amount of ill will.

One of the most visible ways of recognizing the value of employees is by soliciting their ideas for improvement. It could be a program as simple as a suggestion system that is actually utilized. The suggestion system at Toyota generates 1.5 million suggestions annually, and an astonishing 95 percent of the suggestions are implemented. The message such an effort sends to employees is readily apparent: individuals and their ideas are very important.

If people really are an organization's greatest asset, then they should be treated accordingly. Any asset depreciates over time and human assets are no different. An individual's knowledge base will gradually become out of date unless it is nurtured, maintained, and developed. Just as depreciation charges allow for reinvestment of equipment, a firm should also continually invest in the development of its workforce. Unfortunately, too many firms appear to be locked into the do-more-for-less mentality that stifles workers' motivation.

Skills

The skills of workers should never remain static. The skills should evolve, getting better and better as technology and the environment change. Such development is nothing more than a commitment to life-long learning. As individuals' skills improve, the individuals are more capable of contributing to organizational improvement. Unfortunately, few organizations fully understand the linkage between knowledge development and continuous improvement.

The average amount of time spent annually in training and development for each worker is about one week in U.S. firms. In the typical Japanese firm, each worker spends about three weeks in training and development annually. Which of those two investments in human assets best exemplifies that a firm's people are truly important? U.S. managers often respond that the Japanese have low turnover rates so they get better return on their training expenditures. With higher turnover rates, U.S. firms can't afford to invest so much in training because many of the employees will soon be gone. Again, such thinking is fallacious. If employees are treated as a valuable asset, turnover will decline and a better return will be generated by training expenditures.

Shared Values

The final element of McKinsey's 7-S framework is shared values, and it is more ambiguous, more subtle than the others. For each of us as individuals, defining our dominant or subordinate values is a difficult task. Not only is it difficult to define our own values, but it is even more difficult to identify how those values influence our behavior. Exactly why do you like the clothes you wear, the food you eat, the activities you choose to be involved with, the music you listen to? Inherently, the reasons are found in your values, beliefs, and personality.

Organizationally, much the same situation occurs. Organizational values gradually evolve and emerge as part of the day-to-day decisions. Far too often, organizational values are allowed to develop spontaneously. They are not part of a planned organizational effort. And when values gradually emerge, they may not reinforce the organization's goals and strategies. Most commonly, naturally emerging values simply reinforce the status quo, traditional way of doing things.

Innovation and continuous improvement must be instilled as part of an organization's core values. The concepts must permeate a firm's philosophy statements, top management actions, and training programs, as well as all of its systems. The whole organization must be continually learning, plus searching for the best business practices.

7-S in Brief

The primary implication of this 7-S discussion is that the whole organization must be tightly focused on customers. Developing one or two customer-driven programs will be grossly inadequate. Only when all 7-S's are aligned toward continual improvement of delivered customer value will real success be achieved. Becoming customer driven is not just the result of a set of activities. Being truly customer driven is a fundamental business philosophy that must permeate every dimension of corporate culture.

SUMMARY

Nothing in the business environment is static. Turbulence, chaos, rapid change, fierce competition, and demanding customers challenge businesses continually. The relatively stable business environment of the 1960s and 1970s, in which strategic planning was the vogue, gave way to the transitionary 1980s. Clearly, in the 1990s, economic power rests with consumers and customers amid the typhoon of change.

While organizations must have some enduring, guiding goals that shape the decision-making process, it should be noted that flexibility, adaptability, responsiveness, creativity, and innovativeness are the survival characteristics for the 1990s. It means that firms must continually improve product quality to better meet consumer and customer expectations. It means that firms must continually improve service quality to dazzle both the end consumers and the intermediate customers. It means that price must be justified by product and service quality in the competitive context. And it means that firms must improve their customer satisfaction measurement programs and better integrate the program's information into the firm.

The new environment charges firms to better develop partnerships with customers and consumers by integrating them into the organization. The arm's-length, us-versus-them mentality must quickly fade. Customer retention should be a part of an ongoing tracking program so that the precise reasons for customer defections are known. The annual profitability of customers should be tracked continually. While fairly easy for industrial products firms, this area may be more challenging for consumer goods firms.

Every one of these elements must be comprehensively ingrained throughout the organization. Trying to improve when three or four S's reinforce the old behavior will yield nothing but chaos. The whole organization must focus on continual improvement, taking many small steps throughout, instead of undertaking periodic great leaps. If you personally do not continually improve individually, your career will stagnate, or worse. If your firm doesn't continually improve, it will drift slowly but surely toward extinction, toward that pot of hot water. With economic power resting squarely in the hands of consumers, who are continually increasing their expectations and demands, you can be absolutely certain that good enough never is.

For that reason, this book has focused on *processes* for improvement. Customer satisfaction measurement is a process to drive the continuous improvement of product and service quality. Value-based pricing is a process for guiding pricing decisions. Supplier partnering is a process for integrating the value-added chain. *Kaizen* is a managerial philosophy advocating continual improvement of all organizational processes. Explicit in every discussion was the idea that every process must be centered on delivering good value to the customer. Being truly customer driven is clearly the most important success factor of the 1990s.

APPLICATION IDEAS

1. How does your organization cook frogs? Are changes gradual, continuous, and proactive? Or do changes tend to be sporadic and reactive?
2. Are all of the seven S's aligned and harmonized to encourage organization change, innovation, and creativity? Or do the seven S's reinforce the status quo?
3. Which is most important in your organization—innovation or continuous improvement? Has your organization developed strategies to carry out both?

APPENDIX A
A Baldrige-based Self-Diagnostic Questionnaire

SELF-ASSESSMENT QUESTIONNAIRE

The creation of the Malcolm Baldrige National Quality Award by the U.S. Department of Commerce is viewed as one of the most visible and positive actions by government in recent years. Certainly the Baldrige award has focused the spotlight on the critical role of quality in international competitiveness. But winning the award is not the ultimate goal of most firms that apply for the award.

The real benefit of the Baldrige award is its required introspective, structured self-assessment process. Applying for the award requires that a comprehensive, critical analysis of an organization's processes be conducted. The analysis begins with top management and includes all functional areas as well as all levels of the organization. This hard look in the mirror quickly identifies a firm's strengths and weaknesses.

The template that is used to conduct and evaluate the self-assessment is the list of award criteria. The initial criteria were developed by representatives from the Department of Commerce, the National Institute of Standards and Technology, and private businesses. The original criteria have been improved upon each year based on feedback from examiners and applicant firms, reflecting a commitment to continuous improvement.

Although the criteria continue to evolve, there are currently seven major categories for evaluation, each with a variety of subareas. The major categories have point values associated with each that are roughly indicative of the relative importance of that topic to quality improvement. Point values also are provided for each of the subareas, again based on relative importance. The current categories and the point values are presented in Figure A-1.

The categories and subareas were the basis for the questions in the following self-assessment questionnaire. The topics and the number of questions correspond approximately to the Figure A-1 categories. Although developing precisely identical questions and point values

219

was not possible, the questionnaire is generally compatible with the award criteria.

The questionnaire should not be handed to just one person for completion. Instead, a variety of individuals should each complete the questionnaire separately and then meet to discuss the results. From this meeting, a consensus position for an organization can be reached that would be a fairly comprehensive, composite profile.

Although a profile based on only 100 questions could never present a complete picture of an organization, the profile should serve as a starting point for subsequent discussions and analysis. For example, the profile could provide an agenda for site visits to determine supplier certification or for joint supplier-customer team meetings. Thus, this questionnaire should serve as an important initial step in evaluating quality in your own or a supplier's firm.

Figure A-1 Baldrige Criteria Point Values

1992 Examination Categories/Items	Point Values

1.0 Leadership 90
    1.1 Senior Executive Leadership...45
    1.2 Management for Quality..25
    1.3 Public Responsibility..20

2.0 Information and Analysis 80
    2.1 Scope and Management of Quality and
        Performance Data and Information..............................15
    2.2 Competitive Comparisons and Benchmarks.................25
    2.3 Analysis and Uses of Company-Level Plans 40

3.0 Strategic Quality Planning 60
    3.1 Strategic Quality and Company Performance
        Planning Process...35
    3.2 Quality and Performance Plans.....................................25

4.0 Human Resource Development and Management.......................150
    4.1 Human Resource Management 20
    4.2 Employee Involvement 40
    4.3 Employee Education and Training 40
    4.4 Employee Performance and Recognition 25
    4.5 Employee Well-Being and Morale 25

5.0 Management of Process Quality 140
    5.1 Design and Introduction of Quality Products
        and Services..40
    5.2 Process Management—Product and Service
        Production and Delivery Processes...............................35
    5.3 Process Management—Business Processes and
        Support Services...30
    5.4 Supplier Quality...20
    5.5 Quality Assessment 15

6.0 Quality and Operational Results 180
    6.1 Product and Service Quality Results 75
    6.2 Company Operational Results 45
    6.3 Business Process and Support Service Results..............25
    6.4 Supplier Quality Results...35

7.0 Customer Focus and Satisfaction...300
    7.1 Customer Relationship Management 65
    7.2 Commitment to Customers 15
    7.3 Customer Satisfaction Determination..........................35
    7.4 Customer Satisfaction Results 75
    7.5 Customer Satisfaction Comparison 75
    7.6 Future Requirements and Expectations
        of Customers..35

TOTAL POINTS 1000

QUALITY SELF-ASSESSMENT QUESTIONNAIRE

For each of the following questions, rate your organization on a scale of 0–10. If your organization does nothing in a particular area, rate it 0. If your organization does a little, but nothing significant, you might rate it at 1 or 2. If your organization has a moderate level of performance, you might rate it at 5. If the organization has excellent performance, you might rate it at 9 or 10. Your point rating for each question should reflect how well your organization does in that particular area.

Leadership (90 possible points)

The Leadership category examines senior executives' *personal* leadership and involvement in creating and sustaining a customer focus and clear and visible quality values. Also examined is how the quality values are integrated into the company's management system and reflected in the manner in which the company addresses its public responsibilities.

1. Do senior executives provide leadership through visible involvement in quality-related activities such as creating a customer focus, creating quality values, planning for quality, recognizing employee contributions, and communicating quality values outside the company?

   Not at All   Completely
   0   1   2   3   4   5   6   7   8   9   10

2. Has senior management created clearly defined quality values and communicated those values both internal and external to the company?

   Not at All   Completely
   0   1   2   3   4   5   6   7   8   9   10

3. Do the personal actions of senior management demonstrate, communicate, and reinforce a customer focus and quality values?

   Not at All   Completely
   0   1   2   3   4   5   6   7   8   9   10

4. Are senior executives evaluated on the effectiveness of their leadership and involvement in creating customer-focused quality values?

Not at All   Completely
0   1   2   3   4   5   6   7   8   9   10

5. Are the company's quality values and customer focus cascaded throughout the organization so that all employees understand how their job contributes to each?

Not at All   Completely
0   1   2   3   4   5   6   7   8   9   10

6. Does the company's organizational structure effectively and efficiently enhance the attainment of the company's customer, quality, innovation, and cycle time objectives?

Not at All   Completely
0   1   2   3   4   5   6   7   8   9   10

7. Does management assist in the design and review of work unit quality plans and take action when nonconformance occurs?

Not at All   Completely
0   1   2   3   4   5   6   7   8   9   10

8. Does management establish key indicators to evaluate and improve awareness and use of quality values at all levels of management?

Not at All   Completely
0   1   2   3   4   5   6   7   8   9   10

9. Does the company explicitly include in its quality policies, practices, and values public responsibility issues such as business ethics, public health and safety, environmental protection, and waste management?

Not at All   Completely
0   1   2   3   4   5   6   7   8   9   10

Information and Analysis (80 possible points)

The Information and Analysis category examines the scope, validity, analysis, management, and use of data and information to drive quality excellence and improve competitive performance. Also examined is the adequacy of the company's data, information, and analysis system to support improvement of the company's customer focus, products, services, and internal operations.

10. Does the quality-related database use customer data, internal company performance, and cost and financial data to drive continuous improvement?

Not at All   Completely
0   1   2   3   4   5   6   7   8   9   10

11. Does the company ensure that data are reliable, consistent, timely, and easily accessible?

Not at All   Completely
0   1   2   3   4   5   6   7   8   9   10

12. Does the company continually improve the quality of its data and shorten the cycle time from data gathering to dispersal?

Not at All   Completely
0   1   2   3   4   5   6   7   8   9   10

13. Does the company have established criteria that are used to compare company performance with competitors and best-in-class benchmarks?

Not at All   Completely
0   1   2   3   4   5   6   7   8   9   10

14. Does the company continually improve benchmark data and use the data as a source of innovative ideas and continuous improvement?

Not at All   Completely
0   1   2   3   4   5   6   7   8   9   10

15. Does the company use customer-driven data that are directly linked to continuous improvement of product and service quality?

    Not at All   Completely
    0   1   2   3   4   5   6   7   8   9   10

16. Does the company use operational performance data to establish priorities for short-term improvements in areas such as cycle time, productivity, and waste management?

    Not at All   Completely
    0   1   2   3   4   5   6   7   8   9   10

17. Does the company strengthen the integration of customer, performance, financial, market, and cost data to improve decision making?

    Not at All   Completely
    0   1   2   3   4   5   6   7   8   9   10

Strategic Quality Planning (60 possible points)

The Strategic Quality Planning category examines the company's planning process and how all key quality requirements are integrated into overall business planning. Also examined are the company's short- and long-term plans and how quality and performance requirements are deployed to all work units.

18. Does the company use current and future customer requirements; competitive position; financial, societal, and technological trends; and supplier capabilities as key inputs to the development of both short- and long-term business plans?

    Not at All   Completely
    0   1   2   3   4   5   6   7   8   9   10

19. Does the company ensure policy deployment to all work units and suppliers, allocate resources based on the priorities, and monitor alignment of work unit activities?

Not at All   Completely
0   1   2   3   4   5   6   7   8   9   10

20. Does the company evaluate and improve the quality of its planning process, including the downward deployment of policies, as well as solicit input from all levels of the organization?

Not at All   Completely
0   1   2   3   4   5   6   7   8   9   10

21. Does the company identify, for each market or niche, the key quality requirements necessary to attain market leadership?

Not at All   Completely
0   1   2   3   4   5   6   7   8   9   10

22. Does the company link resource allocation, such as capital equipment, facilities, education, training, and personnel, to key requirements that support quality and performance planning?

Not at All   Completely
0   1   2   3   4   5   6   7   8   9   10

23. Do the long-term company plans include significant quality indicators and include projections of competitive position on those indicators?

Not at All   Completely
0   1   2   3   4   5   6   7   8   9   10

Human Resource Development and Management (150 possible points)

The Human Resource Development and Management category examines the key elements of how the company develops and realizes the full potential of the work force to pursue the company's quality and performance objectives. Also examined are the company's efforts to build and maintain an environment for quality excellence conducive to full participation and personal and organizational growth.

24. Are the human resource plans for issues such as recruitment, training, education, involvement, empowerment, and recognition derived from company quality and performance plans?

Not at All   Completely
0   1   2   3   4   5   6   7   8   9   10

25. Does the company strive to continually improve personnel practices and monitor that improvement with key indicators?

Not at All   Completely
0   1   2   3   4   5   6   7   8   9   10

26. Does the company use employee-related data to improve the effectiveness of the entire workforce at all organization levels?

Not at All   Completely
0   1   2   3   4   5   6   7   8   9   10

27. Does the company have specific mechanisms to promote employee contributions and to provide feedback, individually and in groups, on quality and performance objectives?

Not at All   Completely
0   1   2   3   4   5   6   7   8   9   10

28. Does the company have specific mechanisms to increase employee empowerment, responsibility, and innovation?

Not at All   Completely
0   1   2   3   4   5   6   7   8   9   10

29. Does the company have key indicators to evaluate and improve employee involvement at all organization levels, and do those indicators show an increase in involvement?

Not at All   Completely
0   1   2   3   4   5   6   7   8   9   10

30. Does the company conduct skills assessment for all employees and use the results to develop education and training programs that improve quality skills and knowledge?

Not at All   Completely
0   1   2   3   4   5   6   7   8   9   10

31. Does the company provide quality-related training for new and existing employees and track the percentage of employees receiving training and the amount of training hours received by employees annually?

Not at All   Completely
0   1   2   3   4   5   6   7   8   9   10

32. Does the company evaluate and improve the effectiveness of education and training including delivery systems, subsequent job performance improvement, and overall employee development?

Not at All   Completely
0   1   2   3   4   5   6   7   8   9   10

33. Do the company's performance, recognition, promotion, compensation, reward, and feedback systems support quality and performance objectives?

Not at All   Completely
0   1   2   3   4   5   6   7   8   9   10

34. Does the company have key indicators such as cooperation, participation, and employee satisfaction that are used to evaluate and improve performance and recognition processes?

Not at All   Completely
0   1   2   3   4   5   6   7   8   9   10

35. Do quality improvement activities include proactive approaches to health, safety, satisfaction, and ergonomics?

Not at All   Completely
0   1   2   3   4   5   6   7   8   9   10

36. Do employee development efforts support changes in technology, improved productivity, changes in work processes, and company restructuring?

Not at All   Completely
0   1   2   3   4   5   6   7   8   9   10

37. Does the company offer special services to employees, such as counseling, assistance, recreational or cultural opportunities, non-work-related education, or outplacement?

Not at All   Completely
0   1   2   3   4   5   6   7   8   9   10

38. Does the company track key indicators of employee morale such as satisfaction, safety, absenteeism, turnover, attrition rate for customer contact personnel, grievances, strikes, and worker compensation and identify and correct causal factors when problems arise?

Not at All   Completely
0   1   2   3   4   5   6   7   8   9   10

Management of Process Quality (140 possible points)

The Management of Process Quality category examines the systematic processes the company uses to pursue ever-higher quality and company performance. Examined are the key elements of process management, including design, management of process quality for all work units and suppliers, systematic quality improvement, and quality assessment.

39. Are customer and quality requirements addressed early in the design process and integrated into all phases of the production and delivery processes, including the identification of key process characteristics?

Not at All   Completely
0   1   2   3   4   5   6   7   8   9   10

40. Do product designs take into consideration product and service performance, process capability and future requirements, and supplier capability and future requirements?

Not at All   Completely
0   1   2   3   4   5   6   7   8   9   10

41. Does the company evaluate and improve the effectiveness of its designs and design processes so that new product and service introductions progressively improve in quality and cycle time?

Not at All   Completely
0   1   2   3   4   5   6   7   8   9   10

42. Does the company maintain the quality of processes in accord with product and service design requirements by frequent measurement of key indicators and through the use of root cause analysis determination?

Not at All   Completely
0   1   2   3   4   5   6   7   8   9   10

43. Does the company analyze and improve processes to achieve better quality, performance, and cycle time through the use of process simplification, waste reduction, process research and testing, use of alternative technologies, and benchmarking?

Not at All   Completely
0   1   2   3   4   5   6   7   8   9   10

44. Does the company have a system for analyzing product and service performance data and translating the results into continuous process improvements?

Not at All   Completely
0   1   2   3   4   5   6   7   8   9   10

45. Does the company integrate process improvements with day-to-day process management by resetting process standards, verification of improvements, and ensuring use of improvements by all appropriate work units?

   Not at All   Completely
   0   1   2   3   4   5   6   7   8   9   10

46. Does the company evaluate and improve the quality of business processes and support services by focusing on internal customer requirements and deriving performance indicators from those requirements?

   Not at All   Completely
   0   1   2   3   4   5   6   7   8   9   10

47. Does the company have a system to achieve better quality, performance, and cycle time for business processes and support services through process and organizational simplification, use of alternative technologies, benchmarking, and challenge goals?

   Not at All   Completely
   0   1   2   3   4   5   6   7   8   9   10

48. Does the company communicate to suppliers its quality requirements and the principal indicators used to evaluate quality?

   Not at All   Completely
   0   1   2   3   4   5   6   7   8   9   10

49. Does the company monitor supplier performance to ensure that the company's quality requirements are met and give relevant feedback to suppliers?

   Not at All   Completely
   0   1   2   3   4   5   6   7   8   9   10

50. Does the company have specific strategies to improve the quality and responsiveness of suppliers through partnerships, joint training, incentives and recognition, and supplier selection?

Not at All   Completely
0   1   2   3   4   5   6   7   8   9   10

51. Does the company use detailed criteria to regularly conduct a quality assessment of systems, processes, practices, products, and services?

Not at All   Completely
0   1   2   3   4   5   6   7   8   9   10

52. Does the company use assessment results to improve practices, products, and services and to verify that the results lead to effective actions?

Not at All   Completely
0   1   2   3   4   5   6   7   8   9   10

Quality and Operational Results (180 possible points)
The Quality and Operational Results category examines the company's quality levels and improvement trends in quality, company operational performance, and supplier quality. Also examined are current quality and performance levels relative to those of competitors.

To maintain the relative importance weights for each category with those in the Baldrige criteria, the questions in this section are scaled from 0 to 12 instead of the 0 to 10 used previously.

53. Does the company document current levels of performance on all key measures of product and service quality such as accuracy, reliability, timeliness, performance, after-sales services, documentation, and appearance?

Not at All   Completely
0   1   2   3   4   5   6   7   8   9   10   11   12

54. Can the company document trends on all key measures of product and service quality for the past several years?

Not at All   Completely
0   1   2   3   4   5   6   7   8   9   10   11   12

55. Does the company document current-quality-level comparisons with principal competitors in key markets, with industry averages, or with industry leaders?

Not at All   Completely
0   1   2   3   4   5   6   7   8   9   10   11   12

56. When making competitive comparisons, does the company use independent surveys, studies, or laboratory testing?

Not at All   Completely
0   1   2   3   4   5   6   7   8   9   10   11   12

57. When making competitive comparisons, does the company use company-conducted evaluations and testing that are objective and valid?

Not at All   Completely
0   1   2   3   4   5   6   7   8   9   10   11   12

58. When competitive comparisons are made on specific product and service attributes, are the data used to improve company processes?

Not at All   Completely
0   1   2   3   4   5   6   7   8   9   10   11   12

59. Does the company document current levels of operational performance such as use of manpower, materials, energy, capital, and assets?

Not at All   Completely
0   1   2   3   4   5   6   7   8   9   10   11   12

60. Does the company document trends on the operational performance indicators in the previous question?

Not at All   Completely
0   1   2   3   4   5   6   7   8   9   10   11   12

61. Does the company compare operational performance measures with those of competitors, industry averages, industry leaders, and key benchmarks?

Not at All   Completely
0   1   2   3   4   5   6   7   8   9   10   11   12

62. Does the company document current levels of performance on key indicators of quality and performance for business processes and support services?

Not at All   Completely
0   1   2   3   4   5   6   7   8   9   10   11   12

63. Can the company document trends for the key indicators of quality and performance for business processes and support services?

Not at All   Completely
0   1   2   3   4   5   6   7   8   9   10   11   12

64. Does the company make comparisons of performance in business processes and support services with best-in-class benchmarks?

Not at All   Completely
0   1   2   3   4   5   6   7   8   9   10   11   12

65. Does the company document current levels of supplier performance on the key quality indicators?

Not at All   Completely
0   1   2   3   4   5   6   7   8   9   10   11   12

66. Can the company document trends for the key indicators of supplier quality?

Not at All   Completely
0   1   2   3   4   5   6   7   8   9   10   11   12

67. Does the company compare the quality level of its suppliers with the quality levels of competitors' suppliers?

Not at All   Completely
0   1   2   3   4   5   6   7   8   9   10   11   12

Customer Focus and Satisfaction (330 possible points)

The Customer Focus and Satisfaction category examines the company's relationships with customers and its knowledge of customer requirements and of the key quality factors that determine marketplace competitiveness. Also examined are the company's methods to determine customer satisfaction, current trends and levels of satisfaction, and these results relative to competitors.

68. Does the company directly involve customers in determining which product and service attributes are most important to customers and then develop strategies and plans to address them?

Not at All   Completely
0   1   2   3   4   5   6   7   8   9   10

69. Does the company understand how the product and service attributes fulfill basic customer needs?

Not at All   Completely
0   1   2   3   4   5   6   7   8   9   10

70. Does the company constantly seek new and better ways to enhance its relationship with customers?

Not at All   Completely
0   1   2   3   4   5   6   7   8   9   10

71. Does the company furnish clear and complete information to customers to ensure that customers formulate accurate expectations of products and services?

    Not at All   Completely
    0   1   2   3   4   5   6   7   8   9   10

72. Does the company clearly define the roles of customer contact personnel and provide them with full technological and logistical support?

    Not at All   Completely
    0   1   2   3   4   5   6   7   8   9   10

73. Does the company provide easy access to customers who seek assistance, wish to comment, or wish to complain?

    Not at All   Completely
    0   1   2   3   4   5   6   7   8   9   10

74. Does the company proactively follow up with customers to seek feedback for improvement on products, services, and recent transactions?

    Not at All   Completely
    0   1   2   3   4   5   6   7   8   9   10

75. Does the company have service standards that define reliability, responsiveness, and effectiveness of customer-contact employees' interactions with customers?

    Not at All   Completely
    0   1   2   3   4   5   6   7   8   9   10

76. Are the customer-contact service standards deployed to other company units that support customer-contact employees?

    Not at All   Completely
    0   1   2   3   4   5   6   7   8   9   10

77. Does the company monitor the service standards system and use customer information for continual improvement?

Not at All   Completely
0   1   2   3   4   5   6   7   8   9   10

78. Does the company have a system for aggregating, evaluating, and using formal and informal customer complaints and feedback from all company units?

Not at All   Completely
0   1   2   3   4   5   6   7   8   9   10

79. Does the company ensure that complaints and problems are resolved promptly and effectively?

Not at All   Completely
0   1   2   3   4   5   6   7   8   9   10

80. Does the company have specific criteria for the recruitment, selection, and career pathing of customer-contact employees?

Not at All   Completely
0   1   2   3   4   5   6   7   8   9   10

81. Does the company provide customer-contact employees with training that includes knowledge of products and services, listening to customers, soliciting comments from customers, how to anticipate and handle problems or failures, skills in customer retention, and how to manage customer expectations?

Not at All   Completely
0   1   2   3   4   5   6   7   8   9   10

82. Does the company empower, recognize, and reward customer-contact personnel for high performance and monitor their attitudes, morale, and attrition?

Not at All   Completely
0   1   2   3   4   5   6   7   8   9   10

83. Does the company have key criteria to use in regularly evaluating and improving its customer relationship management?

Not at All   Completely
0   1   2   3   4   5   6   7   8   9   10

84. Does the company make a commitment to promote customer trust and confidence in its products, services, and relationships?

Not at All   Completely
0   1   2   3   4   5   6   7   8   9   10

85. Have improvements in the quality of the company's products and services over the past three years been translated into stronger customer commitments, such as expressed or implied guarantees or warranties?

Not at All   Completely
0   1   2   3   4   5   6   7   8   9   10

86. Does the company evaluate and improve its commitments and customers' understanding of them in order to avoid gaps between expectations and delivery?

Not at All   Completely
0   1   2   3   4   5   6   7   8   9   10

87. Does the company measure the key customer satisfaction attributes for each of the major market segments or customer groups?

Not at All   Completely
0   1   2   3   4   5   6   7   8   9   10

88. Do customer satisfaction measurements reflect customers' likely market behavior?

Not at All   Completely
0   1   2   3   4   5   6   7   8   9   10

89. Does the company have a systematic, regular process for gathering valid, reliable, and objective customer satisfaction data?

Not at All   Completely
0   1   2   3   4   5   6   7   8   9   10

90. Does the company regularly evaluate and improve the effectiveness of its overall customer satisfaction program?

Not at All   Completely
0   1   2   3   4   5   6   7   8   9   10

91. Does the company regularly compare its customer satisfaction levels with those of competitors?

Not at All   Completely
0   1   2   3   4   5   6   7   8   9   10

92. Does the company use the comparative assessment of customer satisfaction levels in its continuous improvement process?

Not at All   Completely
0   1   2   3   4   5   6   7   8   9   10

93. Does the company document trends and current levels of indicators of customer satisfaction for major market segments?

Not at All   Completely
0   1   2   3   4   5   6   7   8   9   10

94. Does the company document trends and current levels of indicators of customer dissatisfaction for major market segments?

Not at All   Completely
0   1   2   3   4   5   6   7   8   9   10

95. Does the company document trends and current levels of customer satisfaction relative to competitors for each major market segment?

Not at All   Completely
0   1   2   3   4   5   6   7   8   9   10

96. Does the company document trends in gaining or losing customers from or to competitors?

Not at All   Completely
0   1   2   3   4   5   6   7   8   9   10

97. Does the company document trends in the market share of competitors?

Not at All   Completely
0   1   2   3   4   5   6   7   8   9   10

98. Does the company have a systematic process for anticipating the future requirements and expectations of customers, taking into consideration changing technological, competitive, societal, economic, and demographic trends?

Not at All   Completely
0   1   2   3   4   5   6   7   8   9   10

99. Does the company forecast the changes in key product and service features and changes in the relative importance of those features to current customers and potential customers?

Not at All   Completely
0   1   2   3   4   5   6   7   8   9   10

100. Does the company evaluate and improve its processes for determining customers' future requirements and expectations for current and future products across an extended time horizon?

Not at All   Completely
0   1   2   3   4   5   6   7   8   9   10

SCORING THE SELF-DIAGNOSTIC QUESTIONNAIRE

To determine your score, add the point rating for each question in each section so that you obtain a rating-point total for the section. Calculate the percentage that the rating total composes of the total possible points for each section. The number of total possible points was given in parentheses at the beginning of each section.

The percentage figure for each section will allow you to determine the relative strengths and weaknesses of your company. It is relatively unusual for a company to be highly uniform across each section unless the company scores very high overall. The lower the percentage score for a particular section, the more that area needs attention.

To determine your overall score, total the points for each section. The overall score gives an indication of how your company would fare in a Baldrige National Quality Award evaluation. The following four categories may help in identifying where your company would fit.

800–1030	Excellent-quality performance roughly equivalent to that of Baldrige award winners.
600–799	Good-quality performance that is normally above average in most industries.
400–599	Average-quality performance typified by firms that have started down the road to quality but haven't made major progress yet.
0–399	Below-average quality performance that will lead to problems if quality is not proactively addressed very soon.

APPENDIX B
Supplier Partnership
Diagnostic Questionnaire

The previous questionnaire was designed to create a broad, initial profile of a firm's evolution to total quality management. The supplier partnership questionnaire is narrower and more specialized in nature. It is intended to determine a supplier's compatibility and experience with partnering concepts.

This questionnaire is not intended to be used as a supplier reduction tool. A supplier reduction questionnaire is even broader and more comprehensive than the previous total quality management diagnostic survey, including issues such as facilities, financial position, and labor relations. The questionnaire presented here should be used after supplier reduction has taken place.

The purpose of this questionnaire is to assess a supplier's experience and compatibility with concepts essential to partnerships. As such, it serves as a starting point for identifying areas that need work in formulating the partner relationship. If problem areas can be identified early in the relationship, strategies can be jointly developed to correct any major deficiencies. Therefore, the results of this questionnaire could be analyzed and used as an agenda in initial partnering meetings.

For this questionnaire to be useful, it should not be completed by only one respondent in the supplier firm. Instead, it should be completed separately by a vertical and a horizontal cross section of individuals, preferably members of the partnering action team. Those individuals would then meet to negotiate a composite profile.

SUPPLIER PARTNERSHIP DIAGNOSTIC QUESTIONNAIRE

Top Management (40 possible points)

1. The supplier's top management actively improves long-term relationships with customers and suppliers.

Not at All   Completely
0   1   2   3   4   5   6   7   8   9   10

2. The supplier's top management stresses improving quality throughout the entire supply chain.

Not at All   Completely
0   1   2   3   4   5   6   7   8   9   10

3. Meeting or exceeding customer requirements or expectations is included in the supplier's mission statement, vision, or values.

Not at All   Completely
0   1   2   3   4   5   6   7   8   9   10

4. The supplier's top management emphasizes customer satisfaction as a dominant strategic goal for both internal and external customers.

Not at All   Completely
0   1   2   3   4   5   6   7   8   9   10

Customer Satisfaction (100 possible points)

5. The supplier has a system in place such as quality function deployment to transfer customer requirements and expectations into product and service characteristics.

Not at All   Completely
0   1   2   3   4   5   6   7   8   9   10

6. The supplier has a system in place to anticipate future customer needs and expectations.

Not at All   Completely
0   1   2   3   4   5   6   7   8   9   10

7. The supplier has an effective system for proactive follow-up with customers to determine areas for improvement.

Not at All   Completely
0   1   2   3   4   5   6   7   8   9   10

8. The supplier's top management considers customer relationship management a top priority.

Not at All   Completely
0   1   2   3   4   5   6   7   8   9   10

9. The supplier has a system for infusing customer contact throughout the organization and has empowered employees to resolve customer problems.

Not at All   Completely
0   1   2   3   4   5   6   7   8   9   10

10. The supplier's customer service standards are clearly based on customer requirements and expectations.

Not at All   Completely
0   1   2   3   4   5   6   7   8   9   10

11. Employees with direct customer contact continuously evaluate and improve customer service standards to meet changing customer requirements and expectations.

Not at All   Completely
0   1   2   3   4   5   6   7   8   9   10

12. The supplier regularly monitors customer satisfaction with product and service and compares customer satisfaction levels with competitors'.

Not at All   Completely
0   1   2   3   4   5   6   7   8   9   10

13. The supplier can document positive trends in customer satisfaction levels.

Not at All   Completely
0   1   2   3   4   5   6   7   8   9   10

14. The supplier utilizes best-in-class benchmarking to improve customer satisfaction.

Not at All   Completely
0   1   2   3   4   5   6   7   8   9   10

Quality Planning (30 possible points)

15. The supplier utilizes best-in-class benchmarking to improve internal processes.

Not at All   Completely
0   1   2   3   4   5   6   7   8   9   10

16. The supplier has a system for continuously validating and updating benchmark data.

Not at All   Completely
0   1   2   3   4   5   6   7   8   9   10

17. The supplier allocates resources based on their contribution to achieving quality and customer satisfaction goals over the long term.

Not at All   Completely
0   1   2   3   4   5   6   7   8   9   10

Human Resources (70 possible points)

18. The supplier utilizes cross-functional teams to improve internal processes and has achieved demonstrated successes.

Not at All   Completely
0   1   2   3   4   5   6   7   8   9   10

19. Virtually all of the supplier's employees are empowered to improve processes and service quality, and the majority of employees are involved in quality improvement teams.

Not at All   Completely
0   1   2   3   4   5   6   7   8   9   10

20. The supplier's training and development program is driven by current and future customer requirements and expectations.

Not at All   Completely
0   1   2   3   4   5   6   7   8   9   10

21. The supplier has an active merit-based profit-sharing program that rewards cross-functional team performance and individual performance.

Not at All   Completely
0   1   2   3   4   5   6   7   8   9   10

22. The performance evaluation and reward system is tied closely to the supplier's quality and customer goals.

Not at All   Completely
0   1   2   3   4   5   6   7   8   9   10

23. The supplier has a formal program to evaluate and improve work conditions, employee well-being, and employee morale.

Not at All   Completely
0   1   2   3   4   5   6   7   8   9   10

24. The supplier's commitment to employee training and development is a major corporate objective.

Not at All   Completely
0   1   2   3   4   5   6   7   8   9   10

Information Management (50 possible points)

25. The supplier gathers and integrates both its supplier and customer quality information into the company's decision-making database.

    Not at All   Completely
    0   1   2   3   4   5   6   7   8   9   10

26. The supplier is linked to its suppliers and its customers through electronic data interchange.

    Not at All   Completely
    0   1   2   3   4   5   6   7   8   9   10

27. The supplier routinely uses and correlates customer-oriented data to evaluate internal processes and quality improvement.

    Not at All   Completely
    0   1   2   3   4   5   6   7   8   9   10

28. The supplier continuously evaluates and improves the cycle time to gather, analyze, and use data.

    Not at All   Completely
    0   1   2   3   4   5   6   7   8   9   10

29. The supplier's decision support system supports company quality objectives and focuses on customer-oriented measurement of value and quality.

    Not at All   Completely
    0   1   2   3   4   5   6   7   8   9   10

Management of Process Quality (40 possible points)

30. The supplier's product design decisions are driven by customer requirements and expectations.

    Not at All   Completely
    0   1   2   3   4   5   6   7   8   9   10

31. The supplier's product design decisions include manufacturability, process capability, and its suppliers' capabilities.

Not at All   Completely
0   1   2   3   4   5   6   7   8   9   10

32. The supplier's suppliers, customers, and cross-functional teams are systematically included in all product and process design steps.

Not at All   Completely
0   1   2   3   4   5   6   7   8   9   10

33. The supplier is committed to the continuous improvement of its productive processes and uses statistical process control.

Not at All   Completely
0   1   2   3   4   5   6   7   8   9   10

The Supplier's Relationship with its Supply Base (110 possible points)

34. The supplier has established basic partnerships with the majority of its suppliers.

Not at All   Completely
0   1   2   3   4   5   6   7   8   9   10

35. The supplier has established advanced partnerships with its key suppliers.

Not at All   Completely
0   1   2   3   4   5   6   7   8   9   10

36. The supplier shares openly with its suppliers information and data on all aspects of the business.

Not at All   Completely
0   1   2   3   4   5   6   7   8   9   10

37. The supplier measures its suppliers' performance using lot sampling techniques focused on percentage defective or defects per million.

Not at All   Completely
0   1   2   3   4   5   6   7   8   9   10

38. The supplier gives its suppliers feedback on product and service quality and requests corrective action.

Not at All   Completely
0   1   2   3   4   5   6   7   8   9   10

39. The supplier holds periodic reviews with its key suppliers for the purpose of communicating mutual expectations and requirements, technology trends, and business trends.

Not at All   Completely
0   1   2   3   4   5   6   7   8   9   10

40. The supplier's quality improvement process extends into its own supply base and has demonstrated a positive impact on quality indicators.

Not at All   Completely
0   1   2   3   4   5   6   7   8   9   10

41. The supplier offers training and support to its supply base to help the supply base to continually improve.

Not at All   Completely
0   1   2   3   4   5   6   7   8   9   10

42. The supplier has established with its supply base a supplier recognition and certification program.

Not at All   Completely
0   1   2   3   4   5   6   7   8   9   10

43. The supplier's top management strongly supports partnership relationships with both suppliers and customers.

Not at All   Completely
0   1   2   3   4   5   6   7   8   9   10

44. The supplier is committed to an open, two-way flow of communication with suppliers and customers.

Not at All   Completely
0   1   2   3   4   5   6   7   8   9   10

Supplier's Partnership Experience with Customers (60 possible points)

45. The supplier's goals for quality improvement, continuous improvement, technological advancement, and cost reduction are compatible with its customers' goals.

Not at All   Completely
0   1   2   3   4   5   6   7   8   9   10

46. The supplier has demonstrated a willingness to be flexible and responsive to changes in customer needs.

Not at All   Completely
0   1   2   3   4   5   6   7   8   9   10

47. The supplier has attempted to create an image of trust and reliability with customers.

Not at All   Completely
0   1   2   3   4   5   6   7   8   9   10

48. The supplier has established advanced partnership relationships with other key customers.

Not at All   Completely
0   1   2   3   4   5   6   7   8   9   10

49. The supplier has received advanced certification as a preferred supplier by other customers.

Not at All   Completely
0   1   2   3   4   5   6   7   8   9   10

50. The supplier has demonstrated in other partnerships the ability to reduce the total cost of ownership.

Not at All   Completely
0   1   2   3   4   5   6   7   8   9   10

SCORING THE SUPPLIER PARTNERSHIP DIAGNOSTIC QUESTIONNAIRE

The scoring on this questionnaire is much the same as the previous questionnaire. Each section can be scored individually by totaling the points in a particular section. Then a comparison of actual scoring and the total possible points can be done to determine a percentage score for each section. The percentage scores for each section can be compared to determine where a firm is strongest or weakest.

The scores for each section then can be totaled to give an overall score for a supplier that indicates its degree of compatibility and experience with partnering. The following categories can be used to group the scores.

400–500	The firm is very well suited for and experienced with partnerships. Implementation problems should be minimal.
300–399	The firm has some elements in place but also has some significant weaknesses. Implementing partnerships with this firm should yield good results, but an investment in time is necessary.
200–299	The firm has some major weaknesses that will make partnering difficult initially. The firm will require major changes to really embrace partnerships.
0–199	The firm is not well suited for partnering at present. If top management is strongly committed to partnerships, the firm may have some long-term development potential. Otherwise, the future is bleak.

HOW TO DESIGN A CUSTOMER SATISFACTION MEASUREMENT PROGRAM

Chapter 7 was intended to provide an understanding of why customer satisfaction measurement (CSM) is so important to a firm's long-term survival. That chapter also illustrated briefly how customer satisfaction data could be used to drive a firm's continuous improvement effort by way of the Wonder Corporation example. In order to avoid getting bogged down in technical research design issues, however, the chapter purposely avoided detailed discussion of how to design and implement a CSM program. That is the purpose of this appendix.

Readers are cautioned that the following discussion presents an overview of all of the key issues and at the same time, that space limitations prevent extremely detailed treatment of the subject. There is a forthcoming book by this author that discusses in great detail how to design, implement, and utilize a CSM program.

Designing a CSM program is a sequential, iterative, dynamic process. The process is sequential because certain decisions and issues must precede and guide subsequent decisions. That process is presented in Figure C-1. Each of these steps will be discussed in this appendix.

Designing a CSM program is an interactive process. Invariably, there are unforeseen issues that emerge as each step is taken. In some cases, the new information may require the modification of previous decisions. It is quite normal to cycle through this process several times before a consensus about research design is developed.

The process is dynamic because there is no such thing as a perfect CSM program. Virtually every CSM program can be improved with an expenditure of time and money. And as markets, competitors, and customers evolve and change, the CSM program also must incorporate changes. Though many such changes may be small, say, simply tweaking an otherwise good program to make it better, some firms have come to recognize major flaws in their program and have thrown out the old program entirely. These firms then design a completely new CSM program.

Every firm should develop its own CSM program and custom design it to fit that firm's specific situation. One of the worst mistakes that a firm can make is to simply modify an existing questionnaire from another firm and apply it as its own. There is no such thing as a canned, ready-made questionnaire. Each firm will have different management, products, objectives, customers, and uses for the data, and each of these will influence the research design.

Even though each firm will have a unique program designed to its own needs, the process of designing a good CSM program is generally uniform for all firms. The following 10-step process gives an overview of the key issues that must be considered. If any of the 10 steps are neglected or conducted poorly, the quality of the whole CSM program will be negatively affected.

DEFINE THE OBJECTIVE

Developing good, clear objectives is the first, and probably most important, step in the design of a CSM program. The reasons for developing a CSM program go far beyond simply "finding out what customers think of us," a commonly stated justification. Top management must first clarify, at least very generally, why the CSM program is being implemented and who will actually be using the data. The internal customers, those who actually use the data, have a direct influence on the timing of data gathering, the form of the data, and the data analysis. These issues will become more apparent as we examine the five most common objectives of a CSM program.

Getting Close to the Customer

Getting close to the customer is probably the most common and widespread rationale for developing a CSM program. The virtues of getting close to customers have been touted in the business literature for 15 years. As a result, many managers easily accept this as an objective. And of the five objectives, this objective is also the easiest to attain.

The reason is that this objective involves only *current customers*. The sample frame is easily identifiable and accessible through internal company data, in most cases. The CSM data often can be gathered through the use of a questionnaire composed of closed-end questions that allow

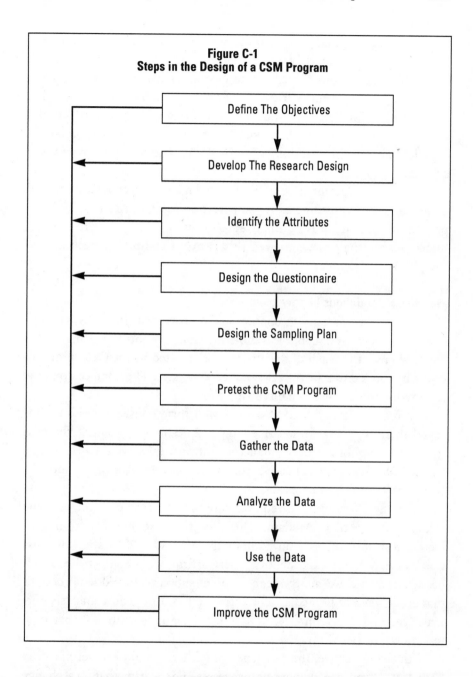

Figure C-1
Steps in the Design of a CSM Program

Define The Objectives

Develop The Research Design

Identify the Attributes

Design the Questionnaire

Design the Sampling Plan

Pretest the CSM Program

Gather the Data

Analyze the Data

Use the Data

Improve the CSM Program

easy compilation and analysis. A closed-end questionnaire is normally easier to administer than other forms. The data can be gathered less frequently—perhaps only every six months or annually—and still yield actionable information.

In some firms, getting close to the customer implies a firm should let customers know that they are important. The act of getting advice, input, and suggestions directly from customers usually clearly conveys this message to customers. Thus, if a firm is trying to communicate that customers are important by including them in a CSM program, *all* of a firm's customers may be contacted. This was the message that Quill Corporation conveyed by sending a Bill of Rights with every shipment to a customer.

The most significant benefit flowing from this objective is improved understanding of customers' needs, perceptions, and priorities. This improved understanding is normally equated with getting close to the customer. As we shall see, however, this is not a completely accurate assumption.

Measuring Continuous Improvement

The objective of measuring continuous improvement is somewhat similar to the previous one, but it is more internally oriented. The major difference here is that each of the attributes evaluated by the CSM program is directly linked to a firm's value-added processes. Thus, the customer is conducting the ultimate quality inspection.

This requires that the CSM data be in a form consistent with the internal metrics of the firm. For example, questions measuring the customer's perception of performance on an attribute would need to be worded and scaled in a manner that yields usable data to the internal customer of the CSM program.

Achieving this objective requires sampling current customers as the primary source of CSM data. This objective also benefits from contacting lost customers as an additional source of CSM data. Lost customers can very quickly identify where a firm has a competitive weakness. This root cause analysis can pinpoint subpar value-added processes that are in need of immediate corrective action. Root cause analysis normally requires a personalized follow-up, such as telephone or personal interviews, to be effective.

With this objective, the frequency of gathering data is determined by how fast a firm can change its processes. For a firm that can change quickly, CSM data may be gathered weekly or monthly to provide feedback. For firms that respond more slowly, less frequent feedback is acceptable. The sampling procedures will be dictated by a firm's internal needs and ability to find and implement process improvements.

Customer-Driven Improvement

The previous two objectives can be achieved predominantly by using structured, closed-end questions. Harnessing the customer's ideas for improvement takes a more qualitative, personalized approach.

Not all customers are equally valuable sources of ideas for improvement. Therefore, a firm must be able to identify which customers are most likely to provide ideas for improvement and include them in the sample frame. Normally, this is done by using a split sample approach. One portion of the sample consists of the group of identified innovators. The other portion of the sample is a random cross section of normal customers.

Whether dealing with innovative or normal customers, the data gathering process must utilize a more personalized, unstructured approach. This is normally done through telephone interviews using many open-ended questions with follow-up probes. To achieve this objective, firms must encourage customers to openly share their ideas and knowledge with the firm.

For rapidly changing products, as in the computer industry, achieving this objective may require frequent customer contact. Innovative customers may be contacted frequently so their ideas can be quickly built into the next generation of products. Capturing innovative ideas early in the design phase is critical to maintaining a high speed to market.

Identifying Competitive Strengths and Weaknesses

To achieve this objective, the firm must measure the customer's perceptions of the competitive alternatives. This type of CSM data is typically of the greatest interest to top management because it provides a measure of the success of a firm's overall strategies. Unfortunately, this objective often requires a relatively complex research design as well.

This objective requires that the sample frame include current customers, lost customers when possible, competitors' customers, and potential customers. Identifying these different customers can be a challenge in itself; once they have been, the questionnaire is usually more complex since several firms are often simultaneously evaluated. This type of research must always be anonymous, which tends to depress response rates because customers don't know who is conducting the research.

Identifying competitive strengths and weaknesses is probably the best way to allocate internal resources. By identifying where a firm is weaker than the competition, that firm can develop strategies to correct the situation. The competitive data are then the guide for implementing and funding various projects.

Linking CSM Data to Evaluation and Compensation

Achieving high levels of customer satisfaction normally results in higher profitability. Recognizing this, some firms have attempted to link performance evaluation and incentive compensation to customer satisfaction. This presents some very difficult challenges.

To achieve this objective, the CSM data must be very precise—capable of detecting small variations in customers' satisfaction levels. Overcoming normal sampling variation requires relatively large sample sizes, which can be costly. It also requires modifications in question structure and the aggregation of several different questions to improve precision.

Since customer satisfaction is normally the result of efforts by the entire organization, all performance and compensation should be very broad based at the group level. Because of the potential variation due to external factors, compensation should be based on underlying trends in the data rather than on a percentage of change at one point in time.

Objectives Summary

Each of these five objectives has different implications for research design. Some firms may choose to pursue one or two of the objectives: a few firms may pursue all five. However, if a firm doesn't specify which objectives it has for the CSM program, the ambiguity will spill over into all aspects of the research design. The more objectives a firm attempts to pursue, the more complex and costly the research design becomes.

DEVELOP THE RESEARCH DESIGN

A research design is an overall description of the CSM program. Normally, it takes several iterations before finalizing a research design that resolves the concerns of reliability, validity, bias, meaningfulness, and desired precision. Ultimately, the research design will describe which attributes will be examined, what the data gathering process will be, who will be sampled, how the data will be analyzed and used, and so forth.

Among the most important research design decisions is how the data will be gathered. The two most common methods are mail surveys and telephone interviews. The primary considerations in making the choice between these alternatives are the objectives, costs, time considerations, staffing characteristics, and data quality.

Mail surveys are well suited for objectives that are compatible with relatively structured, closed-end questions. Mail surveys are less costly for large sample sizes and when the sample frame is geographically dispersed. Because of mail lags, both in pretesting and in actual data gathering, mail surveys take considerably longer to implement. Once the questionnaire has been designed, relatively low levels of staffing are necessary to periodically administer and compile the data, particularly if an optical scan format is used to input the data. Data quality is weakest for mail surveys due to low response rates and lack of control over who actually completes the questionnaire.

Telephone surveys are well suited for objectives that require unstructured feedback from customers. Because they are labor-intensive, however, telephone interviews are more costly, particularly so when the sample size is large. Telephone interviews require more staff with specialized training than mail surveys do, although the actual interviewing can be outsourced to a subcontractor. A significant advantage of telephone surveys is the speed of data gathering. Data quality is usually good because of high response rates and the ability to screen respondents and to use follow-up probes.

A good research design is the result of a whole series of trade-offs. If the objectives have been clearly stated, they serve as the guide for decisions about reliability, validity, bias, meaningfulness, precision, costs, time availability, staffing characteristics, and data quality. With so many considerations, designing the "perfect" CSM program is virtually impossible. But by exercising care and iterating through the process enough times, a firm can easily create a good CSM program.

IDENTIFY THE ATTRIBUTES

The process of identifying the attributes includes the use of information both internal and external to the firm. The initial goal at this step is to dredge up all of the attributes that are potentially relevant to customers. When a firm is initially designing a CSM program, this step is often referred to as "discovery" because a firm discovers for the first time what attributes customers really think are important.

The internal sources for attributes are warranties, guarantees, customer service records, customer contact personnel, and various managers, and although these sources can yield a diverse array of attributes important to customers, the list is usually incomplete. All of these sources have been filtered through the perspective of the firm without direct customer input. The output of the internal search for attributes is often used as input to frame the discussion with customers.

The identification of attributes by customers is usually accomplished through depth interviews and focus groups. With both of these techniques, the goal is to let customers have their say in their own words. In most cases, this process exposes blind spots that have been overlooked by employees of the firm. While the output of such efforts may be somewhat ambiguous, these qualitative approaches allow a more objective reading of the voice of the customer.

Depth Interviews

A depth interview is a one-on-one interview with customers that lasts one to two hours. Normally, about six customers are individually interviewed for each market segment. The interviewer can be an employee of the firm but most often is a professional interviewer. The depth interview is not simply a free-flow discussion with customers. Instead, there should be a specific agenda based on the internal research that guides the interview, but the interview should solicit customer perceptions throughout. Since so few customers are involved in the process, depth interviews should not be viewed as random and unbiased. The customers should be "typical" to the extent possible, and definitely not handpicked, good customers.

The output of depth interviews should be a written report of the attributes and issues raised. A common flow in this process is to use the internal research to develop an agenda for the depth interview. The results of the depth interview are then used to develop an agenda for the focus groups. It is quite common for depth interviews to raise issues that need further exploration in the larger focus group discussion.

Focus Groups

The use of focus groups is so widespread that most readers are familiar with them. Due to the importance of focus groups in designing a CSM program, however, a brief discussion is still warranted. As with depth interviews, an initial purpose of focus groups is to identify a comprehensive list of attributes that are relevant to customers.

A focus group consists of 6–12 customers brought together for two or three hours. The focus group is typically conducted in a room designed expressly for that purpose and is moderated by an experienced professional. Typically from four to six focus groups are held to investigate a specific topic. Focus groups are often observed by managers, either in person, on video, or through the use of a network television system. Focus groups are particularly well suited for developing deeper understanding and insight about customers' perceptions of products, attribute evaluation, and decision processes. Focus groups also serve as useful early warning devices to alert managers to changes in customer needs, often well before such changes become apparent in the marketplace.

The use of focus groups usually adds to the list of attributes generated internally and from depth interviews. For most products or services, a total list of from 30–60 attributes can be identified through the three different techniques. Unfortunately, measuring performance on so many attributes is beyond the scope of most CSM programs. Therefore, the attribute list must be reduced to the most important variables.

Reducing the Attribute List

There are three ways to reduce the attribute list to a workable size. It can be done through managerial judgment, focus groups, or statistical analysis. In some cases, a firm may use all three approaches simultaneously.

Using managers to reduce the list is probably the easiest, fastest, and cheapest way, but it also holds the potential for the greatest bias. If management carefully reviews the depth interview and focus group reports, the potential for bias can be reduced somewhat. The advantage of using managers is that the attributes can be selected based on the ability of each attribute to measure performance of a firm's value-added processes.

Focus groups can be used to reduce the list based purely on the customer's input. The focus group is provided with the total list of attributes and is asked to sort the attributes into the 10 most important attributes, the 10 next most important attributes, and so forth. Because this process is inherently subjective, three or four focus groups should individually complete this reduction effort and the results of each focus group should be evaluated for overall consistency.

The third way to reduce the list is through the use of statistical analysis: Questions measuring a firm's performance on each attribute on the total list are developed, along with several questions measuring overall customer satisfaction. This questionnaire is then administered to a sample of customers. The overall customer satisfaction measures are aggregated to form a dependent variable. The relationship between the dependent, aggregated customer satisfaction score and each of the attributes is analyzed statistically. The most common statistical techniques for doing this are multiple regression and factor analysis. Either technique trims unimportant attributes from the total list and indicates which attributes should remain part of the model.

Regardless of how the total attribute list is reduced, the goal is to identify the attributes of most importance to customers. Since trying to measure performance on 30–60 attributes can be overwhelming, most firms try to end up with a reduced list of 15–25 attributes. This reduced list is then converted into a questionnaire.

DESIGN THE QUESTIONNAIRE

The purpose of the CSM questionnaire is to accurately measure customers' attitudes toward various product and service attributes. The most commonly studied attitudes are performance (how are we doing on this attribute?), importance (how important is this attribute to you?), and comparative (how are we doing compared to the competition?). Unfortunately, the formation of attitudes is relatively complex, and their measurement is equally complex. A variety of factors may influence customer attitudes.

Volatility

Attitudes may be volatile, or unstable, over time. Sometimes the volatility is due to a recent event, such as receiving a high heating bill from a utility or missing a flight on a business trip. Sometimes the volatility may be due to conflict among attributes, as when performance on some attributes is good and performance on other attributes is poor. Most customers experience volatility in attitudes over an extended period of time. A firm should have an understanding of why its customers' attitudes vary, and they should use this information in designing the CSM program.

Bias

Customers' attitudes can be influenced by bias. Bias occurs when customers' responses are influenced by factors others than their true attitudes. Bias can be caused by the cover letter, introductions, question wording, measurement and scaling, or question sequencing.

It is relatively easy to intentionally or unintentionally lead the customer to respond in a certain way. When this occurs, and the bias usually skews responses *positively*, a firm may be getting good-looking results that don't really mirror the customers' true attitudes.

Validity

A number of validity issues are relevant considerations. Construct validity is concerned with whether a question really measures what it is supposed to measure. Convergent validity indicates the appropriateness of aggregating several different questions together for an overall score. Discriminant validity is concerned with different questions' actually measuring different attitudes. Sample validity is concerned with the appropriateness of a particular sample. Each of these validity issues is of relevance when measuring customer attitudes. Fortunately, some types of validity can be measured statistically.

Awareness, Salience, Meaningfulness

Awareness, salience, and meaningfulness can influence attitudes. Greater customer knowledge and experience with a product, or specific attribute, typically lead to greater awareness. Salience refers to how important an issue is to a customer. The more important the product to the customer, the greater the salience. As awareness and salience to the customer increase, meaningfulness also increases. This leads to more clearly formulated and articulated attitudes. Very often, managers may assume that a topic is of importance to customers and that customers should have well-formulated attitudes. In some of these cases, however, the issues may be very insignificant and the customer has no clear attitudes at all.

Reliability

To design a good questionnaire, a firm must consider and measure these types of issues. Volatility, bias, validity, awareness, salience, and meaningfulness all influence the reliability of a questionnaire. Reliability is the ability of the questionnaire to get consistent results time after time. Without a reliable questionnaire, tracking customer attitudes becomes tenuous at best.

Need for Simplicity

The best advice that can be given for designing any questionnaire or any specific question is to strive for simplicity. This applies to all aspects of a questionnaire: the introduction, the directions, the transitions, the wording, and the scaling. The more complex and difficult the task is for the respondent, the greater the likelihood of uncertainty and confusion. Both uncertainty and confusion greatly reduce reliability.

Each question should be as specific as possible, with the rule of only one attribute per question. The more specific the question, the easier it is for the customer to respond. This typically leads to higher reliability.

A Questionnaire is a Funnel

A questionnaire should progress from broader, more general questions at first to more specific, sensitive questions later. There should be very logical progression and flow from the introduction all the way through to the last question. In between, there may be a series of filters and screens that keep respondents from answering irrelevant questions.

For this reason, the first questions are broad, easy-to-answer questions. Questions of critical importance to the CSM program are often in the middle portion of the questionnaire. Demographic questions usually come at the end of the questionnaire because these may be sensitive to some customers. And this type of data remains accurate, even after a respondent is fatigued by completing the whole questionnaire.

Always Have a No-Opinion, Don't-Know Option

Not all customers have an opinion about every attribute. Yet most respondents will attempt to answer a question in some way. To prevent respondents with no opinion from skewing responses, they should always have an out. This implies that most questions should have a no-opinion or don't-know option. It is common for 15–20 percent of respondents to select this option when it is available. Failure to include this option is probably the most common flaw found in CSM questionnaires.

A Mail Questionnaire

A mail questionnaire is more than just a series of questions. The cover letter, introductions, and directions should all be designed to elicit the customer's responses. Indeed, it is very likely that many customers never make it past the cover letter before deciding not to participate. So the first goal of a mail questionnaire is to get a customer to participate. Once participation is obtained, then question sequence and structure become relevant.

A respondent is always educated by completing a questionnaire. This learning process results from a firm's raising of issues to a higher level of awareness by simply asking a question. The implication is that the sequence of questions can influence responses, so the sequential relationship between questions should be carefully evaluated.

There are several types of closed-end question structures that can be used: interval scaled, rank order, forced allocation, categorical. Each of these may require the data to be analyzed in a different way. The design of the questions must be linked to the objectives of the CSM program and to the use of the data.

The most commonly used types of questions are categorical. The customer reads a statement and selects the appropriate response. The most common number of categories is 5 to 7, with a balance of positive and negative options. The following question is a fairly typical seven-category style. The no-opinion category is normally viewed as an additional option and is not counted as one of the seven categories.

How would you rate the quality of your in-flight meal?

Among the Best	Better Than Most	Slightly Better Than Average	About Same as Most	Slightly Worse Than Average	Worse Than Most	Among the Worst	No Opinion
☐	☐	☐	☐	☐	☐	☐	☐

Recently, there has been an increase in the use of expectations questions. These questions attempt to measure how closely a firm's performance met the customer's expectations. The following is an example of an expectations question.

How did the service that you received compare to your expectations?

	Much Better Than Expected	Somewhat Better Than Expected	Same asn Expected	Somewhat Worse Than Exepcted	Much Worse Than Expected	No Opinion
Check-in	☐	☐	☐	☐	☐	☐

These types of questions have some significant advantages over interval-scaled questions in that responses are more varied and less biased. However, these types of questions are somewhat harder to design.

While open-ended questions often appear on mail surveys, respondents don't usually respond well to this type. If any response appears at all, it is normally in the form of just a few words. If open, free-flow customer input is desired, a telephone interview is a far better approach.

A Telephone Questionnaire

Because of speed and the ability to solicit unstructured customer input, gathering CSM data by telephone is increasing in popularity. Telephone interviews tend to be shorter, to use more open-ended questions, and to be more flexible than mail surveys. The key advantage is the ability to let the customers have their say.

The most common problems with telephone questionnaires are that they are often too complicated and overwritten, not conceptually clear, too demanding, and too long. Many managers want hard numbers, and telephone questionnaires are often too structured. A telephone questionnaire should have a totally different design from a mail questionnaire.

A further challenge for telephone questionnaires is that they must be designed with both the interviewer and the customer in mind. The questionnaire must be easy to administer so the interviewer is able to capture all of the responses accurately. And the questionnaire should have an easy flow to maintain the customer's interest.

The primary purpose of the introduction is to obtain the customer's participation, since about 70 percent of refusals come after the introduction but before the first questions. The first few questions should flow directly from the introduction and draw the customer into the interview. The rapport and tone of the interview are normally established in the first few questions as well.

When closed-end questions are used, they should be shorter and less wordy than mail questionnaires. Normally, four or five options are provided in categorical questions, for example. Closed-end questions are often combined with open follow-up probes to find out *why* a particular response was chosen.

There are two types of open questions. With completely open questions, the interviewer must try to type the customer's response verbatim. For long, complex issues this can be very difficult. If the interviewer can't keep up with the response, the interviewer must filter the response to capture the key points. Verbatim responses are particularly good for identifying the terms and vocabulary used by customers in describing the various attributes. To overcome the difficulty of capturing verbatim responses, some open questions may have precoded response categories.

The most common responses to open questions can be identified in preliminary research or in pretests. The common responses are then used to develop precoded categories. The interviewer can check the appropriate category as the response is given, removing the difficulty of trying to get a verbatim transcript. The problem with precoded categories is that all responses don't neatly fall into place. Thus some potentially rich ideas may be lost. The views of the customer and ability of the customer to respond should be considered throughout the design of a questionnaire. Once the questionnaire has been designed, however, the next step is to formulate the detailed sampling procedure.

DESIGN THE SAMPLING PLAN

The design of the sampling plan should flow from the objectives. The objectives should indicate *who* is surveyed, how frequently the CSM data are gathered, and the size of the sample. For some firms, the "sample" may actually be a census of *all* customers.

From the population of all customers, a sample frame of the most appropriate individuals must be identified. For example, let's assume that a firm has 100 customers, also businesses. Within each customer firm the most appropriate respondent(s) must be identified. The individuals may be from purchasing, production, or quality assurance departments. A decision must be made about how many individuals from these areas will be contacted. Some firms may contact only one individual per firm; other firms may contact five or six to develop a composite profile.

Once a decision has been made about whom to contact, the frequency of contact must be determined. Some firms gather CSM data weekly; others may do it monthly, quarterly, biannually, or annually. Some firms may survey all customers on a transaction basis—each time a purchase is made. Other firms may survey every 10th or 20th customer on a transaction basis. Some firms may survey the same individuals repeatedly. Other firms may want fresh customers each time CSM data are gathered. The frequency of the gathering of data should be dictated by the objectives of the CSM program, but monthly, quarterly, and biannually are probably the most common intervals.

Sample sizes also are related to the objectives. If a high degree of precision is required, sample sizes tend to be large. For frequent tracking of performance, sample sizes generally are smaller. The number of comparisons and subgroups influences sample size. Normally, at least 100 observations per subgroup should be gathered. So if the goal is to competitively benchmark against three competitors, 100 customers from each competitor should be surveyed, plus at least 100 of a firm's own customers, for a total sample of 400. If a firm wanted to group customer perceptions by size of firm (small, medium, and large) as well as for three competitors (plus the original firm), the firm would have 12 subgroups, for a total sample of 1,200.

Normally, firms gather 500–1,000 responses. This means 500–1,000 usable responses, not an attempt to contact 500–1,000 customers. All sample-size calculations are concerned with only the usable responses. Once the questionnaire and sampling plan have been designed, the next step is to conduct a pretest.

PRETEST THE CSM PROGRAM

A pretest is a test of the entire CSM program, not just a test of the questionnaire. Every aspect of the program must be evaluated, from the questionnaire, to the sample, to the data analysis, to the use of the data by internal customers. Often this iterative process can require several pretests with revisions after each one. The number of pretests can range from one to five, with two being fairly common.

But since every pretest costs money and takes time, there is often a desire to rush through, or even skip, the pretests. This is a serious mistake that can greatly reduce the quality of the CSM program.

There is some debate about whether a pretest should be declared or undeclared. A declared pretest is one in which the customer is informed that it is a pretest, either before or after the questionnaire is administered. When a pretest is declared, the respondent can often provide specific recommendations about how the questionnaire, or process, could be improved. But declaring a pretest removes some of the reality, because the customer knows it is not a "real" survey. When a pretest is undeclared, it is up to the researcher and interviewer to identify the problems and take corrective action.

The sample for the pretest should be representative of the desired sample frame for the entire CSM program. Though actual sample size for a pretest is a subjective managerial decision, normally 25–75 customers are included, with 50 being a reasonable average. The larger the ultimate sample for the CSM program, the larger the pretest sample size.

The pretest should examine the sample frame to determine if the designated respondent is really the best one. All aspects of the questionnaire, including the introduction, wording, scaling, and measurement, must be evaluated.

Once the data-gathering portion of the pretest is complete, the data should be analyzed using the same techniques and procedures as the full CSM program. This ensures that input procedures, format specifications, and statistical techniques are appropriate. It is quite common to change the question wording and scaling to accommodate the use of a specific statistical analysis.

As a final step in pretesting, the output of the data analysis should be passed along to the users of the data. These internal customers could then see if the data are what they really expected. Including the internal users of the data also increases behavioral buy-in to the whole CSM program.

GATHER THE DATA

Once the CSM program has been designed and pretested, gathering the data is a relatively simple, straightforward step. This step is simply the implementation of the research design.

If the data are being gathered by telephone interviews, it is often enlightening for managers and users of the data to listen in on the interviews. For many, it is their first opportunity to really hear the voice of the customer. Most managers come away with an increased respect for customers.

A variety of fieldwork problems often emerge during data gathering. For telephone surveys, strategies must be developed for no answers or busy signals (how many callbacks?), desired respondent not available (on vacation, out of town), refusals by secretary, and disconnected or nonworking numbers. If a particular individual is not available, should someone else in the department be allowed as a substitute? All of these types of decisions can influence data quality.

ANALYZE THE DATA

There are two different types of data analysis that are used in the design of a CSM program. The first types of data analysis are done when the CSM model is being developed initially. Because a large number of variables are being examined simultaneously, most of these techniques are some form of multivariate analysis. The most commonly used techniques for model building are factor analysis, multiple regression of some type, discriminant analysis, and multivariate analysis of variance. Recently, some research firms have begun using LISREL to identify the relationships among attributes in CSM modeling. These techniques are complex and often intimidating to managers not familiar with advanced statistical tools. Fortunately, once a CSM model has been developed, the second set of techniques is usually much simpler.

For ongoing evaluation and tracking of changes in customer attitudes, a firm's use of means, proportions, and weighting factors, along with simple cross-tabulations, is normally sufficient. Most managers can easily understand these types of analyses because they are common in statistical process control. The Wonder Corporation example in chapter 7 illustrated how these types of analytical tools can be used. There is usually no need to baffle the user of the data with overly complex statistical analysis.

The use of good statistical analysis typically adds credibility and objectivity to the CSM data. If several different types of statistical analysis point to the same conclusion, managerial uncertainty will be lessened.

With the increasing power of personal computers and accompanying software, the circulation of CSM data throughout the company is much easier. This allows the users to massage the data in ways that best fit their specific needs. Very often, the widespread availability of CSM data leads to additional education and seminars for mangers so they can analyze the data themselves.

USE THE DATA

The real purpose of CSM data is to serve as the driver for a firm's continuous improvement efforts. Therefore, CSM data should be linked to a firm's critical valued-added processes. For the most significant benefits, this process improvement effort should be the responsibility of cross-functional, empowered teams. Again, the Wonder Corporation example in chapter 7 demonstrated how CSM data could be linked to cross-functional process improvement teams. Since this issue has been previously discussed, the subject will not be taken up again here.

It should be pointed out, however, that some organizations have hundreds of cross-functional teams focusing on process improvement, with many of themusing CSM data as the ultimate measure of conformance quality. Other organizations have over 80 percent of their workforce involved in cross-functional teams, many using CSM data.

IMPROVE THE CSM PROGRAM

Just as all processes should be subject to continuous improvement, a firm's CSM program also should be reevaluated and improved. As stated initially, no CSM program is perfect. Every program can be improved in some way.

Some firms have found that as their customer satisfaction understanding has matured, the old CSM program becomes inadequate. The old program is then usually replaced with a newer, more sophisticated program that better serves the firm's needs. Throwing out the old program and installing a new one can render a historical database useless.

When large changes are made, it is often useful to overlap the old and new programs for a few data-gathering periods. This allows the new program to be calibrated to the old program so that historical trends can be meaningfully calculated. After equivalency evaluations are made, the old program is then discarded completely.

But regardless of whether the changes are major redesigns or minor adjustments to a CSM program, the CSM program should be continually reviewed for improvement. As a CSM program gets better, the data will become more valuable and actionable for the internal users.

It is also quite common for a firm to begin with one objective for a CSM program and then gradually add others. As each additional objective is added, the program must be modified. The key idea to keep in mind is that a CSM program is a *process* for gathering customer-driven data. Accordingly, a CSM program should be the subject of cross-functional process improvement efforts.

INDEX